MORE THAN A MODEL SHOP
STOCK . ADVICE . LAYOUTS

REASONS TO VISIT

- Open 7 days a week
- Own large carpark
- Refreshments available
- Working layouts in T, N, 009, H0 and 00
- Huge range of stock in gauges from T to G
- Most major manufacturers stocked
- Chip fitting and repairs undertaken
- A warm welcome guaranteed
- Mail order Service
- Good quality second hand bought and sold
- Short walk from Burnham on crouch station
- Layouts under construction
- Over 2000sq ft of pure Model Railways

01621 786 198
Flair Rail . Unit 6 & 7 . Springfield Nursery Estate
Burnham on Crouch . Essex . CM0 8TA
info@flair-rail.co.uk
www.flair-rail.co.uk

WELCOME

Flair-rail, one of the UK's largest model railway stores based in Essex within a small riverside town, Burnham on crouch which in itself offers alot to you as a visitor!

But here at flair-rail you will find among many other things; Award winning working layouts available to view and on permanent display plus a myriad of model railway equipment to purchase from all sorts of manufacturers and suppliers.

FLAIR - RAIL IS AN ALADDIN'S CAVE FOR THE MODEL RAILWAY ENTHUSIAST

AWARD WINNING WORKING LAYOUTS

Award winning working layouts available to view and on permanent display plus a myriad of model railway equipment to purchase from all sorts of manufacturers and suppliers.

Flair-rail is an Aladdin's cave for the model railway enthusiast (or the coach load of hobbyists!) with supplies in gauges from T scale to G scale!

You can spend as long as you like looking at the shop and layouts without being pestered or if you prefer we are always happy to help!

Refreshments available including light confectionery and warm drinks! A large free car park is situated right outside the door and a warm welcome guaranteed inside the door!

SHOP ONLINE

You can view our online gallery, find out information about our business and look at the latest bargains in our online shop.

Visit now at
www.flair-rail.co.uk

LATE NIGHT SHOPPING **WEDNESDAYS**

ONE OF THE
UK'S LARGEST
MODEL RAILWAY STORES
BASED IN ESSEX

Visit us online **www.flair-rail.co.uk**

RAILWAY
FLAIR - RAIL
MODELLING

RAILWAY
FLAIR - RAIL
MODELLING

NEED HELP?

Technical assistance and advice on tap, just ask away and we will do everything we can to help!

Come in and ask about anything from which locos ran where to how digital works and a demonstration!

OPENING HOURS

Open 7 days a week with late night shopping Wednesday night.

So whether your completely new to the hobby or a life long enthusiast, you will find many things of interest here at Flair-rail!

Monday	9.30am - 5.30pm
Tuesday	9.30am - 5.30pm
Wednesday	9.30am - 5.30pm
	8.00pm - 10.00pm
Thursday	9.30am - 5.30pm
Friday	9.30am - 5.30pm
Saturday	9.30am - 5.30pm
Sunday	10.00am - 2.00pm

LATE NIGHT SHOPPING **WEDNESDAYS**

01621 786 198
Flair Rail . Unit 6 & 7 . Springfield Nursery Estate
Burnham on Crouch . Essex . CM0 8TA
info@flair-rail.co.uk
www.flair-rail.co.uk

Visit us online **www.flair-rail.co.uk**

Call us on **01621 786 198**

Visit our shop : Unit 6 & 7 . Springfield Nursery Estate . Burnham on Crouch . Essex . CM0 8TA

GAUGEMASTER.com

The Online Home of The Engine Shed

PUBLICATIONS

GM350 Gaugemaster Scenic Guide	£1.00
GM351 Full Colour Catalogue 2009/10	£2.95

DIGITAL CONTROL

PRODIGY ADVANCE2 WIRELESS SYSTEM
DCC03 Wireless Starter Package	£445.00
DCC13 Wireless Walkaround	£155.00
DCC51 Wireless Conversion Set	£235.00

PRODIGY ADVANCE2 DCC SYSTEM
DCC02 Starter Package	£244.95
DCC11 Extension Plate	£32.95
DCC12 Walkaround Controller	£109.95
DCC55 Wired PC Interface	£39.95

DCC DECODERS & ACCESSORIES
DCC20 Standard Decoder	£19.95
DCC21 Small Decoder	£26.95
DCC22 Micro Decoder	£29.95
DCC23 6 Pin Micro Decoder	£29.95
DCC30 Accessory Decoder	£49.95
DCC40 Auto Reverse Module	£34.95
DCC50 Booster	£144.95

ANALOGUE CONTROL

COMBI Single Track Controller	£34.95

CASED CONTROLLERS
100M Single Track Unit	£69.95
100MO Single Track O Gauge Unit	£74.95
10LGB 2.5 Amp G Scale Single Track Unit	£79.95
P Single Track with Inertia	£79.95
D Twin Track Unit	£79.95
DS Twin Track Inertia	£139.95
DF Twin Track with Feedback	£79.95
TS Three Track with Inertia	£139.95
Q Four Track Unit	£144.95
SELECT Single Track Unit	£77.95
LT-OO Tester/Controller	£169.95

PANEL MOUNTED UNITS
100 Single Track Unit	£27.95
U Single Track with Inertia	£34.95
UF Single Track with Feedback	£29.95
D Twin Track Unit	£42.95
UDS Twin Track with Inertia	£55.95
UDF Twin Track with Feedback	£46.95
UQ Four Track Unit	£69.95

HANDHELD CONTROLLERS
W Single Track Unit	£29.95
WS Single Track Unit with Simulator	£47.95
WF Single Track Unit with Feedback	£29.95
GM75 DIN Plug for Above Units	£2.25

MODULES/UNCOUPLERS

EM-1 N Gauge Uncoupler	£7.50
EM-2 Frets (20) for EM-1	£3.95
SS-1 Super Shuttle Unit	£26.95
SS-2 Station Stop Unit	£31.95
TLU Tension Lock Uncoupler	£9.75

TRANSFORMERS

UNCASED TRANSFORMERS
T1 Output 2 x 16v AC 1.25A	£17.95
T2 Output 1 x 18v AC 2.5A	£17.95
T3 Output 1 x 24v AC 1.25A	£19.95
T4 Output 2 x 12v AC 1.25A	£19.95

CASED TRANSFORMERS
M1 Output 2 x 16v AC 1A	£39.95
M2 Output 1 x 18v AC 2.5A	£44.95
M3 Output 1 x 24v AC 1.25A	£44.95
M4 Output 1 x 12v AC 1.25A	£44.95
M5 Output 1 x 12v AC 5A	£69.95
M8 Output 1 x 20v AC 5A	£79.95
M12 Output 1 x 22v DC 5A	£79.95

WALL MOUNTED TRANSFORMERS
WM1 Output 1 x 18v AC 1.1A	£11.95

CUTOUTS
GM41 Thermal Cut Out 1A	£3.50
GM42 Thermal Cut Out 2.5A	£3.50

POINT CONTROL

POINT CONTROL SYSTEM
PCU1 Cased Point Control Unit	£94.95
PCU2 Slave Point Control Unit	£44.95

CAPACITOR DISCHARGE UNIT
CDU Capacitor Discharge Unit	£11.95

POINT MOTORS
PM-1 SEEP Point Motor with Switch	£4.50
PM-2 SEEP Point Motor	£4.25
PM-4 SEEP Latching Point Motor w/Switch	£5.25

SWITCHES
GM510 Toggle Switch Non Latching	£2.15
GM513 Push to Make Switch Black	£2.50
GM514 Push to Make Switch Blue	£2.50
GM515 Push to Make Switch Green	£2.50
GM516 Push to Make Switch Red	£2.50
GM517 Push to Make Switch White	£2.50
GM518 Push to Make Switch Yellow	£2.50

TRACK

GM18 N Gauge Rail Joiners (24)	£1.95
GM19 OO Gauge Rail Joiners (24)	£1.95
GM45 OO Re-Railer	£4.25
GM46 N Re-Railer	£3.95
GM66 Track Pins (Hornby Style)	£2.25
GM67 Extra Long Track Pins	£2.25
GM90 OO Black Sleeper NS FlexiTrack(100)	£145
GM91 OO Black Sleeper Stl FlexiTrack(100)	£145
GM92 N Black Sleeper NS FlexiTrack(100)	£185
GM93 OO Black Sleeper NS FlexiTrack(24)	£62.95
GM94 OO Brown Sleeper NS FlexiTrack(24)£65.95
GM95 OO Black Sleeper Stl FlexiTrack(24)	£40.95
GM96 N Black Sleeper NS FlexiTrack(24)	£49.95
GM97 OO Brown Sleeper NS FlexiTrack(100)	£255

BALLAST & UNDERLAY

GM114 OO Granite Ballast (500g)	£2.75
GM115 N Granite Ballast (500g)	£2.75
GM117 OO Granite Ballast (200g)	£1.75
GM118 N Granite Ballast (200g)	£1.75
GM200 OO Ballasted Underlay (5m)	£19.95
GM201 N Ballasted Underlay (5m)	£19.95

TRACK CLEANING

HF-1 High Frequency Track Cleaner	£29.95
HF-2 High Frequency Double Track Cleaner£39.95
GM27 Value Track Cleaning Rubber	£3.75
GM37 OO/HO Track Cleaning Pads (3)	£4.75
GM39 N Track Cleaning Pads (3)	£4.75

ROAD & ROADWAY

GM43 OO/HO Adhesive Roadway (1m)	£6.50
GM44 N Adhesive Roadway (1m)	£6.25

HO/OO DIECAST

GM300 Mercedes L319 Van	£2.75
GM301 Mercedes CLK Coupe	£2.75
GM302 Mercedes Sprinter Van	£2.75
GM303 BMW X5	£2.75
GM304 BMW 5 Series	£2.75
GM305 Mini Cooper New	£2.75
GM306 Porsche 911 Carrera	£2.75
GM307 Alfa Romeo 147 GTAA	£2.75
GM308 Alfa Romeo 156 GTAA	£2.75
GM309 Audi TT Roadster	£2.75
GM310 Ford Street Ka	£2.75
GM311 Dodge Viper	£2.75
GM312 VW Beetle RSI New	£2.75
GM313 VW Mini-Bus	£2.75
GM314 VW Beetle Original	£2.75
GM315 Jaguar E Type	£2.75
GM316 Jaguar Mark II	£2.75
GM317 Porsche 356A	£2.75
GM318 Range Rover Sport	£2.75
GM319 Land Rover Discovery 3	£2.75

CORK PRODUCT

GM130 Cork Sheet 1/16" (3 x 2m)	£4.75
GM131 Cork Sheet 1/8" (3 x 2m)	£8.75
GM133 OO/HO Cork Railbed (5)	£6.95
GM134 N Cork Railbed (5)	£5.95

MOD-ROC & PLASTER

GM100 Mod-Roc (2.75m)	£3.75
GM119 Fine Modelling Plaster (1kg)	£4.25

GRASS MATS

GM20 Spring Grass Mat (100 x 75cm)	£6.95
GM21 Summer Grass Mat (100 x 75cm)	£6.95
GM22 Autumn Grass Mat (100 x 75cm)	£6.95
GM23 Gravel Mat (100 x 75cm)	£4.95
GM38 Spring Grass Mat (240 x 120cm)	£29.95

FLOCKS & SCATTERS

GM101 Light Green Scatter	£1.50
GM102 Mid Green Scatter	£1.50
GM103 Dark Green Scatter	£1.50
GM105 Spring Green Scatter	£1.50
GM109 Black Scatter	£1.50
GM110 Earth Brown Scatter	£1.50
GM116 Grey Tarmac Scatter	£1.50
GM150 Light Green Fine Foliage	£2.55
GM151 Dark Green Fine Foliage	£2.55
GM152 Mid Green Fine Foliage	£2.55
GM153 Light Brown Fine Foliage	£2.55
GM154 Brown Fine Foliage	£2.55
GM170 Spring Grass Flock	£2.55
GM171 Summer Grass Flock	£2.55
GM172 Moorland Grass Flock	£2.55
GM173 Meadow Grass Flock	£2.55
GM193 Puffer Bottle Scenic Applicator	£3.75

ROUGH GRASS

GM190 Light Green Rough Grass	£7.50
GM191 Dark Green Rough Grass	£7.50
GM192 Beige Rough Grass	£7.50

TREES

OO/HO SCALE BULK VALUE PACKS
GM120 Deciduous Trees (25)	£17.95
GM121 Mixed Trees (25)	£17.95
GM122 Fir Trees (25)	£17.95
GM123 Small Fir Trees (50)	£29.95
GM124 Deciduous Trees (25)	£17.95
GM125 Fir Trees (25)	£17.95
GM126 Park Trees (25)	£17.95

OO/HO SCALE STANDARD TREES
GM180 Plum Trees (3)	£6.50
GM181 Plum Trees in Blossom (3)	£6.50
GM182 Fruit Trees (3)	£6.50
GM183 Apple Trees (3)	£6.50
GM184 Birch Trees (3)	£6.50
GM185 Weeping Willow Trees (3)	£6.50
GM186 Poplar Trees (3)	£6.50
GM187 Pine Trees (3)	£7.95
GM188 Beech Trees (2)	£6.95

BUILD YOUR OWN TREES

SEAFOAM STARTER PACK
GM195 Seafoam Tree Kit	£17.95

LEAVES
GM156 Light Green Leaves	£2.95
GM157 Mid Green Leaves	£2.95
GM158 Dark Green Leaves	£2.95

LICHEN

GM164 Light Green Lichen	£3.95
GM165 Dark Green Lichen	£3.95
GM166 Assorted Lichen	£3.95

HEDGES

GM160 Light Green Hedging	£5.95
GM161 Dark Green Hedging	£5.95

FENCING

GM145 OO/HO Country Fencing Bulk Pack	£8.75
GM146 OO/HO Garden Fencing Bulk Pack	£8.75

SCENIC STARTER PACK

GM194 Scenic Starter Kit	£24.95

BACKSCENES

LARGE SIZE - 2744 x 304mm (108" x 12")
GM701 Valley Backscene	£6.95
GM702 Countryside Backscene	£6.95
GM703 Open Field Backscene	£6.95
GM704 Village Backscene	£6.95

SMALL SIZE - 1372 x 152mm (54" x 6")
GM751 Valley Backscene	£3.95
GM752 Countryside Backscene	£3.95
GM753 Open Field Backscene	£3.95
GM754 Village Backscene	£3.95

BRICKWORK

OO/HO STONE WALLING
GM30 Plain Grey Stone Walling	£7.95
GM31 Stone Walling with Buttresses	£7.95
GM32 Grey Stone Walling with Arches	£7.95

OO/HO TUNNEL PORTALS
GM197 Stone Tunnel Wall	£7.50
GM198 Single Tunnel Mouth	£13.50
GM199 Double Tunnel Mouth	£18.50

ACCESSORIES

WIRE & SOLDERING
GM01 Low Melt Solder 70 Degree (200g)	£3.15
GM02 Solder 180 Degree (200g)	£3.15
GM03 White Metal Flux (60ml)	£4.95
GM04 Brass Flux (60ml)	£4.95
GM06 Solder Wire 145 Degree	£3.30
GM11 10m Wire	£1.75
Select from *Black, Blue, Brown, Green, Grey, Orange, Pink, Red, White or Yellow*	
WIRE 100m Reel	£7.25
Select from *Black, Blue, Brown, Green, Grey, Orange, Pink, Red, White or Yellow*	

ELECTRICAL ACCESSORIES
GM12 Connecting Leads Ring/Pin (Pair)	£3.95
GM13 Connecting Leads Pin/Joiner (Pair)	£2.50
GM14 Pin Connectors Hornby Style (6)	£2.50
GM15 Ring Terminals (5)	£1.50
GM16 Connecting Leads Gaugemaster (5)	£3.95
GM28 Crocodile Clips Red/Black	£1.10
GM29 Knob for Rotary Switch	£1.95
GM74 Diodes 1A (2)	£2.00
GM77 Terminal Block 12 Way Poly	£1.50
GM79 2.1mm Socket for WM1	£0.90
GM86 Small Magnets (10)	£4.75
GM87 Medium Magnets (10)	£5.00
GM88 Large Magnets (10)	£6.50
GM89 Fuses 5A (5)	£1.75
GM99 Reed Switches (10) & Magnets (5)	£12.50

SWITCHES

GM501 DPDT Slide Switch	£1.10
GM502 DPDT Slide Switch Centre Off	£1.10
GM503 SPST Toggle Switch	£1.85
GM504 DPDT Toggle Switch	£1.95
GM505 DPDT Mini Toggle Switch Centre Off £2.50
GM506 DPDT Mini Toggle Switch	£2.10
GM507 SPST Mini Toggle Switch	£1.90
GM508 SPDT Mini Toggle Switch	£1.90
GM509 SPDT Mini Toggle Switch Centre Off £2.15
GM511 Point Motor Switch for G Scale	£2.75
GM512 Push to Break Switch (5)	£5.50
GM519 Rotary Switch 1 Pole 12 Way	£2.50
GM520 Rotary Switch 2 Pole 6 Way	£2.75
GM521 Rotary Switch 3 Pole 4 Way	£2.75
GM522 Rotary Switch 4 Pole 3 Way	£2.75

LIGHTING

12v GRAIN OF WHEAT BULBS
GM69 Yellow (5)	£3.50
GM70 Red (5)	£3.50
GM71 Clear (5)	£2.95
GM72 Green (5)	£3.50
GM73 Orange (5)	£3.50

LIGHT EMITTING DIODES
GM80 3mm Green (5)	£1.75
GM81 3mm Red (5)	£1.75
GM82 3mm Yellow (5)	£1.75
GM83 5mm Green (5)	£1.50
GM84 5mm Red (5)	£1.50
GM85 5mm Yellow (5)	£1.50
GM76 Resistors 1000 ohm (10)	£1.25

TOOLS

GM600 A2 Cutting Mat	£19.75
GM601 A3 Cutting Mat	£10.50
GM602 A4 Cutting Mat	£5.25
GM603 A5 Cutting Mat	£3.25
GM604 Round Nose Pliers	£7.75
GM605 Flat Nose Pliers	£7.75
GM606 Side Cutters	£7.75
GM607 Half Round Cutters	£7.75
GM608 Bent Nose Pliers	£7.75
GM609 Stainless Steel Tweezers	£7.95
GM610 Double Ended Pin Vice	£4.75
GM611 Saw Set 1 with Handle	£10.50
GM613 Trimaway Knife	£5.25
GM614 Stainless Steel Scalpel & Blades	£5.25
GM615 Plastic Scalpel & Blades	£5.25
GM616 Cutting Knife & Blades	£7.75
GM617 Pick Up Tool	£5.25
GM618 Magnifier Tweezers	£5.25
GM619 Precision Lubricator	£4.25
GM620 Locking Forceps Straight	£5.25
GM621 Locking Forceps Curved	£5.25
GM624 Swivel Top Pin Vice	£5.25
GM625 Curve Tweezer Reverse Action	£3.95
GM626 Straight Tweezer Reverse Action	£3.95
GM627 Blunt End Tweezer Reverse Action	£3.95
GM628 Locking Fine Tweezers	£3.95
GM629 Cutting Nippers (3)	£3.75
GM630 Screw Top Mandrels (3)	£3.95
GM631 Slitting Discs & Mandrel	£3.95
GM632 Budget Needle File Set	£5.25
GM633 Glass Fibre Pencil 4mm	£4.25
GM634 4mm Glass Fibre Refills (10)	£6.25

TOOLS (Ctd)

GM635 2mm Glass Fibre Pencil	£7.7_
GM636 2mm Glass Fibre Refills (5)	£5.2_
GM638 Cutting Broaches 0.6-2.0mm	£11.7_
GM640 Archimedian Drill	£5.2_
GM641 HSS Jbbrs Drills 0.5mm (5)	£3.9_
GM642 HSS Jbbrs Drills 0.8mm (5)	£3.9_
GM643 HSS Jbbrs Drills 1.0mm (5)	£3.9_
GM644 HSS Jbbrs Drills 1.2mm (5)	£3.9_
GM645 HSS Jbbrs Drills 1.5mm (5)	£3.9_
GM646 HSS Jbbrs Drills 1.8mm (5)	£3.9_
GM647 HSS Jbbrs Drills 2.0mm (5)	£3.9_
GM648 Microbox Drills 0.3-1.6	£9.9_
GM649 Microbox Drills 61-80	£9.9_
GM650 HSS Jbbrs Drills 0.3mm (5)	£3.9_
GM651 HSS Jbbrs Drills 0.4mm (5)	£3.9_
GM652 HSS Jbbrs Drills 0.6mm (5)	£3.9_
GM653 HSS Jbbrs Drills 0.7mm (5)	£3.9_
GM654 HSS Jbbrs Drills 0.9mm (5)	£3.9_
GM655 Spare Blades for GM614	£1.8_
GM656 Spare Blades for GM616	£1.5_
GM657 Small Multi Clamp	£11.2_
GM658 Mini Snip	£9.9_
GM659 General Purpose Cutter	£3.2_
GM660 Pick N Place Twin Pack	£6.9_
GM661 Pick N Place Small Tool	£3.9_
GM662 Pick N Place Medium Tool	£3.9_
GM663 Pin Pusher with Wooden Handle	£7.9_
GM670 Deluxe Sable Paintbrush Set (5)	£7.9_

OTHER USEFUL GADGETS & GIZMOS
BX1048 Swinger Mini Organiser	£14.9_
LC8055 Mini Task Lamp with Base & Clamp£29.9_
LC8098 Magnifier Organiser Table Lamp	£59.9_
MODELSTRIP Paint Stripper	£4.3_
PKN1050CM 50 Pice Knife Set & Mat	£19.9_
PKN8008 Rotating Cutting Mat (31x31cm)	£19.9_
PSC4706 Laser Scissors	£3.9_
RTRC07 Cordless Rotary Drill Set	£47.9_
RTRC12 Single Speed Rotary Drill Set	£29.9_
RTRC18 Variable Speed Rotary Drill Set	£39.9_
RTRC40 Mini-Jigsaw Set	£39.9_

XURON CORP

XU2175B Standard Track Cutter	£12.7_
XU2175M Vertical Cut Track Cutter	£13.2_
XU2193 Hard Wire Cutter	£15.2_
XU410T High Precision Shear	£9.9_
XU420T Angled Precision Shear	£14.9_
XU440PET Photo Etch Shear	£13.9_
XU450S Tweezernose Serrated Pliers	£14.9_
XU501 Wire Stripper	£11.9_

DELUXE Materials

GLUES
DL02 Super Phatic	£3.7_
DL09 Scatter Grip	£4.6_
DL10 Speedbond PVA 112g (4oz)	£3.5_
DL11 Speedbond PVA 500g	£8.2_
DL12 RC Craft Glue 112g (4oz)	£3.7_
DL24 Plastic Magic	£3.9_
DL27 Tacky Glue	£3.7_
DL28 Scenic Spray Adhesive	£4.6_
DL57 Roket Card Glue	

SUPERGLUE
DL15A Roket Cyano Hot	£3.8_
DL15B Roket Cyano Rapid	£3.8_
DL15C Roket Cyano Max	£3.8_
DL15D Roket Cyano Odourless	£4.5_
DL17 Roket Blaster (Cyano Curing Agent)	£5.1_
DL18 Rocket Powder (Cyano Granules)	£4.5_

EPOXY
DL03 112g (4oz) Speed Epoxy	£9.2_
DL05 28g (1oz) Speed Epoxy	£5.6_
DLAD-5 4min Speed Epoxy 71g (2.5oz)	£5.6_
DLAD-39 4min Clear Tough Epoxy 224g	£12.5_
DLAD-40 4 min Speed Epoxy Syringe 28g	£3.9_
DLAD-50 1hr Clear Epoxy 224g	£11.5_
DLAD-51 20min Clear Epoxy 224g	£11.9_
DLAD-53 20min Speed Epoxy 71g	£9.2_

SCENIC PRODUCTS
DL16A Solid Water 90g (Resin/Hardener)	£6.9_
DL16B Solid Water 180g (Resin/Hardener) £19.5_
DL16C Solid Water 350ml (Resin/Hardener)£17.9_
DL19 Scenic Water 100ml (Gel)	£5.9_
DL19A Scenic Water 250ml (Gel)	£11.9_
DL25 Scenic Snow	£12.9_
DL26 Scenic Rust	£12.9_
DL29 Scenic Fibres	£4.9_
DL30 Scenic Snow Flakes	£10.9_
DL31 Scenic Shovelled Snow	£10.9_
DL32 Glue N Glaze	£4.9_

ACCESSORIES
DL06 Pin Point Bottle Kit	£3.7_
DL07 Micro Tips & Tube	£3.9_
DL08 Pin Point Glue Syringe & Tip	£4.5_
DL21 Model Lite Filler	£6.2_
DL23 Pin Flow Applicator	
DL48 Glue Buster	
DL49 Tacky Wax	
DLR2G Glue Stand	

YOU DO NOT EVEN NEED A STAMP TO POST YOUR ORDER
The Engine Shed - Freepost BR792 - Arundel - West Sussex - BN18 9BR

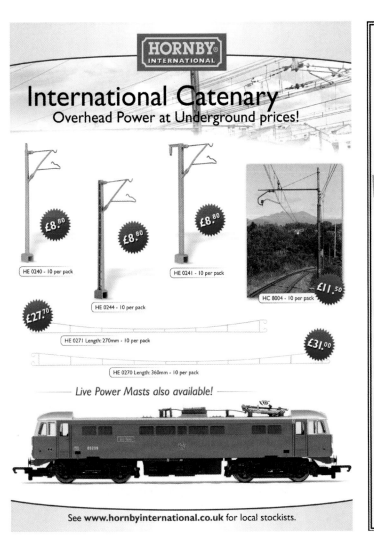

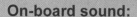
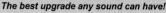

30

CONTENTS

90

82

42

Crowds watch the Red Arrows on August 20, 2009, as 67 025 (with 67 005 bringing up the rear) departs Dawlish with the 2Z64 15.30 Exeter St Davids-Newton Abbot. The 67s had been taken off their normal Taunton-Cardiff duties to run Exeter-Newton Abbot reliefs (with one trip to Paignton) for Dawlish Air Show Day - a very different scene to that described on pages 132-137! Bernard Mills

WELCOME

BRM Annual No.5

It hardly seems a year since the last *BRM Annual* was on sale - well, it's actually a bit earlier this year to coincide with the second National Festival of Railway Modelling at Peterborough! Last year's show proved to be a great success, so I hope you enjoy both the next 'Natfest' show as well as the fifth *BRM Annual* which has now established itself as something of an institution in the hobby. Once again it is packed with inspirational layout features, practical articles and, as always, a large dose of nostalgia!

Tony Wright presents a photo-survey of the Gresley Beat showing developments over the layout's lifetime - then watch the 'Beat' in action on our FREE cover-mounted DVD! Another inspirational layout in the making is Liverpool Lime Street in EM gauge which you can also read about along with Welwyn North, Elvinley Junction and Darley Dale - the last two both large N gauge layouts.

Of course not everyone wants a large layout so Peter Marriott is on hand to show you how to build a micro layout for under £250 in less than a week! And if the thought of building a layout doesn't appeal, why not try to win the BRM micro-layout in our easy-to-enter competition on page 148?

Measuring little more than 4' x 2' it can be set up and running in lesss than ten minutes.

George Hinchcliffe helped found the Gauge O Guild and Gainsborough MRS, saved *Flying Scotsman* then got involved with Steam Town, Carnforth. He talks to Pater Marriott about his long and varied career in the hobby beginning on page 64. Peter also looks into why it seems impossible to get new liveries on some models. It's all a question of being 'licensed to model' as Peter finds out on page 82.

Keeping on the prototype side Nigel Burkin raids his photographic archive looking at shed visits in Scotland and diesels in action around Teesside, while Michael C Shaw takes a 1930's train ride along the Devon coast - it certainly would have been a vastly different scene to that shewn in our header photograph!

Until next time, Happy Modelling!

CONTACTS

British Railway Modelling
The Maltings, West Street,
Bourne, Lincolnshire PE10 9PH

Published by
Warners Group Publications plc
01778 391187
Fax: 01778 425437 (editorial)

Printed by
Warners (Midlands) plc

Publisher
John Greenwood
email: johng@warnersgroup.co.uk

Editor
John Emerson
email: johne@warnersgroup.co.uk

Assistant Editor/Photographer
Tony Wright
email: tonyw@warnersgroup.co.uk

Editorial Assistant
Richard Wilson
email: richardw@warnersgroup.co.uk

Group Advertisement Manager
Patrick Raphael Sisko
01778 391114
email: patsisko@warnersgroup.co.uk

Sales Executive
Jane Cottam
01778 395002
email: janec@warnersgroup.co.uk

Production Secretary
Pat Price
01778 391115
email: patp@warnersgroup.co.uk

Ad Design
Sarah Machin
01778 392076
email: sarahm2@warnersgroup.co.uk

Head of Design and Production
Jayne Thorpe
email: jaynet@warnersgroup.co.uk

Designer
Andrianna Curtis
email: acurtis@warnersgroup.co.uk

Designer
Ryan Housden
email: ryanh@warnersgroup.co.uk

Editorial Secretary
Jean Waterfall
email: jeanw@warnersgroup.co.uk

Track Plan Illustrator
Ian Wilson at Pacific Studio

Subscriptions
01778 392002

Trade Account Sales
Natalie Cole
01778 392404
email: nataliec@warnersgroup.co.uk

UK/Overseas Newstrade Sales
Andrew Stark
01778 391194
email: andrews@warnersgroup.co.uk

Newstrade Distribution
Tom Brown
01778 391135

ISSN 0968-0764

READERS' LAYOUTS ALBUM

Since January 2007, we have had the pleasure of viewing and publishing photographs of a large number of layouts and projects from *BRM* readers, many of whom have gone on to feature in a full 'Layout Focus'. We therefore present a short review of some of the layouts which have reappeared as full features plus six new worthy entries. We're always on the lookout for more, as railway modellers we always tend to dismiss our efforts, usually without justification, so why not share your enthusiasm with other like-minded readers? Remember we pay £25.00 for each picture published and do remember to include your name and address on all emails, letters, disks and prints. Write to Richard Wilson, *British Railway Modelling*, The Maltings, West Street, Bourne, Lincolnshire PE10 9PH or email: richardw@warnersgroup.co.uk

Peterborough

Gilbert Barnatt's layout was one of the first to feature in the then new 'Readers' Layouts' section in the January 2007 issue. He was lucky in that his initial photograph was taken by Tony Wright! The layout will be featuring in *BRM* shortly, Tony has revisited the layout to take more photographs as Gilbert has now scrapped Peterborough to build Peterborough Mk.2.

Spotting at Troughbrook Central

My layout, Troughbrook Central, depicts the North Derbyshire section of the GC main line in the '50s/'60s. A spotter at the end of Troughbrook's platform can expect to see lots of scruffy freight engines from Staveley, Darnall and Annesley or further afield shifting heavy mineral trains - any of one of the 2-8-0s of Messrs. Robinson, Thompson, Riddles or Stanier with the odd 9F thrown in. In between these they might well catch a K3 or a V2 on fast fitted freight or one of Darnall's B1s tearing through on the 'South Yorkshireman'. A Gresley 'namer' might just find its way into the book before the day is out and there's always the chance of something a little more exotic on the York-Bournemouth.

Nick Bailey, Darlingtoname

Nick's excellent layout will be appearing in a future BRM.
RW

THE GRESLEY BEAT

Tony Wright presents a pictorial tour of this outstanding OO gauge model railway, built over the last few years by Cliff Parsons and friends.

You'll probably be reading this before you take the time to look at the DVD fixed to the front of this latest *BRM Annual*. If you are, and you subsequently have access to a DVD player/computer, please take a 30 minute or so time out to view the presentation where you will see The Gresley Beat in moving action. And yes, I know we've done it before, but that was in the layout's exhibition infancy. Much more has been achieved since then (though it's not yet complete), making it, in my opinion (and the opinion of many others, too), one of the most outstanding layouts on the exhibition circuit today, or at any other time.

It's also appeared before on several occasions in the pages of *BRM* (most recently in this year's October issue where the modelling of the grass was described), but, again, much of that has featured work in progress. Here, I hope I can show a much more complete picture, though a few images included are not the most recent and are

presented for comparative purposes.

I have to admit that I'm in a very privileged position with regard to photographing and describing model railways. Very often, I'm given exclusive access with a 'lineside pass', and trains are stopped on demand for me to take a shot. I've probably taken pictures of hundreds (perhaps a lot more than a 1,000?) of layouts in the last 20 years during my time as a freelance photographer and latterly as *BRM*/Warners photographer (my publisher thinks there's enough material for me to write a book about my model railway/ photographic experiences - look out for it early next year). Many of these layouts would qualify amongst the 'best ever', and, where I've poked my lens in their direction, I hope I've done them justice. Several have become or were already my own favourites - personal interest/scale/gauge/period - you know the sort of things. Obviously, my prejudices and likes/dislikes become part of any equation, and I'll probably be accused of too much of that sort of thing by attempting to write about Cliff Parson's OO masterpiece. The masterpiece which takes its name

from the famous aural experience when a Gresley three-cylinder steam loco passed by a spectator. But, even taking my (blinkered?) preferences on board, where a layout is so well done, so evocative and so inspirational, does it matter which railway it represents?

Though The Gresley Beat is definitely based on prototype practice and appearance, Cliff will be the first to admit that it isn't an absolutely *accurate* depiction of the 'Ladykillers' environment around the tunnels immediately to the north of King's Cross, most incongruously called Belle Isle. It might suitably be called an *impression*,

though I believe it's a lot more than that. Despite the fact that the main running lines are (at least) two few in number, Holloway flyover isn't in the right place in comparison with the North London line and Top Shed is on the *wrong* side of the line, you really couldn't mistake this location for anywhere else. Indeed, despite these *mistakes*, in my opinion, it's just as convincing as the Model Railway Club's equally superb Copenhagen Fields, which depicts the same area of the southern end of the ex-GNR main line. The latter is modelled in 2mm finescale (and has also featured regularly in *BRM*) and Cliff's is *only* in OO gauge. I say 'only' with tongue firmly in cheek, for such is the overall excellence of the scene before the viewer's eyes that the gauge is irrelevant. It is *so* convincing, and, anyway, how many finest gauge 4mm layouts have been even *started* on this scale, let alone contemplated? Please, despite numerous assertions to the contrary, somebody prove me wrong and actually build (for exhibition use), a full-scale main line in true-scale 4mm: ft

gauge - 50+ locomotives (mostly multi-wheeled, outside cylinders/valve gear), 200+ coaches, 400+ wagons - within a non-Methusalah-length lifetime. Then, ask me to photograph it. It will be my pleasure!

You could argue, too, that the Beat team's chosen period (the LNER in the 1920s/'30s) is a bit ambiguous and too-wide ranging. Agreed, it does produce anomalies - A1s in original condition alongside A4s, as well as the original, water tube-boilered, battleship grey W1 alongside a V4 (the latter not built until the 1940s, anyway). And, if you go into the '40s, why not a B1? But, that's the work of Edward Thompson, and this layout is called The Gresley Beat for a good reason. None of the master's successor's work is given track room. If there's *Great Northern* running, it's the 'proper' one, similarly so with *Cock O' The North*. However, the work of the master's predecessors is certainly in residence, with Ivatt and Stirling locos rubbing shoulders with the more illustrious Pacifics and V2s produced by the great man himself. But these anomalies don't matter in the overall scheme, because this layout is a celebration of the LNER's heyday - that wonderful time when steam ruled the rails, liveries were in harmony with the things on which they were applied, graffiti was unheard of and Britain was still 'Great'. Ah - the powers of nostalgia!

As mentioned, it's been my delight to be able to photograph so many model railways, and it's been my great pleasure to take pictures of The Beat on numerous occasions, often 'snapped' at exhibitions, but more often with the enjoyment of Cliff's hospitality at the layout's permanent home in deepest Kent. Indeed, having a purpose-built premises to house the layout is ideal but, remember, The Gresley Beat is designed primarily as an exhibition layout, and it's already been seen (and is to be seen) at many of the country's top shows. The viewing public is invited to spend some time observing what happened in the past. On first viewing the layout, to the left, on the longer side, trains emerge from Oakleigh Park tunnel from the north, bringing coal, fish and various commodities. These use the upper level (though any coal will be for King's Cross goods only, Ferme Park, its normal destination, being 'north' of the model). Some of the freights will use the widened lines through Farringdon, for destinations south of the Thames. On the lower level (the fast lines on the model), can be observed the crack expresses and inner and outer suburban

The classic scene under the cenotaph coaling tower at Top Shed sees Class A4, 4482 *Golden Eagle* taking fuel on board ready for its next run north. The loco is representative of one of the general-purpose A4s, introduced in 1936/'37, finished in the standard LNER express passenger (lined apple green) livery of the time, and is a much-modified Bachmann product. In the centre left background, behind the shed, can be made out the top of the water-softening tower, and in the right background St Pancras gasworks dominates the horizon. Cliff himself built the coaler - urban 'scenic' modelling at its best!

BELOW: One of the earlier shots (taken five years ago) replicates the scene looking underneath the flyover at the foot of Holloway Bank, with a brand new V4, No. 3402 in the guise of 'Bantam Hen' heading a running-in turn back to Doncaster as a Gresley A1 heads for Leeds on the first leg of the 'Queen of Scots' Pullman's journey to Glasgow Queen Street.

RIGHT: The same scene at a higher angle showing the area around the signal box substantially complete. How this superb 'grassy'/foliage effect was achieved was fully described in the October '09 edition of *BRM*. One of the 'Coronation' A4s (still minus Class A headlamps, Rupert!) heads the train of the same name on its late-afternoon journey to Edinburgh Waverley, first stop Newcastle.

Gresley Beat Track plan

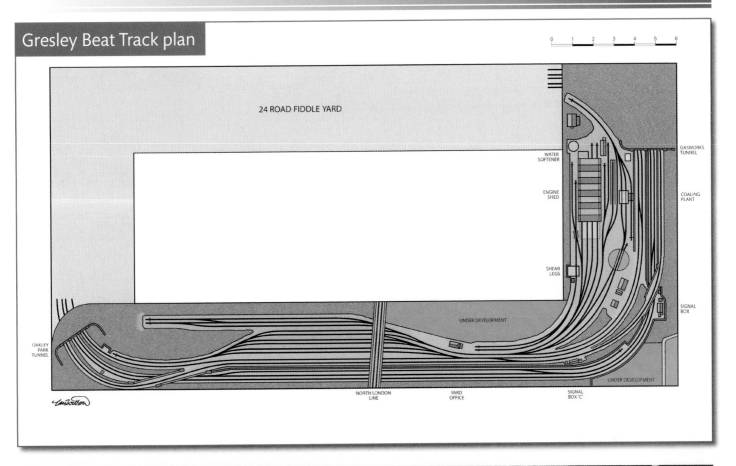

24 ROAD FIDDLE YARD

WATER SOFTENER

ENGINE SHED

SHEAR LEGS

GASWORKS TUNNEL

COALING PLANT

SIGNAL BOX

UNDER DEVELOPMENT

OAKLEY PARK TUNNEL

NORTH LONDON LINE

YARD OFFICE

UNDER DEVELOPMENT

SIGNAL BOX 'C'

ABOVE: We're adjacent to the North London Line's overbridge here with a heavily-weathered Bachmann K3 overtaking one of the pair of P1s (part scratch-built) as both head south (the K3's destination being King's Cross itself, and the P1, King's Cross Goods and Mineral. The 2-6-0 is on the Up Leeds TPO set (built by Steve Banks), and the P1 on one of the heavy coal trains that attempted to feed the capital's insatiable appetite for the stuff.

BELOW: Scenic work is almost complete in this area now (picture taken in August this year) as we view the north portals of Gasworks Tunnel, the ridge pierced (as through the nearby Copenhagen tunnel) at different levels. A J50 and N2 head back to the 'Cross for their next duties as an Ivatt 'Long Tom' plods northwards with returning mineral empties from Goods and Mineral.

ABOVE: Brian Longhurst's superb Cemetary Station dominates this scene as an 02/2 prepares to go on shed. 'Grassing' has now been fully accomplished in the foreground, and the jig-built telegraph poles are so appropriate to the environment. The actual funeral building lasted but a short time in its intended role, latterly being used for many years a furniture store, before demolition in the early '60s. The stained glass windows are illuminated for effect.

BELOW: A similar scene to that opposite, but taken five years ago, and included for comparative purposes. Yes, it's the same 'Long Tom' still plodding on but through a scene devoid of finished grass and even the beginnings of the gasworks. What it also shows is the amount of time needed to fully finish individual areas on a model of this size, and isn't it nice to see the loco now carrying a headlamp?

Another of the general-purpose A4s, this time 4493 *Woodcock* is turned on the 70' vacuum-operated 'table at Top Shed. The quality of Geoff Taylor's buildings is axiomatic, and the general air of dirt and grime has been captured perfectly.

Looking along the full stretch of the longer scenic side we observe the Up 'Flying Scotsman' on the last lap of its near-400 mile journey from Scotland. The yards are strangely empty (I arrived earlier for photography than Cliff's team expected), though it does give a full impression of how much has already been achieved. Compare this scene with the one opposite, top.

ABOVE: Taken in 2004, this view is also included to show for comparative purposes the enormous amount of progress made since the layout first appeared on the exhibition circuit. The Necropolis station is a bit more than a shell, but many parts of this large overall area are just just beginning in terms of scenics. That said, right from the start, for exhibition use, The Gresley Beat has been fully operational and has always provided full value for punters.

BELOW: One of my favourite 'Beat pictures, and there's not even a train in sight. One almost expects Mrs Wilberforce to appear around the corner, followed by the Ladykillers, all of the Guiness gang with murder in mind! Yes, I know the famous Ealing film dates from the '50s but the scene is so much the same. Geoff Taylor's building fit in so well, one is almost 'there', looking south towards a distant Top Shed with its definitive structures, through some typical ex-GNR somersault signals. The gas lamps, period vehicles, walls, fencing and retaining walls are captured to perfection. Everything is so subtle and delightfully observed. Nothing is overstated or 'out of place' and colours are so naturally muted to the extent that this view should really be in black and white. It's wonderful!

services. Expresses modelled include the 'Coronation', 'Silver Jubilee', 'Flying Scotsman', Leeds quin set, Leeds TPO and the 'Queen of Scots', all in their delightful liveries of varnished teak, two-tone blue, silver/grey, as well as the green/cream found on the tourist stock.

On the shorter viewing side can be observed trains passing through Gasworks tunnel (with Regents Canal and the gasworks on top). These will include empty stock, the long-distance expresses, empties returning north and fast freights from King's Cross Goods and Mineral, including the Scotch Goods. There are also many light-engine movements to and from Top Shed, in and out of the 'Cross. The slightly 'potted' Top Shed is faithfully modelled, including the famous depot master's house, complete with Ivatt Atlantic weather vane on the roof.

An amalgamation of York Way and the North London Line's bridges form a natural divide between the capital's urban grime and the leafy, outer suburbs, the latter still representing 'work in progress'. To the south of the bridges can be seen the lugubrious 'Necropolis' station, provided originally as the starting point for the final journey of the dead and their bereaved relations/ friends to the new cemetary near Barnet.

I'm told that the baseboards are constructed from 6mm ply, giving an overall dimension of 30' x 15'. Two sides of this rectangle are modelled for viewing, though the fiddle yard deserves to be seen 'in the round' so to speak. SMP trackwork has been used on the scenic sections, with the ever-reliable Peco employed in the fiddle yard.

Stock is mainly kit-built, though with the ever-improving standard available from the likes of Bachmann and Hornby, the need to build locos, coaches and wagons has diminished. However, the more specialist types not available RTR have to be provided *via* kits or scratch-building. The pictures should show where what and which have been employed.

Cliff Parsons, though without doubt the inspiration behind The Gresley Beat, will be the first to admit to the help he's had with this enormous project. As well as his regular 'team' - Derek, Brian, Barbara, Len, Malcolm, Rupert, Roger (of The Who fame), etc, - Cliff has called on the services of some of the top professional model-makers to provide some of the stock (Steve Banks), some of the buildings (Geoff Taylor) and the signals (Mick Nicholson). But this layout is certainly not the product of 'cheque book modelling'. Cliff's successful business has allowed him the 'luxury' of being able to commission work from those professional already mentioned, but the majority has been built by him and his friends.

ABOVE: An Eric Treacy-style view observed from the top of Gasworks Tunnel as the unique W1 'Hush Hush' 4-6-2-2 heads an Up express through the 'trough' at Cliff's Belle Isle. Above, a J39 heads for Goods and Mineral or the widened lines with goods for south of the river.

BOTTOM LEFT: The Regents canal 'flows' above Gasworks Tunnel and was important to the railway as a source of locomotive water for Top Shed. The gasworks' construction is well on the way, and the vegetation is now complete.

All of this has been 12 years in the making so far, with a few more years needed before it's fully completed. By then, The Gresley Beat will have done so many shows as to have earned a well-deserved retirement. Don't worry as to eventually never being able to see it again, for it's Cliff's wish to finally see a museum trust devoted to model railways and railway preservation, based at his premises in Kent. The Beat will be one of the principal exhibits.

Finally, I hope my pictures have done justice to this wonderful layout. As said, this is a pictorial tribute, and I hope the extended captions fill in any gaps in my narrative. My thanks are particularly due to Cliff and his team for all the help given to me on the numerous occasions it's been my delight to take pictures of The Gresley Beat.

By 1968 steam was confined to the north west of England – mainly Lancashire - so I had a few days out in Manchester over the spring and summer. Unique to Patricroft shed and working into Manchester Exchange were Caprotti Standard Class 5s. My brother and I took a trip out to Patricroft and found 73143 in the platform of the station, minus all plates but with plenty of added dirt! Sad and depressing – but great days for me!

MEMORIES are made of this!

Is your modelling influenced by childhood memories? John Cockcroft asks the question and also took the photographs.

I am old enough to remember steam trains! As a small child I can remember being lifted up onto the footplate of a huge LNER pacific at Leeds Central station, and riding on a train on the last day of services on the Queensbury Lines on May 21, 1955! I was only four and illiterate and neither my family or any of my relations were railway enthusiasts. I remember going on holiday to Torquay in 1959 and collecting engine numbers for novelty because unlike at Leeds it was immediately obvious which engines were green - because they were so clean and had polished brass cab window frames and number plates on the cab sides! I went to the Isle of Wight with my parents in 1966 to see the last summer of the O2 tank locos pulling pre-Grouping carriages.

By 1966 I was interested in trains, but had to pick up all I knew from magazines and books because I was not in a club nor was anyone else I knew interested in trains. By the time I became able to consider myself 'at home' in the railway world, Beeching had hacked out most of the interesting secondary and branch lines, and wherever you looked sidings were being ripped up, stations torn down and, worst of all, steam locomotives withdrawn and scrapped at a frantic rate, to be replaced by horrid bland green boxes or railcars. I took lots of photos of the sad decline of steam in 1967 and 1968 and some of my happiest memories are of shed visits and days out to Manchester to see the last bastions of proper railways. It was all very sad.

Someone else's personal memories are actually rather boring and so you must forgive my rambling on about mine. I do it because my experiences and the attitudes they form have a strong, but not exclusive, influence on the things that I am interested in now. Reading many articles in *British Railway Modelling* I conclude that many of the people who have built model railways are also strongly affected by their early memories, and the popularity of models of the last decade of steam is evidenced by the numbers of ready-to-run models of that period produced by the two main manufacturers. So what we remember has some influence on what models we want to make or own. This in turn leads onto the well aired anxiety that our hobby is doomed to decline and fade as the generation that last knew the old steam railway pass from the scene themselves.

What do people who are in their early 40s and younger think? Are they exclusively interested in blue or multi-coloured diesels

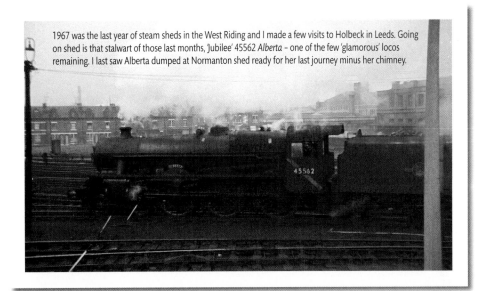
1967 was the last year of steam sheds in the West Riding and I made a few visits to Holbeck in Leeds. Going on shed is that stalwart of those last months, 'Jubilee' 45562 *Alberta* - one of the few 'glamorous' locos remaining. I last saw Alberta dumped at Normanton shed ready for her last journey minus her chimney.

Skipton Shed 1967 - two withdrawn 'Jinties' dumped by the coal stage.

Getting off the train at Manchester Victoria in mid 1968 I was confronted by these two 'Black Fives' in the through roads - the 'Wallside bankers' assisted freight trains up the gradient to Miles Platting. The ugly wooden screen, a trade mark of Victoria, dated from the war when a bomb blew up some of the train shed.

In the summer holidays of 1967 I was encouraged by bolder spirits than I to scale a wall at the back of Holbeck shed in Leeds. As it turned out no one cared about schoolboys sneaking about amongst the locos - it was all doomed anyway and trespassers were like an endless tide. What a place it was with its broken roof and streaming sunlight - I will never forget it and will always be glad of that day.

and electrics running on a 'basic' railway? The real truth is that though modern railways are fast and pretty efficient, they are not really visually interesting and don't seem to do much other than glide into stations and out again. There is no shunting or splitting trains into portions or even many excursions or specials. Though there is a massive variety of liveries they are 'designed' to the point of irrelevance. Are they the food of memory and sentimental reverie of the future?

Personally speaking, I can think of nothing more depressing than modelling such a negative period of railway history than the

1960s – even though I have my most clear and happy memories of that period insofar as steam trains are concerned. Nor have I a sentiment for the trains that took me to university and into the adventures of my 20s – blue bull-nosed 'Peaks' or dead pan Brush Type 4s pulling slab-sided bland blue and grey carriages - I got a car as soon as I could!

I prefer to go back to a time when I have no personal memories and the things that I saw being destroyed were in their vibrant prime! When you could go almost anywhere by train, and that train would be pulled by a different type of engine wherever you

happened to be in the country. Of course the main indicators of the quality of life were in almost every respect worse than now and no one would be more terrified than me if I suddenly found myself trapped in the 1920s! But you see I model things that in my illogical and totally whimsical hobby world I can take at face value – because that's what I want to do. I am of course influenced by my experiences and the things I saw about me when I was young though not in a direct way.

Though I am mindful that this all sounds dead introverted and self-indulgent, I really

Steam ended in the West Riding in the autumn of 1967 but some workings from the north-west still brought proper locos over the border. This is the oil train from Heysham that used to come through in the mid afternoon with a 9F pushing some box or other at Shipley, where I happened to be looking round the station one day and was in the right place to get a shot as the 9F took the south side of the triangle.

haven't got anyone else to experiment with and of course your modelling interests and their origins are much more interesting to you – but are they the same in some ways? So the point of this short piece is to stimulate a discussion and perhaps a survey of what people like to model and how it is influenced by their memories and experiences. Because if the only things that the majority of people like to model are the things they remember then it is probable that the hobby will move away from steam era models. Also, because of the great interest in train spotting in the 1950s and '60s compared to the interests of young people today, there will be a decline in the numbers taking up the hobby.

Or will many modellers take up the hobby as an exercise in historical sentiment and make models of any period from 1830 to 1968 or even later? Is personal memory the vital driver as opposed to other stimulations and influences – perhaps occurring later in life? Is a general interest in history a good start? Or a desire to be creative or make things work? Or a need to take up something that is technically challenging? What influence do preserved railways or memorabilia have?

Why is it that so few women are interested in making model railways? Is the creation of a miniature world in which you are the lord of all things a frustrated outlet for megalomaniacs and control freaks? Why did you become interested? Why do you model what you do? Why not let us know?

By the last year of steam the variety of locos was pretty limited, mainly confined to 'Black Fives', 8Fs, 9Fs, 'Austerity' 2-8-0s and a few standards. At Skipton in 1967 I caught 8F No.48773 still with a smokebox number plate and yellow cabside stripe indicating it was banned from under the wires of the West Coast main line. Not a bad view for modellers as it shows footplate detail really well.

One of the 'Black Fives' in the earlier photo moved off and I got this view of No.44809 by the wooden screen at Manchester Victoria. Obviously some patch-up work had been done on the smokebox because that is the nearest thing in all these photos to a clean loco. Anyone want to model this odd looking weathering pattern?

Easter 1967; I cycled to Skipton to take photos of locos around the shed which was accessible from a road alongside without trespassing. Unfortunately I was not used to the light meter on my new camera which registered the sky and not the locomotives - resulting in silhouettes! However, dumped by the old coaling stage were two withdrawn 'Jinties' and I took the photo looking down from the wall top with no sky – the only usable photos for a 40 mile bike trip. That taught me!

In the early months of 1968 I went for an interview at a teacher training college near Preston and travelled by train – making something of a meal of the day with a long stop at Preston. The station pilot was this Ivatt 4MT 2-6-0 with an LMS goods brake van.

A bright sunny day in Manchester! Conditions were ideal for taking locomotive photos on our visit to Patricroft shed, and here is another shot of a Caprotti Standard Class 5, this time 73133. No one challenged our trespass and everything was almost eerily quiet. The smell of ash, oil and steam will always remain with me - but I would model the shed in 1923 with LNWR locos catching the sun and LMS standard locos yet to come and no thought of diesels to spoil the illusion!

I sometimes walked the three miles to Bingley in the hope of catching the Heysham oil train passing through in 1968. To the west of the station was a wooden crossing which offered an excellent place to photograph trains. My dislike of diesels was refined and purified during the 1960s -partly why I like to go back before they ever polluted any part of my ideal model railway world!

An overall view of the layout showing the window style box design of the light box and supports.

TERRIFIC TRI-ANG HORNBY

Richard Deas tells the story behind his collection and the subsequent layout it inspired.

Although I didn't realise it at the time, a single Christmas present I received in the mid-1960s set my life on a path I am still following to this day. Santa brought me a train set and that was the moment my interest in both model and full-sized railways started. I was around seven or eight years old at the time, but I can still remember the joy of unwrapping the package and the realisation of its contents. It was in fact a Tri-ang Railways RS.29 Holiday Express Train Set, which contained a B12 locomotive, two Mk.1 crimson and cream coaches and an oval of Super 4 track. Dad, who was a cabinetmaker, had made a 5' 0" x

2' 6" purpose-built baseboard with folding legs. Over the next few months a few small accessories were added as money permitted, then for my birthday the following June, my parents bought me a green R.152 diesel shunter.

The following years saw a slow but steady growth in my train set and I can remember saving my pocket money for many months to buy a third locomotive from our local Co-op, which at that time had a large model railway department. This loco, a Tri-ang Hornby R.59 2-6-2 3MT, was cherished for many years. This was a time when money was tight and if you wanted something you had to save up for it. This encouraged

you to look after your toys; a habit that has stayed with me all of my life. At that time we lived around 100 yards from the East Coast Main Line in Retford and when I was 12, we moved house. Much to my delight, our new residence was even nearer to the ECML with our rear boundary fence backing directly onto the former goods yard in Babworth Road. Even better, there was enough room in the garden for a shed. After a few months, my Dad had cleared out the 10' x 6' timber shed and my model railway now had a permanent home for the first time.

My model railway continued to expand, with the addition of further locomotives, rolling stock and track. All of these items

were purchased from the pages of the Tri-ang Hornby catalogues of the day, and I can still remember the excitement as the date for the publication of the next year's edition approached. These catalogues included all of the inspiration required to sustain a young boy's interest in what was then a very popular hobby. My best school friend during this period was Stephen Searson, and we would spend alternate Saturdays in each other's shed, playing trains. Over the years, we expanded and honed our modelling skills, eventually building kits and modifying ready-to-run locomotives into classes that weren't otherwise available.

During the early '70s, my modelling interest changed direction and I started modelling in N gauge. A slow change of gauge eventually saw the last of my OO gauge equipment part-exchanged for the smaller scale models. Over the next 30 years, I produced three large N gauge exhibition layouts, Littleton, Littleborough and finally Littlewood. All appeared in the *Railway Modeller* and at many, many model railway exhibitions all over the country.

An unexpected encounter changed the direction of my hobby yet again in 2001. We were on a railway club trip to Crewe Works and on the way, our coach called at the Brookfield Garden Centre. Now, this is no ordinary Garden Centre as it contains a large narrow gauge steam railway and a model shop. Whilst browsing around the shop I found a Tri-ang R.59 2-6-2 tank locomotive in excellent condition. I simply couldn't resist

it and handed over the cash immediately. My fellow club members and my wife Christine thought I had gone mad. Although I didn't realise it at the time, this loco was to be the start of my resurgent interest in the Tri-ang Hornby era. A few months later, while we were on holiday in the West Country, I found a Tri-ang Hornby *Flying Scotsman* and a few Super 4 series points in a model shop. The memories flooded back and I decided to start collecting in earnest. What surprised me the most were the memories evoked by the actual smell of the locomotives. The aroma of a warm X04 motor or heated smoke oil has the power to transport you back in time. Over the next few years I visited local swap meets and spent many hours on the Internet searching for more items for my collection. Without doubt, the best source of collectable model railway items is eBay; over 60% of my collection has been obtained from this online auction site. It's not always the cheapest, but you can get almost anything there if you are prepared to be patient.

As I gathered more items, I realised that there was more to collecting than just the models themselves. The history of the company and the stories behind the products are equally fascinating. One book in particular has proved to be an invaluable source of information. *The Story of Rovex, Volume 2 1965-1971* by Pat Hammond is a mine of information. Covering all aspects of the Tri-ang Hornby brand, including extensive product descriptions and the story behind the company, this book is an absolute must

for anyone interested in this particular era of model railway manufacturing in the UK.

The Tri-ang Hornby name emerged following the acquisition of Meccano Ltd (owners of Hornby-Dublo) by Lines Bros Ltd (owners of Tri-ang Railways) in 1964. Some of the former Hornby-Dublo models did appear in Tri-ang Hornby catalogues, these locomotives and wagons being marketed under the name Tri-ang Wrenn. During this period, apart from the Tri-ang Wrenn items, all of the products were produced in the Tri-ang Hornby factory at Margate in Kent. This arrangement continued until Lines Bros Ltd itself failed during August 1971. Dunbee-Combex-Marx acquired the whole business and dropped the name Tri-ang to create Hornby Railways.

In 2004, I realised that sufficient items had been acquired to make a reasonable display layout and decided to create my fourth exhibition layout. This one, however, would be a total departure from my previous three exhibition model railways. This would be a collection layout and I wanted it to display many of the items I remember seeing in the Tri-ang Hornby catalogues between 1965 and 1972 but could not afford at the time. From its conception, I wanted to create the feeling of the period and display the models without the distraction of scenery. It was therefore decided to build a quite basic train set, the type of layout to which any young enthusiast of the period would have aspired. The layout is constructed on three 4' 0" x 3' 6" plywood baseboards making a

The 'Battle Space' train is always of interest at exhibitions. This comprises a Sniper Car with ducking sniper, satellite launching car with flying satellite, the large bomb carrier, searchlight wagon with working searchlight, and the red exploding wagon which actually explodes. What more could a small boy want?

General view of the station area.

total size of 10' 6" x 4' 0". Each baseboard is covered with ¹⁄₁₆" thick cork sheet to give a good surface upon which to lay the track. The two outer baseboards are supported on separate cross-braced trestles and the third, central unit is supported from the two outer baseboards. The perimeter of the layout is fitted with an edging strip made from ¼" plywood and on the front there is a light box to illuminate the railway. To make the layout stand out at a show, I decided to recreate the distinctive look of a Tri-ang Hornby window box on the front of the layout. To achieve this, the shape of the window, complete with all of the curves was cut from ¼" plywood and painted with colour matched red paint complete with the yellow perimeter stripe and Tri-ang Hornby logo. Of course, being portable, the light box has to split into manageable sections and be capable of easy assembly at an exhibition. The layout is painted in the colours of the Tri-ang Hornby boxes of the period. The exterior of the box is red with yellow highlights, while the inside is yellow, similar to the box interior packaging.

During the Tri-ang Hornby period the track changed from Super 4 to System 6, don't ask me why there was no '5', there just wasn't. All of the track used on the layout is Super 4 with steel rails. To be honest, I really like this old track; it was the first to use the 'standard' geometry that we still use to this day. It is solid and reliable enough to be set up and taken apart many times and yet it still looks very good. Indeed the sleeper spacing is more to scale than the modern track produced today. The main problem is finding good quality examples of Super 4 as rust has taken its toll of the steel rails over the years. Steel was used for the rails so that locomotives fitted with Magnadhesion could haul longer trains. The chassis on these locomotives were equipped with

The engine shed area with the 75 Ton breakdown crane in the siding. Originally part of the Hornby-Dublo range, this Co-Bo diesel, can be included in my collection by virtue of a Tri-ang Hornby sticker on the old Hornby-Dublo box.

magnets, which acted through the wheels to the steel track. This effectively increased the weight of the relatively light plastic-bodied locomotive, greatly improving its haulage capacity. I was lucky to find a job lot of good quality track at a swapmeet in Doncaster a few years ago and this has formed the basis of this layout. All of the points are electrified using the appropriate surface mounting point motors. These clip on to the side of the point, so that when laid on carpet, as was often the case, the young modeller did not need to dig a hole in the Axminster. To improve the reliability of the control of the trains, I have used modern transistorised controllers and push button switches on a separate control panel to operate points. The point motor circuit is also fitted with a CDU, which improves reliability and eliminates any possibility of burning out one of the point motors. At the back of the layout is a three-tiered display unit upon which I can display a large selection of locomotives and rolling stock. Below the display unit are the automatic exchange sidings, three on the inside and two on the outside track. The loops on the outside track are split into two sections; so four trains can be operated on that track. These automatically change the train every time they disappear around the back, ensuring that there is always something new to see. I try to run the trains in the formation they appeared either in the boxed train sets or the images in the catalogues. Over the past few years the layout has been exhibited at quite a few events, some collectors events and some model railway exhibitions. I must say that the response from visitors has been very positive,

Stephenson's *Rocket* locomotive and period coaches was an attractive and unusual part of the Tri-ang Hornby range until 1969. Although small, its specification included 'Magnadhesion' and smoke.

especially at traditional model railway shows. At a recent show, I spent almost the whole of the event chatting to visitors, sharing memories and information. Many say that they used to have 'this' or 'that' as a kid and point out the models which were part of their childhood. Some even say they still have their old trains in boxes in the loft. The feedback at shows is very encouraging and proves to me that I am not the only one for whom the models from Margate formed an integral part of growing up.

The locomotives, which if I were honest, are my main passion, are the heart of any model railway and this collection is no exception. I have tried to collect as many of

the ones I either had as a child or wanted, but could not afford. So, of course there is a B12, a 08 diesel shunter and a 3MT tank loco together with as many of the rest of the range as I can find. I have even managed to purchase some of the Tri-ang Wrenn range, which as a child, were far outside the range of my pocket money. The Tri-ang Hornby range of models was designed to be played with, and most were; sometimes to the point of destruction. The majority of the production was injection moulded plastic, so a fall onto the floor could sometimes spell the end for a model. So although many items were produced in vast quantities over the years, surprisingly few survive in 'mint

The station area with a Class 3F tender locomotive at the head of 'The Midlander'.
The display unit over the fiddle yards is visible along the back.

boxed' condition. Most of my collection is in good running condition as I am a firm believer that these models should be enjoyed for what they are, working models. I must admit that I have been amazed by the quality and reliability of the models produced at Margate. I have not yet found any loco that can't be brought back to life with only a small amount of TLC and a few spare parts. Don't forget that most locomotives on the layout are around 40 years old and they still run as well as they did when they left the factory. I wonder if in four decades time, we will be able to say the same about the models we purchase today? The range of models produced at Margate was vast and included many working accessories, which had great play value. Items like the Royal Mail coach, which collects and delivers mailbags, electric turntable and giraffe car, where the giraffe automatically ducks down to avoid overhead obstructions, still fascinate the observer. Some locomotives even had smoke and a 'chuff-chuff' noise. One item which always catches the eye is the Battle Space Turbo Car. A large motor connected directly to a big yellow fan at the rear powers this unusual vehicle. A streamlined futuristic bright red plastic body with a yellow point at the front covers the four-wheel freewheeling chassis. Applying power causes the propeller to spin and the car to move forward at high speed. Unsurprisingly, very few have survived in good condition, as high-speed derailments and visits to the floor would have resulted in a high mortality rate. I suppose such a model could not be produced today, as it would fall foul of modern health and safety regulations. In a time before the batch production we see today, a model could

remain in production for many years and in some instances decades. The original 'Princess' for example, was produced for over 20 years - originally made by Tri-ang, then Tri-ang Hornby and later Hornby Railways. During this period the locomotive was continually refined and developed until it was finally replaced by a totally new version of the same prototype. Toward the end of the Tri-ang Hornby era, locomotives like the 9F pointed the way to the future with their finer scale wheels and more accurate appearance. Indeed so good was this loco that it remained in production well into the new millennium.

Another thing I like about these old models is the fact that in many ways, the young owner was encouraged to do his own maintenance and repairs. Manuals about care and operation were included with each model and service sheets were available to explain the construction. There was even a range of CKD (Completely Knocked Down) kits available. These included all of the parts required to assemble your own locomotive or coach, all you needed was a screwdriver and even this was in the kit. All of these innovations encouraged the owners to become aware of how things worked and how to repair them when they didn't. These basic skills are part of the basic building blocks of childhood and can help you in later life either in the home or work environment.

In collecting these models I have realised that although thought by some as simply 'playing with trains', there is far more to it than that. I think that when you get to a certain age, you begin to reflect on a time when life was simpler (and better?); the summers were always sunny; the snow fell in the winter and you bought your gas from the

gas board and electricity from the electricity board. It's a way of turning the clock back to the happy, carefree days of childhood. I suppose my recently acquired rose-tinted glasses may help. It's sort of a mid-life crisis, some buy a sports car, some a motorbike, for me it was toy trains. Whilst in almost every way, today's models are far more detailed and accurate, they somehow don't seem to have the charm of the products of the Tri-ang Hornby era. Looking back at the range today, you really appreciate the quality of the design. These models were obviously built to a price, but their design and construction was very ingenious, simple and effective. What's more, they still work very well today, long after their projected lifespan. Ideas such as 'Magnadhesion', smoke units, steam sound and the vast range of working accessories are an essay in good design practice.

Whilst on holiday in Kent a couple of years ago, we visited the former purpose-built Tri-ang factory in Margate. Although it appears the same from the outside as it did when it was built, inside it is little more than a warehouse, distributing the current Hornby range which, like so many things these days, is now made in China. This is a far cry from the time when, so proud of the facility in which the models were produced, Tri-ang organised factory tours so that visitors could see the manufacturing process from raw materials to finished models. As a draughtsman, I would have particularly enjoyed the tour of the drawing office. There was also an excellent service department where damaged items could be sent for repair. This was a time when after-sales service was paramount and great pride was taken in keeping the trains running and the customers happy, a philosophy which, at least Hornby, still retain.

Anyone interested in these models should consider joining the Tri-ang Society. They are a very friendly club and have members

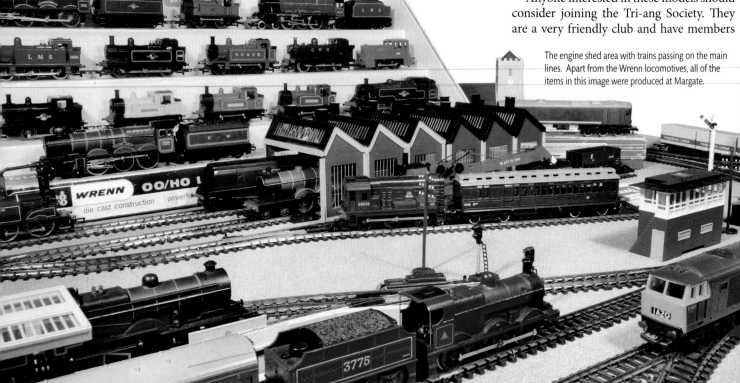

The engine shed area with trains passing on the main lines. Apart from the Wrenn locomotives, all of the items in this image were produced at Margate.

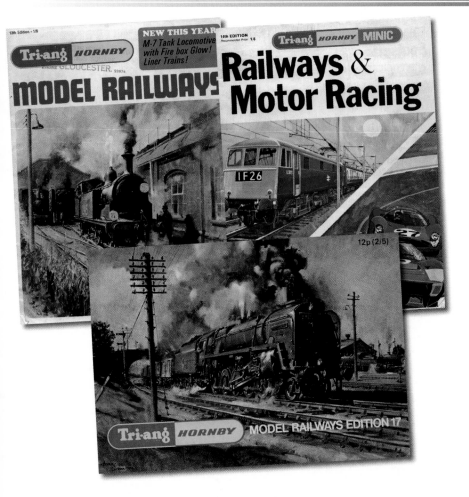

BUILDING THE HORNBY BRAND

1951 Lines Brothers buy Rovex Plastics Ltd, producers of Rovex Scale Models trains - move to purpose-built factory at Margate

1952 Rebranded Tri-ang Railways

1958 Acquire Mini Models (introduced Scalextric in 1952)

1964 Acquire Hornby-Dublo after collapse of Meccano

1965 Taken over by Lines Bros (parent company of Rovex Scale Models), renamed Tri-ang Hornby

1967 Some Hornby-Dublo tooling acquired by G&R Wrenn Ltd (subsidiary of Lines Bros) - becomes Tri-ang Wrenn

1971 Tri-ang Group collapses - Rovex Tri-ang acquired by Dunbee Combex Marx

1972 Rebranded Hornby Railways

1976 Rebranded Hornby Hobbies

1980 Management buy-out from Dunbee Combex Marx - rebranded Hornby Hobbies Ltd

c.1997 Rebranded Hornby plc

2004 Acquire Spanish manufacturer Electrotren in £5.3m deal

Acquire Lima group (including Rivarossi, Jouef, Arnold and Pocher) for £6.3m to form new Hornby International brand

2006 Acquire German scenic manufacturer Heico Modell for £135,000 - rebranded Hornby Deutschland

2008 Acquire Airfix and Humbrol in £2.6m deal

Acquire Corgi (including Bassett-Lowke) for £8.3m

Hong Kong based Kader Manufacturing Trust (owners of Bachmann, Graham Farish and Lilliput) acquire Sanda Kan Industrial - Sanda Kan factories produce model trains for Athearn, Atlas, Life-Like, Lionel, Märklin, Walthers and Hornby

2009 Attempt to recreate Barnstaple to Bideford line with 'Top Gear' presenter James May disrupted by vandals dropping 2p pieces on track and stealing batteries - a record breaking ten miles of Hornby track laid!

who specialise in the products of the Tri-ang factory including the short-lived TT railway system and even the O gauge 'Big Big' trains. Creating my collection, and building and exhibiting the layout have given me many hours of pleasure and during the process I have made many friends. What more can you ask for from a hobby? For a further look at the layout visit: www.trianghornby.net.

Useful addresses
■ **The Tri-ang Society**
PO Box 226, Sale, Manchester M33 4XY
www.tri-angsociety.co.uk

Record breakers – more than 300 railway enthusiasts gathered to recreate the disused railway line between Barnstaple-Bideford on August 27, 2009, using three pallets of Hornby track! 'Top Gear' presenter James May filmed the feat for his new series 'James May's Toy Stories'. Despite attempts to disrupt the project, ten miles of track was laid on the Tarka trail. James May (standing) looks on as Hornby's Simon Kohler and his team lay track at 'Barnstaple Junction'.

TEES-SIDE DIESELS

Steel, mineral and chemical traffic has kept a variety of diesels at work on Tees-side for many years. **Nigel Burkin** presents a selection of images taken around the River Tees, from Sectorisation to the present day.

Tees-side is rich in modelling opportunities if industrial modelling, particularly modern heavy industry, is your thing. With the Durham coal fields to hand, a deep water estuary for shipping, a chemical industry based on petrochemicals and the mining of anhydrous minerals such as rock salt, anhydrite, gypsum and other associated minerals, Tees-side soon became an important industrial base with many top companies located there.

Rail traffic became dominated by the large Dorman Long steel complex at Redcar, east of Middlesbrough which has despatched huge quantities of semi-finished steel products during its operational life time. The complex, adjacent to Teesport, is huge with a great network of internal railways for the movement of slag, molten metal and steel for various finishing processes. BR and latterly EWS has been heavily involved in the rail movements associated with this works including inter-works flows to Skinningrove on the Boulby line south and east of Saltburn, the pipe mill at Hartlepool, the former, now closed, rail mill at Workington and steel for Scotland to mention a few.

The adjacent port takes deliveries of minerals for export from the nearby Boulby potash mine which is transported in covered hoppers, which in the past included the 'green giants' and a variety of hoppers taken from other flows until they fell apart from corrosion. Many redundant hopper wagons and containers ended their days on this traffic.

Chemical traffic originates from all over the various chemical plants on both sides of the river estuary: Wilton on the south bank

A general view of Tees Yard and the depot buildings taken on December 20, 1995. Present in the yard was a train of chemical tank wagons including Distillers carbon dioxide tanks, 56 111 in Load haul livery with potash hoppers and an unidentified Class 56 facing the opposite direction with more covered hoppers used on the potash circuit. Tees Yard remains a very busy location today although you should pick your time and day to make a visit!

together with Seal Sands, Port Clarence and Billingham Haverton Hill on the north have all despatched anything from single tank wagon loads to block trains. The large storage facilities at Seal Sands often saw block trains of tanks with 'spot traffic' flows, one-offs which were real bonuses to find when out taking photographs because some of these locations may not see rail movements for many days. Chemical traffic could include nasties such as hydrocyanic acid traffic, lesser hazards such as carbon dioxide and a whole host of things like chlorides, caustics and petrochemicals. The variety was huge but not being an industrial chemist, knowing the exact nature of some loads is outside my knowledge.

Today, the bulk of chemical traffic is transported in container tanks or containers fitted with internal bags for the carriage of powders and pellets. Such containers include the 30' IFF, UBC and IBC 'Bulktainers' for which a kit is available in 4mm scale. The bulk tank trains are rarer now, although

Bringing the story up to date is this view of EWS 66 002 *Lafarge Quorn* hauling a train of chemical 'Bulktainers' into Tees Yard from the Middlesbrough direction on January 30, 2009. The yard behind the locomotive is used for the marshalling and storage of wagons awaiting their next assignment. EWS/DBS has much more minimalist servicing facilities at this location resulting from the closure of Thornaby depot.

Class 47s were common motive power for chemical traffic and Freightliner trains in the Sectorisation era. 47 361, photographed between duties at Thornaby on September 24, 1989, was a regular in the area, being based at Thornaby (note the Kingfisher logo). The name *Wilton Endeavour* was associated with the area.

Metals Sector allocated 37 202 was also present on the depot at Thornaby on September 24, 1989. Class 60s were still on the drawing board at this time!

Block steel trains were dominated by Class 37s which had been subject to heavy general repair in the 1980s. Class 37/5 locomotives were a common sight around Tees-side and on block steel trains working from the area. In a line were 37 503, 37 512, 37 667 and 37 668 at Thornaby on September 24, 1989.

One location that would make the basis of an interesting layout is Belasis Lane at Billingham on the north side of the river. A sprinkling of snow lies on the ground in January 1996 as 56 033 with Transrail badges gains the double track section opposite the signal box with a short train of chemical tank wagons.

Philips petroleum still operates block trains of petroleum from Port Clarence.

To round up this summary, mention should be made of the Railfreight Terminals at Middlesbrough Goods which see deliveries of various freight traffics including road salt, steel and anything else that may be handled by Dawsons and Cobra Railfreight. Unfortunately, the Castle Cement terminal on the site is no longer served by rail. Freightliner has a container terminal on the Wilton site which sees regular trains. Many chemical flows now utilise this service together with container services operated by EWS/DBS. Scrap traffic originates from Thompsons at Stockton whilst limestone is delivered to the steel plant at Redcar from Hardendale Quarry and previously Redmire in North Yorkshire.

Such a broad, if sometimes infrequent traffic base has seen a wide variety of locomotives based in the area together with an interesting selection of visiting locomotives on a day-to-day basis. The basic traffic patterns amounts to local trip workings operating from the Tees Yard hub, being marshalled and laid over in the main yard until departure time is reached. Block trains were not remarshalled in Tees Yard; in effect, passing through or simply being held in the yard until departure time. Most departures and arrivals were during the late afternoon and evening for overnight runs, some of them quite long distance trains going as far as South Wales. Whilst Thornaby depot was an important location for locomotive overhaul and maintenance, it's now a shadow of its former self given that the freight flows are divided between several companies with maintenance facilities elsewhere.

When I lived in the Durham area between 1988 and 1995, I chased trains around the Tees-side industrial complexes whenever I could. I was fortunate enough to catch some unusual or infrequent workings, some of which are presented here. I do wonder why the Tees-side area has not attracted more modellers than it has because there are some fascinating locations and the variety of wagons that could be modelled is pretty vast. Such locations worthy of models would be Belasis Lane at Billingham, Saltburn with its branch off to Boulby, Seal Sands and the Railfreight terminals at Middlesbrough Goods - all offer opportunities. Some tank wagons and covered hopper wagons would have to be scratch-built or cross-kitted whilst steel traffic enthusiasts will be able to build a fleet of BAA and BBAs using plastic kits from Cambrian. BDAs and BYAs are available from Bachmann.

Tees-side is a little appreciated area for freight and worthy of more investigation to look at its modelling potential.

Two Class 37s, with 37 358 leading, haul an empty potash train away from Tees Port bound for the mine at Boulby in February 1995. The trains consists of 'Green Giant' bogie covered hoppers. The Redcar steel making complex in the background is unmistakable!

Shunting engines found employment in Tees Yard and at the surrounding terminals and chemical sites. In September 1989, Class 08 shunter No.08 770 was allocated to Thornaby and adorned with the Kingfisher logo.

Typical of the spot traffic flows of chemicals is this trip working from Tees Yard to Seal Sands with 37 066 in charge, taken from the platforms of Thornaby station on December 20, 1995.

English Electric experimental gas turbine 4-6-0 GT3 is seen at Marylebone on July 19, 1961. **Colour Rail (Ref:210283)**

GT3 - OR HOW TO BUILD A MODEL WITH SCANT INFORMATION

Building the Golden Arrow kit of the unique English Electric gas-turbine 4-6-0 in OO gauge by **Richard Irven**.

I have always had a soft spot for GT3. It had such a short life and yet it had some strengths that could have been developed. GT3 ended its days quickly cut up on the orders of the government of the day because it was shown up in a newspaper as having cost a lot of money and yet after just three years was already considered redundant. I have wondered for years when I would find the time and skill to scratch-build it. Thanks to Golden Arrow I do not have to.

This is not a Tamiya-style kit. Golden Arrow kits do look to be lacking in detail when you take them out of the box but they are designed to be detailed up by the modeller to whatever level they wish to. I have built several of their kits and with

a little patience they can be made into decent models of some of the more unusual prototypes. The few parts provided all fit together well and so the majority of this article is about how you can add the details to the kit. You will need to cut back any flash and fill any holes before you start. Take care with the resin as it is brittle and it can shatter off in sections if you are a bit ham-fisted.

To go with the pieces from the kit you will also need to lay your hands on a Hornby 'Black Five' chassis and a 'Britannia' tender chassis. This sounds expensive but there are suppliers of engine bits, and it seems the less of an engine you want, the less you pay. I used East Kent Models and they were very helpful,

even removing the unnecessary valve gear on the chassis so that I did not need to.

The other thing you will need to do is find as much information as you can. There is not very much, due mainly to the short life of the loco itself, and some of it is conflicting. I found two drawings of GT3 - on one it shows one brake per wheel and in the other two. It is a minefield that only studying photos will help clear up. Again, there are few of these.

The chassis

There is very little to do here, especially as the cylinders and valve gear were already missing. The back end needs the frames extended to make up the gap from the end

of the 'Black Five' chassis and the back of the loco. I just used suitable thickness Slater's 'Plastikard' sheet to do this. I also used plastic rod to make up the outside brake rigging. It's held in place by wire drilled through the rod and fed through the brake rigging supplied with the chassis. You could also use brass rod here instead, and some would say that was better as it could be thinner and yet more robust, that would be your call though. I did use a spare piece of brass in order to fabricate a front piece for the bogie. This is important as it is very visible.

The body

This is a model with little external detail so it is important to make the most of what is there. The pieces supplied fitted well to make up the main superstructure. It is worth drilling out the air scoop(?) at the front and whilst you are at it also drill out the windows and the grille sections on the tender, too. It is worth fabricating a cab interior as it is very visible through the large side windows. A word of caution with the glass, you must avoid touching it as it fogs with fingerprints and needs time to dry out. It is also brittle, and I broke one piece but Chris at Golden Arrow kindly sent out a new set for a charge that really only covered the cost of postage back to me. The cab interior had a sloped desk about 4mm deep, about half height against the backhead and two seats just in front of the doors. Due to limited information, I do not know what was actually on the console.

Small grab handles for the running plate were made out of 0.5mm brass wire and the handrail knobs were fitted into pre-drilled holes. You'll also need to make up the very visible front steps above the front buffers. These also have the added advantage of firmly securing the handrails which otherwise might hang vulnerably out at the front of the loco. This is quite easy to do. I cut a piece of brass sheet 3mm x 4mm and

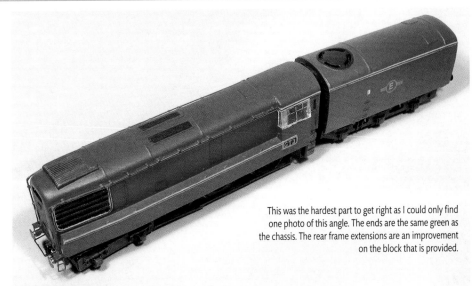

This was the hardest part to get right as I could only find one photo of this angle. The ends are the same green as the chassis. The rear frame extensions are an improvement on the block that is provided.

drilled a hole through for the handrails and soldered it securely. The steps were made from folding 0.5mm brass wire to give two vertical sides of 9mm and a bottom side of 3mm, but do remember to leave some wire beyond the 9mm verticals to bend back to give you some surface to solder or glue to the underside of the brass plate. In order to form the second step, I soldered a wire across the vertical uprights 3.5mm from the bottom and then cut and filed back the excess. Do all of this before fitting the oval buffers of your choice. The last thing that needed adding to the body are the 'skids' above the bogie. Again, these are very visible on the prototype, so have to be fitted. I made them out of brass, 44mm long, bending down 2mm at each end to a 45° angle. They're supported off the underside of the running plate by lengths of plastic rod. Once the interior painting was completed, I fitted the back half of the cab and then used filler to fill the gap on the roof line, because on the real thing the roof was a continuous piece.

The body needed little further work. I fitted a door handle from 0.5mm brass

wire, and used the same wire for the steps in the cut outs up the tender side. Small brass washers were fitted along the bottom edge of the body. After painting, I fitted a Modellers' Mecca corridor connection between tender and cab. It makes such a difference.

The 'tender'

The tender chassis needed a bit of work. After removing the steps and sieve boxes from the frames, I made new steps to fit under the steps on the tender body side. These need to be 3mm wide x 5mm high with a step at the top and bottom. There is also a 4mm long flat step above this, I made this out of brass sheet with the back edge folded over to give a larger surface to glue to. The chassis also needed lengthening so that it fitted the body. You are supplied with a lump to extend the chassis, but the real frames are thin so I used plastic sheet. This allowed me to fill the lightening holes at the back of the frames and re-drill in the correct location. I re-used the buffer beam by prising it off the frames and re-attaching it to the new rear frames.

A broadside view which shows the value of weathering models. The transfers are not perfect but are a near match. Producing the right ones was beyond my capabilities. This photo illustrates the benefits of fitting a cab interior and crew. They are needed because of all that glass. Take care - you can see the glass marks easily.

This picture clearly shows the tender steps and circular additions on the tender body. The pipe from the tender to the cab is very obvious so had to be modelled.

Finishing

The prototype photos show a variety of colours and no one could tell me which was correct, neither a signalman who worked on the ex-GC at the time nor a friend who saw the engine at Marylebone - he was more interested in the V2 that was next to it. The colour ranges from an orange, through a chocolate brown to a dark maroon red. The kit's instructions suggest a red spray paint, available from Halfords. I did not think that it looked correct compared with the photos, even taking into account the different ageing effects on old film. I mixed one part yellow and two parts Railmatch dark brick for the body and yellow with a drop of black mixed in

for the chassis. Do make enough in one batch to paint it all, and to do the touch-up painting of the roof once the filler has been applied.

The lining is black on yellow loco lining from Fox with the yellow band painted on first to widen it. It really should be yellow with a green centre line but it was a dark green and almost looked black. Correct branding transfers do not exist, so I cut the middle out of a Modelmasters' large BR tender emblem and used an HMRS 'Pressfix' large letter 'E' from a sheet of LNER loco lining. It says British Railways rather than English Electric and the 'E' is not quite the right style but no one makes the transfers as yet.

Conclusion

Overall, this kit goes together easily and with a little extra work makes into an excellent model of an interesting prototype. It can be made for a shade under £100.00 overall, and this compares very favourably to the limited edition runs of early modern traction prototypes being brought out by the RTR manufacturers.

BRM highlighted this GT3 body kit in the August 2008 issue. It can be obtained from Golden Arrow (Chris Meachen), 392 Harold Road, Hastings, Sussex TN35 5HG, price £55.00 post free. Tel: 01424 445334. email: c.meach@tiscali.co.uk

BELOW The front end is improved by the modelling of the steps and pipework. A goalpost is a simple but effective coupling.

GT3

Experimental locomotive designed and built for British Railways by English Electric at Vulcan Foundry, Newton-le-Willows, to demonstrate re-use of redundant steam locomotive frames with gas turbine power plant. Overtaken by dieselisation and scrapped at Wards, Salford, in February 1966. The two other experimental gas turbine locomotives of the time were Brown-Boveri No.18000 (GT1) - known as the 'Kerosene Castle' - withdrawn by 1959, and Metropolitan Vickers BR18100 (GT2), both originally ordered by the GWR in the 1940s. No.18100 was withdrawn in 1958 and later converted to 25kV for crew training (renumbered E1000), finally being scrapped in January 1973. Only No.18000 survives, at the Railway Age, Crewe.

Engine: 2,700hp EM27L recuperative gas turbine
Driving wheel diameter: 5′ 9″
Tender capacity: 2,000 gallons fuel oil, 1,750 gallons water
Weight: 123 tons

KEY

1: Engine. **2:** Engine driven auxiliaries gearbox. **3:** Alternator. **4:** Fuel pump. **5:** Lubricating oil pressure pump. **6:** Lubricating oil scavenge pump. **7:** Starter motor. **8:** Transmission gearbox. **9:** Power turbine balance gear. **10:** Air intake filter. **11:** Exhaust chimney. **12:** Batteries. **13:** Driving cab. **14:** Vacuum brake ejector. **15:** Air motor driven exhauster. **16:** Brake cylinders. **17:** Electric driven pump set. **18:** Electric driven cooling pump set. **19:** Train heating boiler. **20:** Oil cooler. **21:** Oil tank. **22:** Fuel tanks. **23:** Water tank. **24:** Oil suction filter. **25:** Oil pressure filter. **26:** Fuel oil filters.

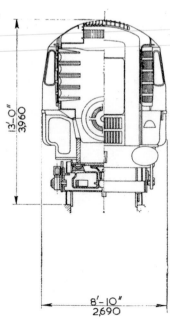

13′-0″
3,960

8′-10″
2,690

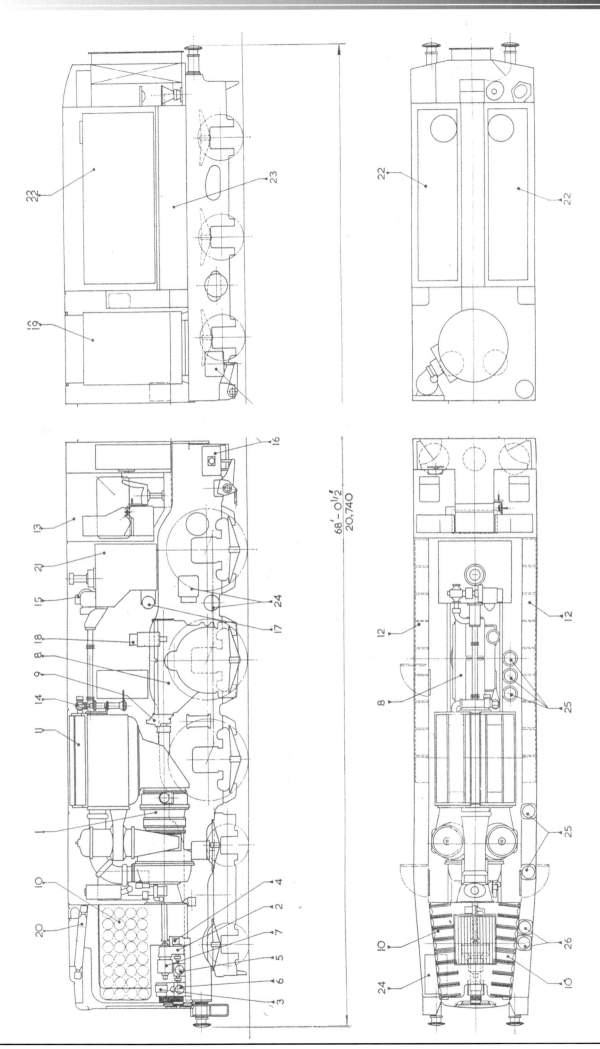

WELWYN NORTH
CAPTURING THE PAST
IN OO

This loft-based recreation of a section of the
ex-GNR main line in the home counties is described by **Chris Worby**.

The prototype 'Deltic' roars
through Welwyn North.

I blame my late father! I place the cause of my personal obsession firmly in his hands. Any tendency for a compulsive interest in steam and things mechanical can be traced back to factors that I had no control over and was a mere recipient of.

It's late 1951, a young couple out in London, perhaps Christmas shopping. They are standing at the window of 112 High Holborn. He turns to her and says 'I hope it's a boy!' Well perhaps Bassett Lowke must share some of the blame.

The child that arrived soon after the commencement of the second Elizabethan era stood no chance. He was taken to see the Great Northern Ivatt Atlantics double head to Doncaster (September '53) before he could utter too many words. Awdry stories were read at bed time, by day tales of the the graceful Stirling 'Eight Foot' single's revival in the '30s were told, and of *Green Arrow's* first run out of the 'Cross. There were the weekend walks with the family dogs that always included lineside paths and the opportunity to see 'Streaks', 'Footballers'/ 'Sandys', 'Concrete Mixers' and many others,

including ancient, asthmatic wheezers (J50s and J52s). Early lessons in numeracy were reinforced with a blue-covered pocket book where engine numbers all started with a 'six' and round-topped fireboxes ruled.

I suppose by adulthood the problem was out of control and the only treatment was self-administered exposure to 1:1 steam; dabbling in 1:12 ; and of course building/ accumulating 4mm models.

Welwyn North is, I suppose, my way of trying to recapture something that now seems to belong to a remote and distant by-gone world. It is, in fact, my first serious attempt, after many false starts, at building a pretty complete and scenic layout. Whilst I have grown to admire a wide range of locomotives, even those with brass safety valves, or cast bar frames, all very different from my childhood diet, like many enthusiasts, that early exposure is where I return for the motivation to get on and complete something.

I am fortunate to have a pretty reasonable space at my disposal (24' 0" x 12' 0"), so building something to recapture the 1950s and for me the southern end of the East Coast Main Line seemed a pretty automatic decision. Besides, I'd dallied over the years with the four 'B's - buying, botching, butchering and building a collection of locos with a GN/ER bias, I suppose in the hope that one day I would knuckle

down and get on with building a proper layout for them to run upon.

Previous attempts had always stalled or failed through being over ambitious, not having sufficient time, skills issues, and resources. Few got beyond the rudimentary track-laying stage. I decided that approaching that critical half century, I ought to be focused and get on with the project, that despite distractions and attractive alternative commitments, I would set some time aside each week for layout work. I would even do the boring repetitive tasks (wiring/ballasting in my case) through to completion.

I went through the debate about fictitious locations and what-if stations versus basing the model on an actual place. One of my weaknesses in the past could be put down to the lack of boundaries your imagination sets. In my case I think this was contributory to previous failures because of a tendency to generate grandiose schemes. I decided that an actual place would be an excellent constraint, particularly if I chose a simple prototype. The 'KISS' acronym comes to mind (Keep It Simple, Stupid). Clearly, it would have to allow my East Coast/Great Northern main

Welwyn North Track Plan

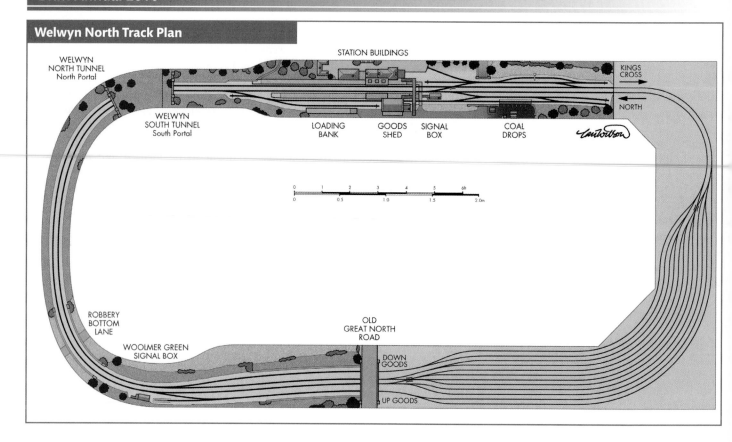

WELWYN
NORTH TUNNEL
North Portal

WELWYN
SOUTH TUNNEL
South Portal

STATION BUILDINGS

KINGS
CROSS

NORTH

LOADING
BANK

GOODS
SHED

SIGNAL
BOX

COAL
DROPS

ROBBERY
BOTTOM
LANE

WOOLMER GREEN
SIGNAL BOX

OLD
GREAT NORTH
ROAD

DOWN
GOODS

UP GOODS

line interests to come to the fore. It was also going to have to be Pacific/RA9 friendly.

The London end of the GN is nearly all four track (paired Ups and Downs), indeed, south of Wood Green it was arguably six plus. The stations were large with extensive goods and coal yards and whilst most seemed to have plenty of tunnel and bridge locations to lend themselves to scenic breaks, on my own I was not going to tackle something approaching the size and complexity of (say) the group that produced Biggleswade. The other factor would be compression which, even with the space available, the greater the width of the model the more

odd and less convincing the outcome if you have to reduce/compress length/distance.

I needed a location that was buildable within my estimated attention span - no point losing interest half way through the project, etc. The Hertford loop stations could have fitted the bill. They were double track, used at weekends for main line diversions, but almost every other train would have needed to have been a suburban. The thought of building multiple pairs of 'Quad-arts' to properly represent traffic over the loop was off putting. So it was back to the main line, In fact there were three options to the south of Hitchin,

The first was Hadley Wood which even in the early 1950s was still only double track. It is hemmed in by tunnels at both ends. It had lost its one siding, that during the war had accommodated a dining car for mess facilities for Kings Cross' out-stationed HQ staff who worked in the evacuated grand houses near by. However, through the '50s the widening programme from New Barnet to Potters Bar to quadruple the main line meant the station became a building site. The changes in this period were quite drawn out but dramatic. You couldn't use the location if you wanted to allow the model to depict a period rather than a specific year.

Because of my collecting/accumulating of models I wanted something that could span and act as a backdrop to cover the period from post-Nationalisation through to the German style deflector-carrying A3s and the first of Finsbury Park's 'Deltics' without being too far off beam.

Next up the line, Potters Bar was a more interesting station than Hadley Wood and it was even the end of a permissive working block, but the same problem of modernisation and change through the '50s meant that it had to be discounted, too. Hence, we now head to milepost 22 (from Kings Cross) and Welwyn North.

To this day, Welwyn Tunnels, North Station, and, most of all, Digswell Viaduct remains a two-track choke for ECML and GN suburban services. It continues to this day to create a headache for the traffic department and train service planners. GNER when they held the franchise wanted the station shut to increase line capacity!

92044 on the Blue Circle Cement train to Scotland.

So, Welwyn North it was to be, a simple two-track station with modest Up and Down sidings mainly for handling coal. It is, and was, in the outer suburban service area so I would not need a brace of 'Quad-arts'. The station's appearance and track layout remained pretty constant post-war, right up to the early '60s when siding rationalisation started and re-signalling gradually swept away the semaphores. I guess the only noticeable visible change in this period would have been the arrival of the blue 'corporate sausage' signage in the early 1950s.

There was no excuse in terms of available material to facilitate research. I still posses (as a registered hoarder) my copy of the *Model Railway Constructor* article on Welwyn North from 1965. There is the Gladwin, Neville and White book on Welwyn's railways and subsequently the station has featured in both *British Railways Illustrated Annual* and magazine.

From a modelling perspective, if I were to model Welwyn North, the only really critical fudge, beyond the usual distance compression, seemed to be what to do at the southern end of the station limits where Digswell Viaduct should be! Well, of course, there have been other compromises, as well as unintended errors that have come to light, particularly as better information has been found.

So, with the philosophical debate behind me, it was time to get modelling. The base or supporting structures for the layout are pretty traditional, although I have tried to keep weight down, given the room is also home to my lifetime collection of railway

The Station Master acknowledges the driver of *Clive of India* as he restarts after an unwelcome signal check.

books and magazines, too. Most boards are 3/16" ply on nominal 2" x 1" framing. Because of its loft space location, parts of the layout have to be removable to access hatches to reach tanks and roof voids. The baseboards/supporting structure is therefore fixed on more or less two walls (one end and side) with the other parts being capable of movement. Inevitably, the fiddle/storage yard occupies the fixed area as that is where most of the stock is stored. The station and the majority of the scenic areas can be disconnected and moved without too much damage to the infrastructure to enable household maintenance, etc.

The station section is on a ply-based box beam type structure with ends cantilevering, this being overall 16' 0" long x 2' 0" wide, and is mounted on castors for mobility. The boards are at two levels to allow for the down coal yard/drops and road under bridge. Most of the other parts of the layout are train set-style flat boards with the scenery rising from them. The other exception is a dropped area to accommodate my five arch representation of (the seven arch) Robbery Bottom Lane Viaduct, just to the south of Woolmer Green Box.

The layout itself is simple in concept, being a double-track circuit with the station

An Atlantic passes under the Great North Road bridge.

on one side and fiddle yard on the opposite side and one end. To give a flavour of the compromises involved, even though this purports to be a model of a real place, the station area modelled represents about a scale quarter of a mile. In reality, the distance from the north end of Digswell Viaduct to Welwyn South Tunnel portal is two thirds of a mile. The country end of the layout extends to the Great North Road overbridge beyond Woolmer Green box, in fact about two miles from Digswell. Of course, the liberties taken in achieving this are considerable. However, it does allow a short section of four-track main line. Partly, this was achieved by shortening and merging Welwyn North and South Tunnels and missing out probably one of the most photographed sections of any line in the country, that short section between the two tunnels.

The track bed comprises mineral-finished roofing felt in the scenic areas. The trackwork itself is pretty varied in origin, accumulated over the years, recovered from previous aborted layouts and projects. It has a very mixed pedigree coming from quite a few manufacturers, generally code 100. I can point out bits from Gem, Graham Farish 'Formoway', even Jouef amongst the predominant Peco 'Streamline'. Operational pointwork is all from Peco. Ballasting is mainly N scale fine, and the whole lot has been spray-painted, generally with an earth brown/terra

cotta colour available from Homebase DIY stores. Areas have been subsequently stained, particularly to represent where engines stood for any length of time.

Turnout switching is achieved through Peco solenoids. I mounted these directly to the underside of the points preferring this to mounting below boards. From an operational standpoint, this initially was fine, but some of the older turnouts plastic bases are beginning to show signs of fatigue bringing unreliability! Visually this shortcut also means having a hole in the trackbed and support boards, which from some angles isn't particularly convincing.

The modelled area doesn't really extend beyond the company boundary fence. Indeed, the fencing for almost all the layout is part of handling that awkward point where the backscene meets the layout. The backscenes themselves are simple sky, painted with a hint of distant trees, I like to think inspired by the late Bert Collins approach on his rendition of Hitchin.

Embankments and what countryside there is relies on using built-up polystyrene recovered mainly from white goods packaging, covered with plaster, painted and then overlaid with what is meant to look like grass but is in fact green kitchen abrasive pads split/pulled apart and glued over. Various other scenic material and paint has been applied to break up uniformity and disguise joints.

Road surfaces are from fine wet and dry paper, and in some of the yard areas a grey tile joint filler.

Signalling is scenic or non-working, built using Ratio components. The splitter at the south end of the station limits actually disappeared pre-Nationalisation, being relocated to the southern end of the viaduct. However, it lives on as a distraction at the end of the scenic section. Ground signals are also non-working and are from 'Detail Counts'.

One of the advantages of basing a model on an actual location is that the buildings required don't need to be invented. Even if plans aren't available, something at least with the basic elements of what was there can be constructed. Their location in relation to the railway is prototypical and if they are railway buildings in practical terms they are correct! The only downside personally relates to my own skills and tendency to compromise in the interest of finishing and getting on with the next job. Reverting to the four 'Bs', most of the buildings on my representation of Welwyn North are as a result of my butchering activities. I am much happier starting with some components, perhaps a kit and then augmenting these with other materials, chopping/cutting to produce a facsimile of a prototype.

The main station building is unsurprisingly based around the Modelyard Kit of Welwyn North with a 'Plastikard' roof and additional

It's 1961 as Finsbury Park's first production 'Deltic' passes under the Great North Road Bridge.

detail. The Down waiting room has its origins in a Peco kit. Wills components form the basis of the bridge sections of the coal drops, the station forecourt garages, Woolmer Green' box and the Great North Road overbridge. Heljan/Knightwing parts provided the superstructure for Welwyn's 'box, and the footbridge steps are pure Hornby.

I don't suppose my approach is particularly frugal. I've plenty of bits in the scrapbox for that next scheme. I excuse my way of doing things with the old adage that life isn't long enough - the model is a representation, not dead scale, etc, etc.

As a digression, when attempting to replicate a prototype you inevitably turn up a few interesting nuggets as part of the learning process. My excursion was no exception.

Welwyn North is the last surviving original-style station from when the line to London King's Cross was built. Indeed, even my own native Wood Green (now Alexandra Palace) was once just a two-platform station very similar to Welwyn, even to having the raised coal drops. Welwyn is unsurprisingly as a result of its survival on the National Listed Buildings schedule, but is, in reality, boarded and very tired looking.

It was, evidently, the last place on BR to have a shunting horse. As modellers we perhaps forget that way-side stations in the country relied on horsepower to move wagons around. I don't know what the duties

were at Welwyn but it would be interesting to know if it included moving wagons from the Up to the Down side and vice versa. Perhaps on our motive power wish-lists that seem to pre-occupy modellers annually, we should be asking Bachmann or Hornby to come up with the horsepower solution for our yards?

Welwyn, even in late Victorian times was already hot London commuter property. The large, single storey building on the Up platform originally provided covered stabling for the horse-drawn carriages of the well healed. The concrete garages in the forecourt (modelled) and similar ones in the Down goods yard later provided garaging for well-off season ticket holders to leave their Humbers, Wolseleys, Armstong Siddeleys, Rileys and Rovers by day.

Reverting to the fact that an awful lot of modellers focus on building up a collection of locomotives (the persistent collecting or spotting gene perhaps) and a hunch that many of us opt for the fictitious location to bring together diverse types that in reality never or hardly ever rubbed shoulders, I thought it would be interesting to tabulate the loco types (steam and diesel) you could have seen at Welwyn North between Nationalisation and 1963. I would suggest that the table on page 52 demonstrates that reality can be more surprising than your imagination. Indeed, careful selection of location and time frame can allow quite alien types to appear justifiably

on a prototype-based model. Clearly, many of the locos weren't around at the same time, but if your model is a back drop and you don't have a 'Deltic' on the Up line passing an Ivatt C1 on the Down you can get away with it, at least in the privacy of your own home or with other consenting adults.

I suspect even this list is incomplete. If you go a little more up to date on the one offs (ie: later into the '60s) you can add a 'Castle'; rebuilt 'Merchant Navy', and even a K4.

Visiting my 4mm Welwyn North today you can probably see most of the steam types in the regular columns and some from the occasional and one offs. Engines, as well as the tail ends of trains, are lamped, and crews populate most footplates. As my locos have been acquired or built over the years there is quite a range of standards. I guess the sources of my motive power can be distributed across my four 'Bs' acronym:

Bought: more or less as out-of-the-box perhaps with some minor additions.

Botched: as above but repainted re-numbered/detailed (ie: no longer of interest to collectors).

Butchered: usually mounted on a proprietary chassis with a chop up of body parts to produce something otherwise un-available. An example is my W1 comprising two Hornby A4 bodies, a Bachmann A4 chassis, chopped old Tri-ang A3 tender and other bits from the scrap box.

It's 1949 as *St Simon* brings a late-running sleeper out of Welwyn South Tunnel.

Built: in my case ancient Wills and K's kits on proprietary chassis, right through to Nu-cast and Little Engines kits.

Behind the locos you could see a range of trains:

Expresses: these are in fixed sets of six to eight coaches, drawn from Gresley, Thompson, Stanier and BR Mk.1 types of Bachmann, Hornby, Kirk, Coopercraft, Lima, Replica, Mainline and Trix pedigrees. Carmine and cream predominates - there are a few teaks and a couple of all maroon rakes, including a shortened seven-car 'Talisman'.

Pullmans: six-car 'Master Cutler' set and an eight-car 'Harrogate Sunday Pullman' set

Suburban/secondary: five-coach Bachmann inner suburban set, six-coach mixed BR/Gresley outer suburban set, and a 'Quad-art' pair still in construction.

Parcels/vans: 20 plus wagon version of the 'Scotch Goods', 21 wagon set of ancient Dublo wagons that is a challenge to the hauling capacity of all but my old Hornby 9F with a white metal kit-based BR1F tender body, and two mixed parcels sets.

Freight/goods: two mineral sets, one empty (Down), one loaded (Up), 20 wagon 'Presflo' Blue Circle cement set, mixed part-fitted freight including brick wagons, a pick-up goods, and two engineers' trains.

Under construction is a version of the 'Ashburton Pullman', which carried North London's rubbish out to the brick pits at Ayot in Bedfordshire. In fact, it left the main line just before Welwyn North for the Dunstable Branch. Its journey started on what is now the site of the Arsenal Football ground. Enough said, but this must have been one miserable job for the rostered guard!

Given the East Coast Main Line was renowned for most expresses exceeding eleven coaches, and Up minerals usually 60 wagons long, Down empties being 80, you can see another area of compromise.

TABLE 1: LOCOMOTIVE TYPES SEEN AT WELWYN BETWEEN 1948-1963

Steam	Regular	Occasional	One off/Specials
2-10-0	9F	-	WD
2-8-0	O2, WD	O1, O4	38XX, Stanier 8F
4-6-4	W1	-	-
4-6-2	A1, A2, A3, A4 BR 7MT	-	Rebuilt 'Princess Coronation' Unrebuilt 'Merchant Navy'
4-6-2T	-	A5	-
4-6-0	B1, B2, B17	B16, BR 5MT Stanier 'Black Five'	GW 'King', Rebuilt 'Royal Scot' B12, Stanier 'Jubilee', BR 4MT
2-6-4T	L1	BR 4MT, Fowler 4MT	-
2-6-2	V2	-	-
2-6-0	K3	K1, K2, Ivatt 4MT, BR 4MT	-
0-6-2T	N2	N1, N7	-
0-6-0	J1, J6, J15	J39	-
0-6-0T	J50	J69	-
0-6-0ST	J52	-	-
4-4-2	C1	-	GN Ivatt C1/C2
4-4-2T	-	-	C12
4-4-0	-	D16	GW *City of Truro* MR Compound
2-4-0	-	E4	-

TABLE 2: REGULAR DIESEL TYPES SEEN AT WELWYN

EE Type 4 (Class 40); EE 'Deltic' prototype and production (Class 55); EE 'Baby Deltic'; DP2; Falcon; Lion; Brush Type 4 (Class 47); EE Type 1 (Class 20); NB D61XX Type 2; BRCW Type 2 (Class 26); BRCW Type 3 (Class 33); Brush Type 2 (Class 31); BTH Type 1(D82XX); BR/Sulzer Type 2 (Class24/25); EE 350hp (Class 08/11); Gardner 204hp (Class 04)

Operation tends to be simplistic and sequence-based. The 12-track fiddle/storage yard was conceived with four roads Up and four Down, the centre four being reversible. Each track holds two trains. As one leaves, that behind is drawn forward, the departing train soon arriving in the space vacated. In practice, the reversible roads feature hasn't been used, so sessions tend to be arranged with eight Up and four Down roads or vice versa depending on the time of day I am implying. Main line traffic often ran in what appeared to the linesider as pulses of activity in the pre-diesel era before the advent of the modern high-speed railway.

With hindsight, though, I would have organised the yard as two simple unconnected sets of loops. The other improvement I would make is to increase the number of loops to 16, although more would be a serious reach problem given access is from one side only.

I have to say thanks to Tony Wright for the great photos and for the work he and others have put in over the years to give encouragement to those with a north of London interest.

So to the future, there is plenty to do fixing some of the layout's construction shortcomings. I ought to set about improving running reliability, too. I could re-vamp the fiddle yard, even finish the 'Quad-art' kits I've had for ages, but then there is 1:1 and even the 1:12 live steam action which I have been neglecting!

N2/3 Class 0-6-2T heads a suburban set.

Aristocraft Dash 9 in BNSF colours heading on to Candy Box roof with a mixed train of freight cars. The inner loop can be seen returning back across the market on the right-hand side of the picture.

MODEL MARKET

Club secretary **Eddie Reffin** describes the project to return a model railway to Inverness' Victorian Market by Inverness & District MRC. Photography by Graeme Elgar.

An important part of Inverness, Capital of the Highlands, has received a boost with the return of model railways to the Old Market Hall after a gap of three years. The Model Shop that traded in the market for many years had become a magnet for young and old alike, who would gaze upwards and watch the LGB trains go by on the elevated layout. When the shop finally closed, following retirement of the owner, the railway was packed up and taken to Ireland.

Fast forward to 2008 and an approach was made to the Inverness & District Model Railway Club by Inverness Business Improvement District (BID) and the Market Traders Association to see if the club would be interested in helping to restore the 'railway in the sky' with the aim of promoting the market in the run up to Christmas and

beyond. A proposal was put to the members of the club in an Extraordinary General Meeting and after much discussion, broad agreement was reached amongst club members that the club should and would want to be the drivers of the project. By the time funding was secured for two circuits and a time delay shuttle, it was late October and the Christmas deadline loomed close! Fortunately, the range of skills within the club meant it was able to call upon various members to carry out the work, including joinery, wiring and planning of the layout in the remaining available time.

Making a start
The project commenced in early November, falling into a number of different categories. First of all, a survey of the area was carried out to see if anything of the original infrastructure

remained. New baseboards and bridges were soon identified as the main works required in this area. Secondly, a decision would have to be reached on what gauge and type of train that we required to withstand the extremes in temperature in the market.

It became apparent that the 1:29 scale, G scale trains made by Aristocraft and distributed in the UK by Bachmann Europe plc fitted the bill perfectly, due to their durability and reliability which would be vital, as they would be plying their trade for hours at some twelve feet above ground level. Thirdly, working parties were formed to actually carry out the work. Four new bridges and replacement baseboards were constructed in quick order thanks to the club having a joiner in its ranks!

An order for track, stock and accessories was placed, after assessment by the club

Aristocraft C-16 in Colorado Road livery hauling a passenger service made up of three coaches on the inner loop above the old Model Shop. In the background can be seen the large bridge crossing of the outer circuit.

BNSF liveried Dash 9 crossing the bridge above the entrance to the front of the Market. This view gives you an idea of the heights that we were working at and the scale of some of the bridges which had to be rebuilt. The shop on the right is where the Model Shop used to be.

Chairman who had the most experience of large scale equipment. Deliveries of equipment arrived speedily in mid-November so the fun part could begin in earnest. The track laying was found to be surprisingly quick due to the clever design of the Aristocraft product allowing rapid progress of the loops.

Over the next three weeks, all the track and electrics were installed, a task made easier by the fact the team was able gain access to the premises in the evenings when there were no members of the public around. Perspex screens were fitted around the perimeter to prevent any chance of a derailed train from injuring the aforementioned public! With all this work completed slightly ahead of schedule, attention turned to testing the layout ahead of the big day.

Locomotives and rolling stock

The first phase of the project was equipped with the following locomotives:
- Class 66 locomotive
- Santa Fe FA unit
- Rodgers 2-4-2 steam locomotive
- Diesel centre cab switcher
- Steam 0-4-0 switcher

Rolling stock included a set of old time coaches and a variety of freight stock. Plans for future acquisitions include Aristocraft intermodal wagons for the Class 66 locomotive.

The big day

The railway was officially opened by Highland Councillor Jimmy Gray, Provost of Inverness, on December 6, with reporters and photographers from the Press and Journal. Councillor Gray pressed a button to start the layout's first public operations, whilst visitors and club members waited with bated breath to see the first trains running. Right on cue the Aristocraft locos started moving off for the first of many circuits.

One slight hiccup was caused by an over enthusiastic press photographer who managed to leave her camera bag across the track. Luckily the only damage was to her reputation and not the model.

Operation and maintenance

The railway has now settled into its regular pattern of running at the weekends, entertaining countless visitors to the market. All smoke units were turned off to avoid problems with burning out when empty since trains are running for about six hours daily with only weekly maintenance, a tribute to the quality and durability of Aristocraft equipment. The club was given a very successful track cleaning car made by a club member which consists of an open wagon, heavily weighted and equipped with pads which are soaked in isopropyl alcohol (IPA).

Running has been without problems since operating speeds were reduced allowing

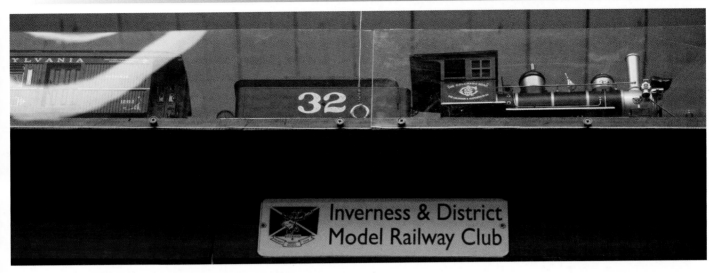

Aristocraft C-16 in Colorado Road livery crossing the short bridge on the inner loop. The Perspex screen is to protect the trains as much as the public.

trains to run slowly through visual areas for the public to better see them. As with all new layouts, there were a couple of teething problems and a couple of derailments -which left one loco running for some time against derailed stock which eventually wore some grooves into the track! Of the first two loops, the outer track uses the widest radius curves possible and 18 metres of straight track. The inner is of smaller radius curves bought from a club member and there is an 8 metre shuttle track using an Aristocraft shuttle unit linked to two end track sections additionally equipped with diodes.

The power supply is mounted on top of the shops, but there is an infra-red switch to enable power to be turned on and off from floor level. A timer was installed to allow auto-starting and stopping of the layout at the end of a day's running. There is no power drop around the layout despite only one set of feeds to each track. All Aristocraft track is assembled by screwing it together at the rail joiners which is not always simple 12' above ground level, due to the small screws being coated in wax which protects the rail joiners when in storage. Otherwise, the track was found to be very straightforward to place.

Some of the retailers in the market would like to hear more noise coming from trains themselves. The locomotives do not have any sound boards fitted due to time and money constraints, though this may become a future project. Conversely, some retailers' premises over which the trains operate have said it can be too noisy. The solution is not yet clear, although one option is to relay the track on sound insulating material.

The club still has some track left and is considering whether to do another loop in another part of the market - funding is becoming available for further expansion.

What next?
Has the project been successful? Well, the main aim has been to reinvigorate this area

of the market and on the whole it has been a success. The local press have run a series of very positive articles on the railway and BBC Alba (a Gaelic Satellite channel) has featured the railway in one of its broadcasts.

Initial discussions have now taken place with a view to extending the railway into the next area of the market with a further two loops envisaged. If this becomes a reality then the club will be in a good position to undertake the work.

If anyone is interested in finding out more about the Market Railway or Inverness & District MRC and its activities, then please visit: www.freewebs.com/invernesssmrc or email: invernessmrc@yahoo.co.uk

Acknowledgements
The Inverness & District MRC would like to thank Dennis Lovett and his colleagues at Bachmann Europe plc for their support, technical help and advice.

The freight service hauled by the Aristocraft Dash 9 in BNSF livery heads across the largest bridge on the line. Built from sheets of plywood, its construction was made more difficult by the fact that it is curved.

Aristocraft Dash 9 in BNSF colours heading towards the Candy Box roof with a mixed train of freight cars. Some of the additional support wires can be seen for the bridge.

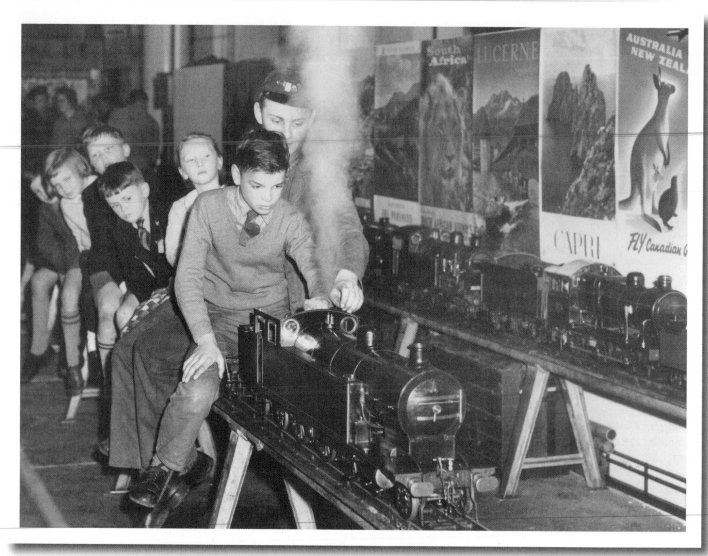

The fascination of steam for boys! A young enthusiast drives an LTSR Baltic tank under the watchful eye of its driver - by 1961 this locomotive had run at the Easter show on a regular basis for 30 years.

THE MRC EXHIBITIONS

For many modellers, the Model Railway Club's Easter show at Central Hall was a 'rite of passage'. Keith Castell, Richard Reidy and Tom Cunnington of the MRC explain the show's origins which date back nearly 100 years! Photography from the MRC Collection.

Some of the very first meetings of The Model Railway Club in 1911 were referred to as 'exhibitions', with members bringing along their models to show to fellow members. On March 13, 1912, one of these meetings in Victoria was made open to non-members, and can therefore probably be considered to be the first ever model railway exhibition. A similar event was held the following year and again on March 18, 1915, at St Philips Hall in Pimlico, and made a small surplus.

The event planned for 1916, which was to have raised funds for the Red Cross, was cancelled, no doubt due to the hardships caused by the Great War

GP Keen (after whom the MRC's headquarters is named) was elected Chairman in 1921, and to achieve his aim of a permanent base for the Club he worked tirelessly to build up funds, mainly through the medium of exhibitions. 1924 saw the first real changes with a two-day show at Easter in Kingsway Hall that netted a

profit in excess of £3. This display included models and demonstration tracks and also a passenger carrying one upon which ladies were specifically not permitted to drive the miniature steam locomotives!

By 1925 the profits had risen to nearly £24 and in 1929 the exhibition had expanded to a five day, 3,000 gate affair and the Kingsway Hall was recognised as too small. Caxton Hall, Holborn Town Hall and Australia House were all considered, but on October 21, 1930, the Committee decided to book

the Lower Hall of the Methodist Central Hall, Westminster for the 1931 event. This decision was a major commercial risk, which in the event of financial failure, would fall jointly and severally on individual members' estates, and for their protection the MRC was converted into a company. By 1937 both Upper and Lower Halls at Central Hall were in use, a decision prompted by the unexpected conversion of half the Lower Hall into a restaurant. The generally recognisable post-war exhibition format was thus determined.

Back in the 30s, well-known visitors included Gresley, Stanier, Maunsell and Sir Henry Wood, and no doubt others not recognised by us. The 1939 exhibition was held in the shadow of a deteriorating international situation on a personal decision of Keen with six working layouts and displays from visiting clubs.

The annual exhibition returned in 1947 and continued in Easter Week at the Central Hall. In 1951, as an example, 37,000 people visited the show. The shows were set up on Maundy Thursday and Easter Saturday, and open to the public from Tuesday to Saturday, as no activity was permitted in the halls on Good Friday or Easter Sunday.

As the 1960s progressed it was mooted that the Central Hall would soon not be available and representatives from the Royal Horticultural Society (RHS) called upon then chairman and exhibition manager John Anning to offer the facilities of the New Horticultural Hall, that wonderful art deco piece of architecture in what was then a public transport desert in Westminster, but not far from the original exhibition of 1912 in Victoria. The initial move to the RHS Hall was a success, although the traditional Easter Week had to be attenuated somewhat and the Bank Holiday days utilised.

Mindful of the necessity of maintaining an Easter presence in the market place assurances were sought from the RHS that these dates would be guaranteed. But after a short period the RHS reneged on the agreement and when arranging the 1968 Show the Club was told that Easter was not available as there was a flower show and that the MRC could have August or November, take it or leave it. August was chosen and an excellent exhibition mounted including both the Club's OO and O gauge layouts.

The MRC was used to having queues right round the hall during shows but on the first day the queue was cleared in 15 minutes, a literally ashen faced treasurer

reporting the predicted disastrous gate to Anning. The financial loss was heavy: so much so that the Club was forced into amalgamating with the trade's 'Hobby Show' (which had filled the autumn slot for

A large crowd forms at Central Hall for the 1953 exhibition, and a leaflet for the 1949 Easter show at Central Hall (above).

ABOVE: A display of Great Western models, date unknown but certainly post-1934 when the GWR introduced their 'shirt button' device.
BELOW LEFT: In 1978 members of the Gauge One Model Railway Association won the Hornby Trophy with their 35' x 22' live steam layout. G1MRA Chairman and MRC member Francis Dobson (centre), inspects one of the magnificent locomotives on display. With him are Mike Hick (left), in charge of electricals, and G1MRA Secretary Stan Roberts - the Hornby Trophy is displayed in the background.
BELOW RIGHT: MRC Chairman G P Keen shows a schoolboy the smallest and largest locomotive in the 1930 exhibition, held in the Kingsway Hall.

a major London show) with the exhibition being underwritten by others and operated by the Club. This continued for some years until the trade tired of the administration and passed the exhibition company to the MRC for a nominal £46. In the meantime the show had returned to the cramped conditions of the Central Hall that had, incidentally, remained available. The public and profits had, however, returned allowing much needed improvements to Keen House, notably to the heating and catering departments.

In recent years rock musicians including Phil Collins, Rod Stewart and Jools Holland have been regular visitors to the shows. Rod Stewart always came on his own – he told the Manager that it was one of the few venues where he was confident that he would not be pestered by fans (nuisances)?

In the early '80s, with Central Hall and the show bursting at the seams, the Club was approached by Argus Specialist Exhibitions Ltd, a commercial concern, who had connections with, and economical access to, the exhibition spaces at the then new Wembley Exhibition Centre and suggested a joint venture, the International Model Railway Exhibition (IMREX) in which the MRC had a 51% stake.

IMREX in 1983 was a roaring success, way beyond the Club's wildest expectations. As the second IMREX approached a newly elected treasurer took one look at the projections, stated that it was a late Easter (historically always poor for the exhibition), and predicted a loss. The other show managers didn't take the warning seriously enough and went ahead with a monster eight-day event. The sun shone, almost no-one went to one of the best shows ever mounted and the loss was almost exactly that predicted £20,000 (almost £50,000 today). The immediate solution favoured by some was to allow the exhibition company to go into insolvency, but to the Club's credit this view did not prevail and it was thought more appropriate to allow creditors to be paid in full. A rescue plan was implemented, with one more IMREX at Wembley with a projected technical loss to maintain a presence in the market place, and then move the whole event back to the RHS Halls, but with cast iron assurances

Anne Carter drives a loco watched by envious children at the 1958 show. How different to 1924 when ladies were not permitted to drive the miniature steam locomotives.

LEFT: 'This model railway was of great interest to these youngsters, but not enough to stop them from eating ice creams' says the caption to this photograph taken at the 1957 Easter show. Are Anthony Gosdon (7) of Croydon, Christopher Allen (10) of Billericay, Bryan Pope (9) of Reading, Terry Brooks (13) of St Albans and Robert Shelton (9) of Glasgow still railway modellers?

BELOW LEFT: A very happy exhibitor attends to his magnificent model of an LMS Pacific - named 'Duchess of Brighouse'.

RIGHT: Admiring a large scale model tram at the MRC's 1961 show.

BELOW RIGHT: An extensive Trix OO gauge three-rail layout captures the interest of visitors to the 1955 exhibition.

The Rev. Wilbert Awdry, creator of 'Thomas the Tank Engine', with Tidmouth Junction at one of the Easter shows in the 1980s.

of the Easter dates agreed with the Hall authorities. The Club took out a £30,000 loan secured on Keen House, and took over Argus's share of the exhibition company.

Once back in Westminster the 1986 IMREX broke even, and the next two, benefiting from almost saturation TV coverage, made so much money that all losses were recovered and some £50,000 was spent on refurbishing Keen House including the re-roofing of the Upper (now John Anning) Hall and refurbishing the flat. However, the golden days could not last for ever and as more people travelled abroad over the Easter holidays, the economy slowed and interest in the hobby waned, IMREX went into slow decline despite many attempts to invigorate it. Additionally it was evident that the Club had become a slave to the exhibition, rather than the event being an enjoyable if

Posed concentration - one of the modelling 'demons' with a part built OO gauge Southern tank loco at the 1957 show.

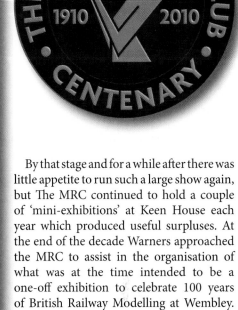

By that stage and for a while after there was little appetite to run such a large show again, but The MRC continued to hold a couple of 'mini-exhibitions' at Keen House each year which produced useful surpluses. At the end of the decade Warners approached the MRC to assist in the organisation of what was at the time intended to be a one-off exhibition to celebrate 100 years of British Railway Modelling at Wembley. The Club organised the 'amateur' side of the show – the layouts, demonstrations and stewards, with Warners organising the trade, publicity, venue and ticketing. Following the success of that show in 2000, the partnership continues to this day with the annual *London Festival of Railway Modelling* on the last weekend in March at the impressive venue of Alexandra Palace.

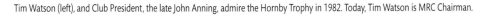

Tim Watson (left), and Club President, the late John Anning, admire the Hornby Trophy in 1982. Today, Tim Watson is MRC Chairman.

A typical publicity shot from the 1950s - a schoolboy inspects a brass-built Southern Railway 'King Arthur' locomotive in 1959.

somewhat exhausting way of raising funds. The scale of the show was so large that whilst the profits in good years were great, the losses incurred caused the Club great difficulties which were tackled firmly and successfully by its management and members.

By 1995 IMREX had reduced to one hall but finally lack of trade support meant that IMREX for '96 had to be pulled. Nearly 30% of the trade support came from one trader and that firm had gone into liquidation – perhaps a reflection on the state of the hobby at that time.

In the midst of the gloom one green shoot was established. Warners, publishers of *British Railway Modelling*, approached the Club very close to the Exhibition opening around 1993 to enquire hopefully rather than confidently whether a stand could be found for their new railway modelling magazine. With a little juggling of the plan (and aided by a cancellation) a stand was found, perhaps to Warner's surprise, and that set up a working relationship which has endured to this day.

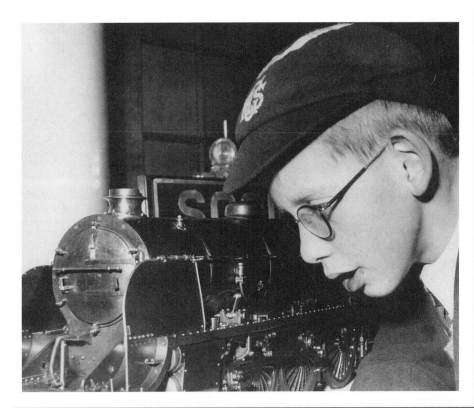

Looking across the locomotive depot and approaches to Fort Fay station with its Lego footbridge in the background.

O GAUGE PIONEER

From founding the Gauge O Guild and Gainsborough MRS to rescuing Flying Scotsman and running Steamtown, Carnforth, George Hinchcliffe has always had railways in the blood as **Peter Marriott** discovers.

Our hobby is full of big names, modellers who have contributed a lot to the hobby. Some of them are well-known personalities to us at model railway shows, others are well known through their layouts and published work rather than their faces. George Hinchcliffe is one of the hobby's excellent modellers who started out with some Hornby trains and track back in the 1930s. In the years that followed he worked with the real *Flying Scotsman* at Steamtown, Carnforth, and was a founder member of both the Gauge O Guild and the Gainsborough Model Railway Society.

Recently I was privileged to visit George at his Lancashire home. What follows is a summary of the many accounts that George was pleased to pass on to readers of *British Railway Modelling*. The accompanying pictures show George's loft layout that appears for the first time in a mainstream model railway magazine.

George first became interested in model railways in 1935 with a few Hornby trains and some pieces of track. Once he had returned to the UK at the end of the

Fort Fay control panel.

Second World War he became interested again to spend time with model railways. George reminded me that in 1948 there was very little model railway equipment

The canal basin at Fort Fay.

100 coaches, 200 wagons and vans, 150 points, around half a mile of track and nine stations. The building of the present model railway commenced in 1953 and covers 2,500 square feet. It needs ten operators to cover all the train movements. The period modelled is from the late 1930s to the end of British Railways steam, with some diesel operation permitted. To learn more about this outstanding model railway visit: www.gainsmodelrailway.ik.com

George has always worked in 7mm scale and when he was Trade Liaison Officer for the Gauge O Guild in the 1950s he remembered that there were just nine companies manufacturing bits and pieces for O scale. Looking at the hobby now he thinks it splendid that there are now O gauge ready-to-run locomotives and rolling stock available plus a host of other parts and accessories.

available for sale, but he still wanted to rekindle his modelling activities, so he responded to an advertisement in a house window to acquire some more Hornby O scale track. It was around then that George became one of the founder members of the Gainsborough Model Railway Society. He still makes regular visits to Gainsborough to see the Society's huge O gauge layout and enjoys meeting different visitors at the club premises. The Gainsborough model railway is reputedly the third largest O gauge model railway in the world. It depicts the East Coast Main Line from Kings Cross to Leeds Central and boasts 125 locomotives, around

ABOVE: George Hinchcliffe at the controls of his loft layout.
BELOW: The goods yard at Fort Fay.

George still enjoys reading the *GOG Gazette*, the journal of the Gauge O Guild, which now has over 5,500 members including over 500 outside the UK. One magazine that George has fond memories of but is no longer published is *Model Railway News*.

Amongst some of the good developments in the hobby that George has noticed are the number of good quality ready-to-run O gauge locomotives, wagons and carriages; motors becoming smaller making their installation into model locomotives easier: ready-to-lay track, and white metal kits and etched parts. We asked George, 'Who were the modellers he had most looked up to?' The names of Jack Ray, W S Norris and James Stanley Beeson were just some that he mentioned. Other people that George knew personally and

For younger visitors here is a wagon load made from Lego bricks..

who appear in George's autobiography *An Obsession with Steam: The Memoirs of George D Hinchcliffe* include Terence Cuneo, Alan Pegler, Bill McAlpine and his family.

Flying Scotsman

Mixed between the Royal Navy and teaching jobs, one of the aspects of Georges' 'railway life' that he is most proud of is his

part in the return of LNER A3 locomotive No.4472 *Flying Scotsman* to the UK from the USA. Whilst the locomotive was on the West Coast of the USA, its owners ran into financial difficulties, which gave Sir William McAlpine a chance to purchase and repatriate the locomotive. Sir William explains: '*I was rung up by Alan Bloom. He and some others had said, we think the Flying Scotsman's in trouble. In fact it had gone bankrupt on its American tour and was becalmed in San Francisco. I suggested we get hold of George Hinchcliffe who had managed it over there on this US tour and who was a school master at the time. He said 'I'll go and see what the situation is,' and off he went. I paid his fare. He phoned me to say, 'If you want to save this locomotive you've got to ring this man in the morning'. Simple as that. I asked myself, do I want a locomotive in San Francisco? So I said, if I buy it can you get it back? Hinchcliffe reckoned he could. Fortuitously he had struck up a conversation with a shipping manager on the plane going over who was intrigued by the Flying Scotsman story and was prepared to arrange shipment of the locomotive home via the Panama Canal. Hinchcliffe, said yes, he could. So I said, if we get it back will you manage it for me? He said, 'Well I'll think about it very seriously'! I didn't honestly*

There is plenty of activity over the railway fence as this scene at Fort Fay shows.

George was not only a founder member of the Gauge O Guild but also the Gainsborough Model Railway Society. The Gainsborough MRS O gauge layout represents the East Coast Main Line from Kings Cross to Leeds Central in the steam era - this is the recently rebuilt Kings Cross on the Gainsborough layout, well worth a visit on one of their Open Days. **Tony Wright**

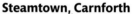

believe him, that he could get it back but he did.' Thanks go to www.railwaypeople.com for permission to use these quotes.

Bill McAlpine paid the debt owed to US and Canadian railways and the cost of the shipping. The *Flying Scotsman* returned to the UK in February 1973. Restoration work followed at Derby. Trial runs in the summer

A busy scene at Westerley Victoria.

of 1973 took place on the Torbay Steam railway and thus Britain's most famous locomotive was saved for posterity.

As part of its golden anniversary celebrations in 2006, the Gauge O Guild provided a 7mm scale model of *Flying Scotsman* to be part the National Railway Museum collection. George Hinchcliffe

presented the engine to the Museum on March 20, 2006.

Steamtown, Carnforth

Not far from Carnforth railway station is what was Carnforth motive power depot where many steam locomotives were based in the UK's steam era. On August 13, 1968, the last run undertaken by a steam engine owned by British Railways took place and began at Carnforth. During the last weeks of steam Carnforth became popular with enthusiasts and in 1969 Steamtown became based at the depot.

George became the Managing Director of Steamtown in 1976. Over the years Steamtown restored and played host to many locomotives including *Flying Scotsman*, *Duchess of Hamilton*, *Lord Nelson* and *Sir Nigel Gresley*.

Sadly Steamtown closed to the general public for safety reasons in 1997. Now West Coast Railway Company (WCRC), a railway spot-hire company and charter train operator, is based at Carnforth.

The home layout

Georges' O scale layout occupies the entire loft area of the home shared with his wife Janet. Co-incidentally (of course) the house backs onto the West Coast Main Line. Janet told me that the first time that they came to view the house she was not

'King Arthur' 4-6-0 No.798 *Sir Hectimere* gets ready to leave Westerley Victoria.

Waiting for the next departure is Albert Einstein!

aware that the railway line was located nearby until George asked her tactfully 'Did you hear those trains dear?' Reason obviously won the day, because the house was purchased and Janet speaks highly of the home too now!

As one enters the 'railway room' there is a hinged duck-under of two main line tracks. The layout measures approximately 40' 0" x 40' 0" with a double track continuous

circuit plus two large terminus stations (one with three platforms, the other with four). The termini are called Fort Fay and Westerley Victoria. George completed the layout about 12 years ago.

The track is Peco 'Streamline' bullhead with all of the points and signals being electrically operated. The main line run is about 160' in length. The track on the layout is cleaned once a year. When I asked George

which company made the signals he replied 'I did. They are all scratch-built and work from relays below the baseboard. Some of the signals feature route indicators'.

There is a turntable at each terminus station – one scratch-built by George, the other built from a Metalsmith kit.

George has 40 locomotives on his layout (all built by himself), over 30 carriages and 'a lot' of wagons (approximately 60). Most of the carriages and wagons at the outer end of the rakes are fitted with Kadee couplings that work from magnets between the rails. Between the other wagons three-link couplings are fitted. The late Fred Newman built many of the carriages while Mike Hanson made many of the wagons.

George goes up into the loft a couple of times a week to 'play trains' but four or five times a year he has a full operating session with four friends – Ian Dawson, Chris Wragg, Robert Booth and John Skelly. When serious operating sessions are taking place, bell codes are used so that the operation of the O gauge system is as life-like as possible. The grandchildren, Callum and Sandy, visit their granddad from Preston to run the trains from time to time.

Mr Hinchfield did inform me that he wears one item of essential clothing on each visit to his loft – a Ffestiniog Railway cap. Apparently this is to protect his head as he moves amidst the roof supports – I must say I was not convinced by this explanation. I think George just likes wearing caps bearing railway logos!

The most recent locomotive built by George is LNER 3442 *The Great Marquess*, being around a year old. At the time of writing George was undertaking a repair job on a locomotive for one of his friends.

George has already earmarked that his locomotives will to go to family and friends once the final whistle blows.

Sir Hectimere at Westerley Victoria again - many of the coaches on the layout were built by the late Fred Newman.

Useful addresses

■ Gainsborough Model Railway Society: www.gainsmodelrailway.ik.com

■ Gauge O Guild www.gauge0guild.com

■ National Railway Museum Home of Flying Scotsman www.nrm.org.uk www.flyingscotsman.org.uk

■ Metalsmith www.metalsmith.co.uk

This page - scenes around Fort Fay station and locomotive sheds.

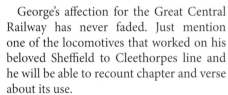

A sense of humour

What struck me about George and his layout was the underlying sense of humour. So whilst the layout was predominantly hand-built there was still place for the wagonload made from Lego bricks to appeal to children visiting the layout.

On the platform at Westerley Victoria is the seated McKenzie family but nearby stands a model of Albert Einstein waiting for the next departure. The footbridge at Fort Fay is made from Lego bricks and some of the buildings on the layout seem to have suffered more fire damage than is usual! George assured me that each of his cameo scenes has a story to tell.

George's affection for the Great Central Railway has never faded. Just mention one of the locomotives that worked on his beloved Sheffield to Cleethorpes line and he will be able to recount chapter and verse about its use.

In conclusion I would like to take the opportunity to say 'thank you' to George and Janet for making me feel at home on my flying visit to Lancashire. I enjoyed the visit – and the opportunity to drive some of the trains on the layout.

Railways are in George's veins. In his 87 years he has worked with some of the most famous of railway personalities and some of the most famous locomotives. But in addition he has helped found two important model railway institutions. I doff my cap to you, sir. The hobby would be a poorer place without you.

'Princess Coronation' Pacific No.6230 *Duchess of Buccleuch* heads an express away from Liverpool Lime Street.

LIVERPOOL LIME STREET

The genesis and construction of this magnificent EM gauge project to recreate Lime Street in miniature is described by **John Holden**.

for the festive period. This involved a trip on the 'Lekky' to Liverpool's Exchange station then a short taxi ride to Lime Street to catch the London train. Imagine that first experience when the taxi went right into the station and along the platform and stopped at the carriage we were to travel in, then getting out of that cab and experiencing for the first time the sights, sounds and smells of this great cathedral to the flanged wheel. Then we entered our carriage and found our compartment. I was left wondering how 'they' knew we had paid for our trip. Suddenly we were somehow safe in a warm cosy cocoon. Looking out of the window all was wet, steamy, cold, and *very* dirty. Water was streaming down green slime on the massive stone wall just outside our window, and I could hear the sound of a wheel tapper out there making his way down the train testing the wheels, whilst I was warm and dry inside with my copy of the *Eagle*.

I could go on, but I'm sure you all recognize the scenario, probably just about 15 minutes or so of my life, but an indelible impression left on my mind forever! These annual experiences led to the inevitable compulsion to build a model of Lime Street.

Lime Street Mk.1

My first attempt was at the age of nine when an 8' 0" x 4' 0" piece of hardboard was placed on some old drums in the cellar and my Tri-ang American outline diesel became the prototype 'Deltic' that had hauled us to London on the 'Merseyside Express'. Not what might be called a model railway, but boy did we have amazing imaginations in those days - or was this the effect of all that NHS orange juice and cod liver oil?

Lime Street Mk.2

Lime Street Mk.2 came along light years later. I was now married, had two daughters, and a very tempting loft in our three bedroomed semi. Although the loft was a great railway room, it would not be possible to model Lime Street as it should be, so a compromise was struck, and the name changed to Line Street.

It was at this time, through a local model railway club I had joined, I met my mate Brian Pickergill. Together over the years, we have visited shows up and down the country. It was on one of these forays that we were converted to EM (more on this later). Brian brings a mechanical engineer's background to Lime Street which has on many occasions 'saved the bacon' in finding ways to do things.

Seven years later and a house move beckoned so all the work so far done was consigned to the bin in two weeks! Oh dear. Would I ever see my life long dream?

Lime Street Mk.3 (My Nemesis)

They say everything comes to he who waits, but surely this was taking it a bit too far! After the usual round of decorating and alterations, and in between other domestic duties, the new loft soon beckoned. This was a far better affair, much larger than the last, and indeed it took a fair amount of time and money to prepare for the inevitable Lime Street.

I still could not model the station properly, but I was not going to make the same mistake again - that is, building the layout into the loft. So I set about making the baseboards as stand alone units, a bit like the old wooden bread trays. These would be inverted, and bolted together and aligned using EM Gauge Society locating dowels and the whole would sit on sub-frames attached to the sides of the loft. This way with another house move, all would not be lost. Each board or module was 4' 0" long by 2' 6" wide.

So now we have just converted the loft, and made these baseboards and what happens? Yes, you guessed it, another house move, this time, into an old derelict Victorian house. Unfortunately for Lime Street this took nearly 20 years to renovate. However, over that period I got some coaches and a few locos built along with attending shows with our demonstration stand.

During that time some significant things came to pass, I began to realize that those baseboards I had built and now had stored at our new home could form the basis of an exhibition layout, no need to worry about fitting it all in the loft, exhibition halls are a little bigger! Suddenly I saw the light, I could have my Lime Street in full! The next significant thing that happened was a chance comment that I was building Liverpool Lime Street to an operator of a layout at expoEM North. The layout was Olive Mount, and the operator was non other than Chris Hewitt. At first I think he thought I was either mad, or from another planet, but eventually he realized I was serious, and since then we have become great friends, and his contribution to this project is immense covering track building and all the buildings that you see on the layout. Literally, he can build a layout faster than I can build a loco!

So there you have it, the story of how this monster came about. One thing I must say is that over the years I have been working on Lime Street I have been surprised that no one else has had a go given the enclosed nature of the station. That is of course up to the time when Lime Street had its second outing as a 'layout under construction', then I found out my good friend Dave Pennington was having a go too. His model is set in the early 20th century, in LNWR

O k, where to start? Well, first, maybe, 'Why Lime Street?' This story I am sure you will find, is another variation on a familiar theme for most of us 'sons of the post war bulge'! I was brought up in the sleepy suburbs of Southport in spitting distance of the old L&Y electric line to Liverpool. Each New Year Mum's treat was a trip to London

Duchess of Buccleuth is about to pass under Brownlow Street as it leaves Lime Street station.

times. So now as he lives south of Watford, we refer to his layout as Lime Street Southern division, and mine as Lime Street Northern division!

OVERVIEW

I've tried to explain how Liverpool Lime Street became the obsession it is with me. I would like to take things one step further and explain how the current Lime Street evolved and why I've done things the way I have.

Over the years I have heard comments made both in print, and verbally, about peoples layouts and I can't help thinking that in some cases the comments are both unfair, and ill informed. If the owners had been given the opportunity to explain their thinking, then people may have understood better where they were coming from. So here we go, and if you don't agree with my thinking, then as Brian would say, 'Each to their own'!

Firstly the layout is built to 4mm/EM standards. Now that's enough for someone somewhere to disagree straight off!

So why choose 4mm/EM? Again, over

time I have seen many articles and 'letters to the editor' about the virtues of all the scale gauge combinations, and for a layout of this size, for me, 7mm was out. Also to produce the level of detail I would want in 7mm, it would take a lifetime to produce one train! I have never done anything

with 2mm so I felt that 4mm offered me the best compromise between the level of detail I wanted, and the ability to produce the section of railway I wanted. As to the OO/EM/P4 debate, well, again I hear good arguments from all camps. My advice to anyone is to listen to all the pros and cons,

The 'Turbomotive' clatters over the station throat pointwork. The large girder bridge carries Copperas Hill over the railway.

No.6202, the 'Turbomotive', threads its way through the tunnels and bridges in the deep cutting on the approach to Lime Street.

take your time, and study carefully the layouts on the circuit in each of the gauges, then go for what *you* think is right for *you*. For what it is worth I have never regretted going EM. Besides, you couldn't meet a better bunch of railway nutters than EM Gauge Society members.

The next fundamental decision was what period I should model. Logically I suppose it should have been the mid-'50s, where all this madness started, but I had rather a liking for the LMS and I had noticed that very few layouts portrayed the period just after the war, I assume because it was

a very drab period in railway history. So being born in 1947, rightly or wrongly I went for the post-war period right up to Nationalisation (does that make me drab too?).

As you will realise, Lime Street is a main line terminus, and therefore is an 'End to End' layout. Also, as a main line terminus, the pointwork in the station throat will be very complex to support quite an intense level of traffic. Hardly your sleepy branch line terminus! To meet the demands stated above, and to reduce operator error, it was obvious that a good deal of 'Automation/ Computer Control' would be required (more on this in a future article).

The first thing to decide was how we were to accept and despatch trains to the station bearing in mind that, again unlike your average country terminus, Lime Street handled some of the longest trains on the LMS. When a schematic track plan was studied it was apparent that the layout would have a very 'thin' middle section where a section of the famous cutting was to be. Indeed the layout would have 'thinned down' from about 6' 0" deep at the buffers, to just 1' 0". It was straight away obvious that some form of 'kick back' arrangement

'Black Five' No.5054 arrives with an Officer's Special.

A bird's eye view of the signal gantry controlling the approach to Lime Street. Built by the author, it is complete with working theatre indicators showing which platform the road is set for.

would be most suitable to 'park' stock between movements to and from the station. This would significantly reduce the overall length of the layout without the loss of the 'full length' trains. This left a choice of either a sector plate, or a traverser to work between the station (*via* cutting), and fiddle yard. It was obvious that the former would be the best option given the length required (10' 0" minimum). The turning of locos would be done by a remotely controlled turntable at the end of the fiddle sidings furthest from the sector plate.

Trackwork would be SMP for the plain track and all points would be hand-built using the 'Ply and rivet' method (he's a good lad that Chris!). You may have heard of the computer system for designing trackwork called 'Templot' - well Brian came up with a simple system using an eight foot length of 3/8" square Perspex. Align the Perspex along the line you want the track to take at one end, then let the Perspex follow into the curve you want, and the Perspex naturally forms a transition from one to the other. We call it 'Tramplot'!

All points are electrically operated by Fulgarex point machines, including the trap or catch points.

One of the early fundamental decisions that had to be made was should the layout be operated from the front or the back? This decision was influenced by my desire to present the layout in the best possible way. Again, over the years visiting exhibitions, I have noted how only a minority of layouts have given consideration to their presentation. In a lot of cases it seems to have been an after thought, or something

The deep cutting walls dwarf an ex-LNWR railmotor.

LIme Street signal box was a large LNWR structure that lasted until 1948 when it was replaced by an 'ARP' style LMS Type 13 box with 97 lever Westinghouse 'L' frame.

of no importance at all, yet some of the most memorable layouts I have seen have also been the best presented.

I see the layout like a stage; the base board front/curtains, lighting pelmets, and each end of the layout (tabs), should form a frame within which the railway should form a scene in which the 'play' is acted out. The whole should be well lit. The sight of beer bellies behind the layout does nothing to make the scene convincing, so the backscene had to go right up to pelmet height. For these reasons, I decided to have

No.6202 was the most succesfull attempt at improving the low thermal efficency of steam locomotives, running nearly half a million miles in 15 years. Rebuilt as 46202 *Princess Anne*, it was damaged beyond economic repair in the horrific Harrow accident in 1952.

the operators at the front of the layout. With a 45' 0" long layout, there is plenty of room for the public to see the layout round the operators, also this way my beer belly is less obvious!

The major disadvantage to this is the ease with which the operators can be distracted. Members of the public, and friends alike, tend to speak to them whilst in the middle of an operating session. This potentially could have catastrophic results, but usually only means the whole job stops for a few minutes till they realize Lime Street has come to a grinding halt! We try to have an extra 'man' on duty to answer any questions that may come up during a show, but this is not always possible.

Returning to the control side of things, as the layout is now primarily built as an exhibition layout, there must be as much movement as possible within the bounds of authenticity to sustain the interest of the paying public, and also keep the operators on their toes! Basically, what has evolved is that there should be one operating position at the fiddle yard/sector plate end of the layout, this being adjacent to where the fiddle yard track meets the sector plate, and a double operating position adjacent to the station throat. Two positions are necessary, to allow simultaneous operation of the station area. The layout is operated under a master card system that is broken down into the constituent parts for each operating position.

Transport of delight

One area of layout design that is rarely discussed is the means by which it is packed and stored for transport both to and from exhibitions up and down the country. This is extemely important. We spend a fortune both in time and money building our little masterpieces, yet so many times one sees them just chucked in the back of a transit! Also one has only a limited time to load the van before setting off for the show, and a limited time on arrival to set up. Then of course there is knock down time when the show is over. No one wants to be last man away, and who gives a damn at 11.30pm when the van has to be unloaded before you get off home to bed? (why on earth do we bother?).

Over the years, I've seen the most ingenious methods employed to achieve the above; some people deserve a medal for their efforts, they are unsung heroes. All this is never seen by the public. In my case I tried to keep pace with this side of things as the layout was built. When the present incarnation of Liverpool Lime Street was planned 30 years ago. At that time bread was still being delivered in wooden trays (bear with me). When I suggested the size and construction of the baseboards, people remarked on the similarity to the humble bread tray. Once while out driving, I noticed a bread van making its delivery, and was impressed with the way all the trays stacked into a metal frame on wheels that allowed a complete delivery to be made in one trip from van to shop. I immediately seized on the idea as the means to transport the baseboards into, and out of an exhibition hall - thus the system was born.

The main parameter is that all baseboards must be the same size and shape (small discrepancies can be catered for). Thus from their dimensions, the dimensions of the frame(s) can be calculated, not forgetting to allow sufficient height for both the depth of the baseboard, and whatever might ultimately be built on top (houses, street lamps, etc.).

Although not essential, it is best to plan the frames so that the top board on the frame is the first to be needed when setting up the layout and last to be replaced on knock down, this keeps the centre of gravity as low as possible, and thus the frame stable. This is not always possible, due to the fact that different baseboards have varying height requirements, and this can lead to an uneconomical size of frame. This is because there is a maximum height you can make these frames due to the head clearance of the type of van you need. We manage with a 3.5 ton Luton box van, so our frames can be about 5' 5" high (don't forget to allow for the wheels in your calculation for the overall height!).

Our frames are made with 1" square section mild steel and the shelf/runners are of 1" x 2" unequal angle mild steel. This is obtainable from numerous steel stockists around the country (good old Google!). There are 3/8" mild steel base plates in each corner of the base of the frames that are drilled to bolt the wheels to. Don't forget to weld small pieces of flat steel bar at the back of each runner to prevent baseboards sliding through. Finally weld two cross braces of flat steel bar diagonally from corner to corner of the lower section of the frame (see refinement 1 below).

The wheels should be as large a diameter as you can get. Ours are 7", again a search on the Internet found a suitable supplier. I would recommend having two wheels at one end of the frame of the fixed type, while the other two swivel. This gives you good control of the frame when steering, remember these things get heavy! The swivel type usually has a brake mechanism, which is useful when lowering the frame on the van tail lift! Rubber tyres are to be preferred as they reduce the vibration when traversing concrete paths, etc. I would point out at this stage that I have no welding skills, and rather than risk the whole thing collapsing with half of Lime Street on it, I found a local metal works to do the welding for me. I just cut all the steel up to the required sizes, bundled it up into numbered packs, and supplied a set of drawings. So if you are good with a MIG welder you could do it cheaper than I did. Finally, there are some refinements I have made to improve the frames further:

1: With the use of the next size down square section steel, you can cut the frames across the middle, and weld in small pieces to form a plug and socket arrangement. This way the frames can be collapsed and stored under the layout during the show,

Unusually for a large exhibition layout, Lime Street is operated from the front.

thus saving valuable floor space in the exhibition hall. The top cross members are treated the same way, thus the frames collapse into five parts.

2: The frames have been 'powder coated', a process that gives an excellent finish, far more durable than paint.

3: The shelf 'runners' have been covered with strips of formica; this allows the baseboards to slide easily into and out of the 'shelves', and preserves the powder coat finish.

4: My wife has made covers out of the blue tarpaulins that you can buy at B&Q. These sleeve over the frames during transit, and as well as keeping the dust off at home, protect the layout when loading/unloading in the rain.

5: I have fitted pieces of foam pipe lagging to each vertical corner at a strategic height to act as buffers when the frames are strapped up in the van.

In conclusion, I would say that the system I have developed is by no means cheap, but you have to consider how many times you are likely to take your layout into and out of an exhibition hall. Every time we have taken Lime Street out since I built them, we

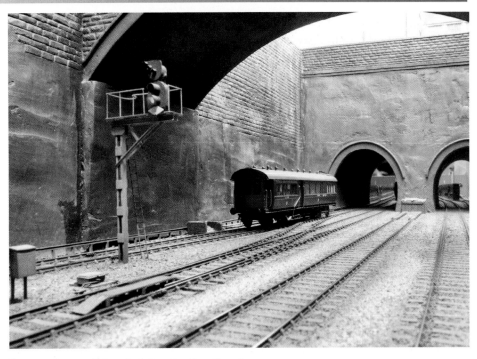

The steam railmotor again illustrating just how deep the cutting walls are.

have said 'Thank God we have the frames!'

They save a considerable amount of time when setting up, baseboards are only removed from the frames when required, so there is less risk of damage on the exhibition floor, to say nothing of during transit. Also, there is less strain on you and your friend's backs! The only drawbacks I can see with the system are the cost, and the fact that you have to hire a van with a tail lift.

The 'Turbomotive' and her eleven coach train arives at the, as yet, unfinished Lime Street station. A lot more work has been carried out since Tony Wright photographed the layout including production of the 78 columns and pillars to support the overall station roof...

North Staffordshire Railway 'B' Class 2-4-0T No.2 is built from a Planit Models kit designed by the late Eric Mullineux.

A 'KNOTTY' QUARTET

A collection of delightful O gauge North Staffordshire Railway locomotives described by **Neil Burgess**. Photography by Ray Lightfoot.

This is a collection of four North Staffordshire Railway locomotives modelled in finescale O gauge for a layout begun some years ago. They are all built using Slater's wheels and Mashima 1833 can motors, driving through gearboxes from Branchlines. The original project to model the 'Knotty' was an idea of my late father-in-law Eric Mullineux, a native of the Potteries, whose father, Arthur, had started work as a lad porter at Cheadle some time during the Great War and who went on to give a lifetime's service to the North Staffordshire, the LMS and British Railways as a goods clerk. Attired in Norfolk jacket and cap, Ray Lightfoot set up his glass-plate camera and tripod in the station yard at Lane End one morning in April 1912 to record this quartet of engines for posterity.

B Class 2-4-0T No.2

These little engines were a development of the 'A' Class, originally designed by C. Clare, the North Staffordshire's Locomotive Superintendent between 1875-82. The 'A' Class originally had driving wheels of 4' 6", with 3' 5" leading wheels and the 'B' Class differed from them primarily in using 5' 6" drivers with 4' 0" leading wheels. Over the years the original 'B' Class were modified with marginally larger boilers - 4' 2" diameter against the original 4' 0" - and received larger cabs. The majority of the class were built under the superintendence of Clare's successor, Luke Longbottom, who oversaw the motive power arrangements from 1882 until his death in office in 1902. No.2 was originally built at Stoke in December 1890, and was rebuilt in this form in 1903. It was placed on the duplicate list, becoming 2A,

in 1923 on the building of the 'New L' class 0-6-2 tank, now the last remaining North Staffordshire Railway steam locomotive, preserved in the National Collection. No.2A was soon renumbered 1447 by the LMS, who withdrew it in November 1930.

Eric Mullineux produced a number of etched kits for NSR locomotives, in both 4mm and 7mm scales, under the 'Planit Models' label. This is one of his kits, originally built by me for his planned layout, though sadly he never lived to see it.

'A modified' Class 2-4-2T No.40

Most of the original 'A' Class engines were themselves rebuilt with larger driving wheels, of 5' 1" diameter with 4' 1" leading wheels. In this form the majority ran until withdrawal, none being absorbed by the LMS in 1923. However, three were rebuilt

The 'D' Class 0-6-0Ts were the most numerous class on the NSR.with 49 being built between 1813 and 1899. The model is built from a Chowbent kit, sadly no longer available.

again, this time as 2-4-2 tanks, the trailing wheels being 3' 6" in diameter, giving them a slightly unbalanced look. Nos.35, 40 and 52 were so altered in 1898, in due course receiving the larger 4' 2" boiler. These

survived the Grouping to become LMS Nos.1455, 1456 and 1454 respectively, all lasting until 1932.

No.40 is another of Eric's kits, with extended frames and bunker.

'D' class 0-6-0 tank no. 32 [3294]

The North Staffordshire tended to build small classes of engines, something which did nothing to help their survival under the tidy-minded LMS, but the 'D' Class of 0-6-

Also built from a Planit Models kit, 'A modified' Class 2-4-2T No.40. The prototype was one of three rebuilt from 'A' Class engines in 1848, lasting into LMS ownership and eventually withdrawn in 1932.

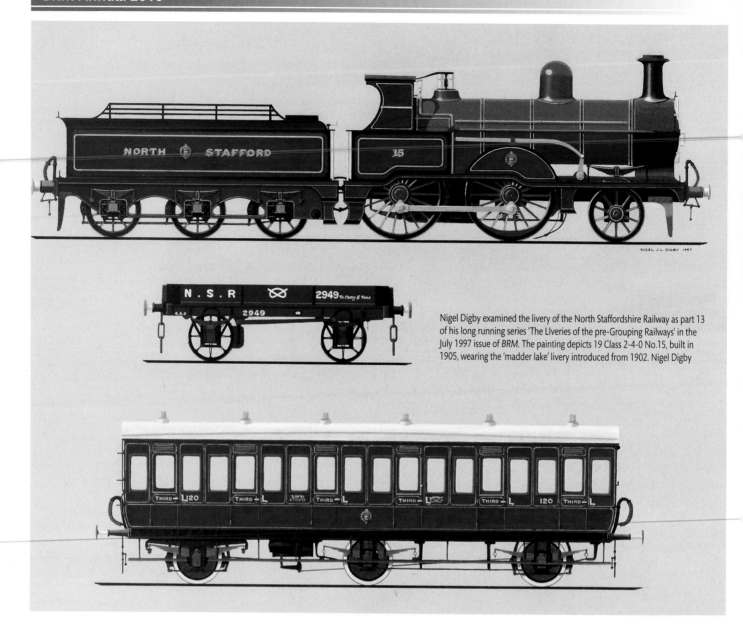

Nigel Digby examined the livery of the North Staffordshire Railway as part 13 of his long running series 'The LIveries of the pre-Grouping Railways' in the July 1997 issue of *BRM*. The painting depicts 19 Class 2-4-0 No.15, built in 1905, wearing the 'madder lake' livery introduced from 1902. Nigel Digby

0 tank engines was the most numerous on the railway, having 49 examples. These were in effect the goods version of the 'A' and 'B' Classes, having 4' 6" wheels and longer side-tanks and were built throughout Longbottom's term of office between 1883 and 1899. They displayed an array of variations in numbers of wheel spokes, cab sizes and widths, while the two boiler sizes found on the 'A' and 'B' engines were also in evidence. All survived into LMS ownership, being numbered 1550-1598 and disappearing between 1927 and 1937. No.32 was built in 1884 and rebuilt in 1903. The model is from the now-withdrawn Chowbent kit.

'M' Class 0-4-4T No.9

Luke Longbottom's successor was John Henry Adams, the third son of William Adams, of North London, Great Eastern and London & South Western railways fame. He had worked previously under Harry Wainwright on the South Eastern & Chatham and had co-operated with William Surtees in designing the 'H' Class

0-4-4 tanks for that company. Adams' locomotives were of a very distinct appearance, clearly differing from those of Clare and Longbottom, and his style was perpetuated by his successor, John Albert Hookham (1915-23). These included higher-pitched and much larger boilers with cylindrical smokeboxes mounted on saddles and having a clearly domed smokebox door fastened with wheel and handle; and also cabs with rounded eaves, much in the style of Deeley's contemporary designs on the Midland. Adams' first design was an 0-6-2 tank, the 'L' class, followed in 1907 by five members of the 'M' class, which were the passenger equivalent of the 'L'. The original two 'M' class engines were built with a vertical plate extension to the main bunker sides, shown here on No.9, the first engine. These plates were later replaced by flared extensions, with which the remaining three had been built from new. In 1920 four more engines, with slightly larger bunkers and other minor differences, were built as class 'New M'. The nine engines were numbered 1431-39

by the LMS and 'M' No.1434 and 'New M' No.1436 (NSR Nos.41 and 15 respectively) achieved the dubious distinction of being the last two standard gauge NSR steam locomotives in main line service, being withdrawn in March and April 1939.

The model is scratch-built with brass main frames and plastic card body. I was very much experimenting with the latter, since it is a material I use extensively in modelling and with which I enjoy working. As long as everything is properly braced and care is

For those with an interest in the prototype or in modelling the 'Knotty', the North Staffordshire Railway Study Group exists to promote research and interest in the company and its history.

The NGRSG meets four times a year and publishes a newsletter, *Loop Lines*, six times per year and *The Journal* bi-annually. For more information contact the Hon. Secretary, David Moore, 6 Pennine Way, Biddulph, Staffordshire ST8 7EJ or visit: www.lnw1.demon.co.uk/nsrsg.htm

taken not to warp the plastic with too much solvent - good principles to observe anyway - there is no reason why plastic should not be used for scratch-building in 7mm scale. I have a double framed 0-6-0 tender engine of Class 'F' in works at the moment, about which Mr. Wright has indicated an interest in hearing when complete, so there may be more reports from Lane End in due course.

Painting and lining

Pre-grouping era models tend to require liveries considerably more elaborate than those carried in later days and the North Staffordshire is no exception, painting and lining everything, including goods locomotives. Until the end of the Longbottom period locomotives were painted in a reddish-brown colour described as 'Victoria brown', passenger coaches having the same colour on their lower panels and off-white on the upperworks. Adams replaced this with a redder colour, described as 'Madder Lake', which was still much browner tinted than the contemporary crimson lake on the neighbouring Midland. Coaches also received all-over Madder Lake, apparently because the company felt using off-white in the polluted atmosphere of the Potteries was too much like fighting a losing battle. Lining was yellow or gold, edged with vermillion and I am reliably informed that the best guide to the Adams livery is the F Moore painting of 'New C' Class 0-6-4 tank No.31 which appeared as the frontispiece to George Dow's *North Staffordshire Album*.

For modellers, Phoenix Precision Paints produce Madder Lake in tinlets, but, though no doubt excellent in many ways, I have found it needs several coats for brush painting and, because of the relatively long periods between use (I can't make models fast enough, in other words) tends to become rather treacle-like, so I have tried an alternative. This is one of the car touch-up aerosols from Halford's, a colour rejoicing in the name of 'Clove brown', which seems to pass muster with the critical eyes of fellow North Staffordshire Railway Study Group members. Hand lining has also been tried, though latterly I have experimented with waterslide lining from Fox Transfers. Here though I discovered that yellow lining is really a bit stark and 'M' Class No.9 will be lined using their 'old gold', which I think might do the trick by producing a more subdued finish. Boiler bands are produced from thin black cartridge paper with the yellow and red lines applied using a bow pen, then stuck onto the boiler cladding with satin varnish.

Observant readers will notice the locomotive lack some details like brakes, vacuum ejectors and injectors, the latter being Giffard type items mounted on top of the tanks in the manner of the Beyer, Peacock engines on the Isle of Man. These sorts of things present no small challenge to the modeller, some of them being almost impossible to find information about and others – such as the injectors – needed a degree of research and occasional good fortune to find. This is one of the attractions

of modelling pre-1923 companies, particularly the small ones. If this brief piece encourages you to look more closely at the 'Knotty', some sources of information are given below.

Further reading

■ *Portrait of the North Staffordshire Railway* Rex Christiansen with R W Miller
(Ian Allan 1997)

■ *The North Staffordshire Railway* David & Charles (1971)

■ *North Staffordshire Album* George Dow (Ian Allan 1970)

■ *North Staffordshire Locomotives* Ken Hopkins
(Trent Valley Publications 1986)

■ *The Knotty* Basil Jeuda (Lightmoor Press 1996)

■ *The North Staffordshire Railway* 'Manifold'
(J H Henstock Ltd. 1952)

■ *Locomotives Illustrated No.135 - North Staffordshire Locomotives* (March/April 2001)

There are also several titles in the Oakwood Press series covering individual North Staffordshire lines.

'M' Class 0-4-4T No.9 is scratch-built, using braass for the main frames and plastic card for the body.

LICENSED TO MODEL

Intrigued as to how manufacturers reach agreement to use logos and liveries on new models, **Peter Marriott** explores a little known topic of great importance to our hobby. Photography as credited.

When modellers see a real train carrying a new livery it is inevitable that some will want to buy a model of it in that colour scheme as soon as possible. Likewise, when a new train operating company takes over a franchise and introduces its own distinctive livery, we modellers are keen for manufacturers to release models in the new livery, or transfer manufacturers to produce the new logos and markings immediately! Railway modellers might be impatient but just why are there delays for us in obtaining models in the latest liveries? Do the manufacturers try hard enough to release the models that we want to buy quickly enough, or is the whole process a lot more complicated than modellers envisage?

I confess to having known nothing about this topic until the editor suggested to me

that I might want to do some research that could form the basis of this article. I have to say that I have found the topic to be more interesting than I envisaged it would be. I have learned a little about the 'behind the scenes' negotiations that take place between manufacturers in the model industry and the numerous companies in the real railway. That said I am not legally trained so I apologise in advance for any incorrect statements that might have been made in this feature. In the course of my enquiries I spoke with model manufacturers in the UK and overseas in addition to speaking to two UK transfer producers. To get the real railway's view on this topic I spoke with CrossCountry to get the view from the other side of the fence. Whilst this magazine is for modellers of the UK scene we have included the section on licensing issues in the USA as it does

show that these issues are not just confined to our shores. In fact you might reach the conclusion that things are rather simpler on this side of the Atlantic! The issues that we wanted to explore in this research were:

- What is a licence?
- Why do model manufacturers and the producers of transfers need a licence to replicate a corporate livery in miniature?
- How long do negotiations take for permission to use a companies' logo or livery?
- Do railway companies seek monetary reward for permission to use their logos and livery on models?

Defining a licence

Before a model manufacturer can use a logo or livery on one of their models they need to approach the owner of that logo or livery to seek permission to use that

corporate identity in miniature. In rough terms, the granting of that permission is called a licence.

So just what is a licence? Basically it is a contract that grants a party explicit rights to use the intellectual property of another company. For example, Virgin Trains may grant permission to Bachmann to use their livery and logos on its model of the Class 57 'Thunderbird' locomotive but Bachmann also had to negotiate for a separate licence to use the 'Thunderbird' nameplates from Carlton International Media because they are the owners of the *Thunderbird* TV series and other media rights. Put another way this is a business arrangement in which the owner of branding agrees that another company may replicate its branding or livery on one of their products.

There is no such thing as a standard licence granted by prototype railway companies to model makers or the makers of transfers. Every licence, arrangement or agreement is unique with its own special requirements that might include a designated time period with financial or other obligations. Licences will permit the manufacturer to sell the licenced products in a particular area of the world.

The trademark of a company may form part of its 'intellectual property'. This can be the company name, an image, a word, a phrase, a symbol, a device or any combination of these that is used to identify a company, its goods and services from those of other companies. We are all familiar with the Nike '√' and the McDonalds big 'M'. These are logos of the parent companies. The same applies to the First Group's 'F' symbol and London Midland's new green, black and grey colour scheme.

Some modellers see the use of logos, etc, on model locomotives as promoting the free advertising of a company's product and its name. They may feel that the prototype company should be grateful that folks want to run miniature trains in that livery but current train operators and railway companies do not always see it that way. They are commercial organisations and it may be the wishes of railway modellers are not too high in their promotional activities or advertising campaigns. How different it was in the days prior to modern privatisation in 1994 when the railway companies almost fought to get their liveries onto models. They saw it as a relatively easy and cheap way to ultimately attract more customers onto their trains. And in the past the application of logos

and livery was not always as precise as it is today. For proof of this, look back at some of the early models carrying the liveries of the pre-Grouping, 'Big Four' and Nationalised operators. Companies like Bassett-Lowke even made models for companies such as the Caledonian and London & North Western Railway to market to the public.

An example of the licensing issues at the time of writing is the new Scotland branding/livery that is owned by Transport For Scotland rather than First Scotland. A licensing request needs to be made to Transport For Scotland for permission to use their logo on future models rather than to First ScotRail (as was the case until recently).

Model manufacturers view

To gain the manufacturers perspective of the licensing minefield we spoke to Dennis Lovett, Public Relations Manager of Bachmann. He has dealt with licensing issues from both sides of the fence because he previously worked in senior positions within the railway industry. He first got involved with licensing when working for Network South East at Waterloo and explains: *'The approach back in the 1980s was somewhat different to now. BR had no licensing issues as far as I can recall, but when Sectorisation came along model manufacturers appeared reluctant to reproduce the new Network South East livery on any of their models. Chris Green, the NSE Managing Director, soon noticed that the model shops were bereft of locomotives and rolling stock in NSE red, blue and grey. I was asked to sort this out and did so by ringing round the model manufacturers at that time and almost pleading with them to produce models featuring the NSE livery. How things have changed since then!'*

But even then things were not without their complications Dennis confesses: *'I*

remember working with Ken Court of Lima on the NSE releases of the Class 50 and Mk.2 coaches. We at NSE supplied all of the livery diagrams, paint samples, etc, to Lima but unbeknown to us the grey on the real locomotive and coaches had been darkened in the workshops as the first ones looked too light when they applied the paint.

Unfortunately no one altered the livery diagrams and Lima got it wrong which was all down to me! They say you learn by your mistakes and that one has haunted me ever since. I remember the samples sitting in the stock cupboard at Euston House – I wonder what happened to them as they would be pretty collectable now!'

As BR was prepared for privatisation, the world of licensing became much more complicated. InterCity was particularly protective of its swallow logo and livery. Dennis followed Chris Green to work at InterCity where his first task was to respond to all the letters from model manufacturers asking if they could reproduce the Inter City livery. *'We kind of owed them a favour for all of the NSE models that they had produced so for the last two years of its existence, InterCity was well represented in model form.'*

After privatisation things changed dramatically. Not all of the new railway companies were as willing to let their logos and liveries appear on models. Well known professional railwayman Chris Green was one person who was in favour of allowing model manufacturers using licenced liveries so when he joined Virgin Trains the issues were quickly resolved for that company and at the Warley Show in 1999 he launched the Graham Farish models in Virgin Trains livery.

'But not all operators were as sensitive to the modeller's requirements. One or two of the train operators, now no longer around, were not only protective of their intellectual property

Class 170/2 No.170102 at Burton on Trent on June 7, 2008, when operating a Nottingham service. This livery has been captured perfectly on a new Bachmann model. Nigel Burkin

RIGHT: BR green liveried D200 acts as standby at Blea Moor on November 24, 1985. Late Pete Walton/Strathwood

but allegedly demanded huge financial returns in return for use of their liveries. When a new franchise operator is announced or a company is taken over, then dealing with licensing issues for railway models is low down the real railway company's list of priorities. Although model manufacturers may endeavour to make contact immediately, it might take several months before an operator responds because they have more pressing concerns at the time' recalls Dennis.

He went on to explain: 'Model manufacturers often have to negotiate from a position where they have to explain who they are and what they do - not everyone understands model railways. Model manufacturers then have to negotiate and, depending on the complexity of the situation, this can take several months. Then an agreement needs to be signed, which can range from one sheet of paper to a document several pages in length. There is invariably a cost involved, which may have to be reflected in the price of the product.

Simply, the more complex the deal the more likely it is to add to the cost of the model. Some agreements take over a year to sign off from the first approach. Once a licence agreement is in place, we can then work with the company concerned to obtain livery diagrams, paint samples, vinyl samples, logo details and signage. But the railway company might still request to see the prototype of the model carrying the livery before finally signing off the miniaturised livery and logos. Only then can production begin on the models.

We prefer to get the agreements in place before announcing any model - it can go wrong and in the past we have, on the odd occasion, had to seek retrospective permission, which is neither good for your health or a company's reputation. The whole area of licensing is one that some modellers fail to

consider. It becomes more difficult every year and more time consuming. I can see why there is considerable growth in models carrying the British Railways totem because these do not require licensing agreements!'

Transfer makers' views

We put the following questions to Mike Watts of Fox Transfers and Precision Decals' John Peck:

BRM: What are some of the difficulties that you have had when approaching train operating companies and others to seek permission to use their logos, livery, etc?

Fox: 'One of the problems we have is finding the right person in a real railway company to talk to about licensing matters. Whilst we may write to CEOs, Public Affairs chiefs and other senior people, only rarely do we receive a response to our initial request. Sadly, they seem to believe that we are just dealing with toy trains and maybe do not take the requests very seriously. Other businesses in the model railway industry will find that the same happens to them.

Where we do find it easier to receive agreement to use corporate identities is where the company has worked successfully with us over a long period of time. The relevant person in the company knows our work (and us) and that makes reaching an agreement so much quicker. They may have already worked with us on some promotional project, but in some cases our contact moves on and we have to go through the whole process afresh on our next approach to them.'

Precision: 'One of the first problems might be in finding the correct person to ask for permission to use their logo or livery once a contact is found. Sadly most of the companies

we approach do not reply. After a reasonable time period we then need to decide if we will go ahead and produce the transfers anyway. If the company did complain that we were using their livery without permission we would, of course, need to stop producing the product.' John Peck continued: 'Recently locomotive 60 040 in DB Schenker colours with advertising for the Army has proved to be very difficult to obtain a licence for. The amount of money the Army were requesting to grant us a licence to produce the corporate identity in miniature was prohibitive for us. Usually we could never have covered our costs on such a short run of transfers, however we came up with a legitimate way to avoid licensing by releasing decal components that require some further putting together on the model to recreate the branding.'

BRM: Do TOCS, etc, seek monies/payment in return for the use of logos etc?

Fox: 'Some companies have requested a lot of money from us to produce their corporate livery. They maybe under the misapprehension that we sell as many products as does the 'Thomas the Tank' name but of course we do not. Some companies require that legal agreements be drawn up with us before they grant us a licence to produce their livery. They may ask that we pay for each part of the legal process. With other companies a 'gentleman's agreement' is all that is needed.'

Mike Watts continued: 'Because of the very commercial nature of present day train operations it is proving quite difficult for us to expand our range of modern image transfers. Actually we find that today modellers who want to apply transfers and detail their models are concentrating on steam era and early BR diesel liveries. Modern image locomotives are well covered by the ready-to-run models emanating from the factories in China with their superb manufacturing techniques. One other trend that we have noticed is the growth in the interest in transfers for the larger scales (predominately O and gauge 1). Sales of etched-brass nameplates are very strong at the moment. We work in close co-operation with the real railway company to ensure that our products match the dimensions and colour, etc, of the originals.'

Precision: 'The few companies that do demand payment for use of their livery, etc, make such projects a non-starter for us. Where licence fees are requested it can make it impossible to produce products without making a huge loss. Our aim is to offer the modellers products that they want at the same time as offering good value for money. Various recent projects for us including Freightliner and 'Thunderbird' logos, along with about 75% of the projects we'd like to have run have had to be dropped because of financial concerns. There are still 'Thunderbird'

One of the more recent liveries to be reproduced on models is Fastline Freight. Fairly new 66 305 is seen at Barrow-on-Soar on September 4, 2008, with a rake of loaded hoppers on a Daw Mill Colliery-Ratcliffe Power Station working. PC Roulston

locomotive models made by Heljan for sale without nameplates because a licence was not obtained to produce the nameplates. Some companies readily offer licences on their intellectual property free of charge. These include Network Rail and Wrexham & Shropshire Railway. We are keen to work with customers like these and are pleased to be able to offer them what is effectively free advertising and improved customer relations for their excellent co-operation.'

John Peck's slant on current trends for his business: 'I now sell mostly modern image new livery products - we find that interest in the older easier to produce subjects, where licensing is not an issue, is falling off. Our 7mm O decal products have never really taken off whilst N gauge has seen a notable increase in interest levels but still as nothing compared to OO. I would put this down to the market interest being in specific subjects rather than scales. If a good model was made available in G scale - like the Aristocraft 66 - then there will be a need for decals for it, after all you do have to put the details on models.'

A real railway company's views
We spoke to CrossCountry to gain the views of a real railway company in this matter and are grateful to Lee West for the time spent on this.

BRM: What are your criteria for agreeing to the use of logos, livery, etc, on model products and what assurances do you seek from manufacturers that your logos will be used correctly?

CrossCountry: 'We are pleased to work with model manufacturers and we invariably say 'yes' to their request to replicate our livery and logo. We always ask to see the prototype of the model carrying our colours before it goes into production - we do this to ensure that the livery, logos, numbering, etc, has been correctly applied and will thus be a good representation of our product. Our licences to replicate our livery are all in writing and the agreement is specific to the particular model and scale. So, for example, Bachmann may come to us and ask for licences to apply our livery to both their N and OO gauge models of the 'Voyager', and Dapol may just come to us in respect of their N gauge 'Voyager'.'

BRM: Do you seek monies/models in return for the use of logos, etc?

CrossCountry: 'We do not seek payment from manufacturers for the use of our livery and logos but we do request that they make a charitable donation to The Railway Children charity in exchange for granting a licence for them to replicate our products. The amount of donation is agreed in advance and will form

part of the licensing agreement. In addition we will usually ask for a small number of the finished models carrying our livery that can be used in our reception area or at presentations.'

Across the big pond
In the USA, the Union Pacific Railroad links 23 states in the western two-thirds of the country moving agricultural products, automotive, chemicals, energy, industrial products and intermodal. The railway has long-haul routes from all major West Coast and Gulf Coast ports to eastern gateways. Union Pacific moves goods across more than 33,000 miles of track employing 47,000 people and operating 7,094 locomotives and 90,877 freight cars.

Union Pacific's trademark licensing program protects the integrity of its names and trademarks by controlling the commercial use of those marks. In response to suggestions from railway modellers and historical societies, the company allocates income generated by their licensing program to support its 'Heritage' programmes, including the railway's steam programme, its heritage passenger fleet and the museum. Union Pacific has licenced dozens of manufacturers to produce and distribute items bearing the company's trademarks, including Union Pacific clothing products that are available at various retailers including Urban Outfitters, Wal-Mart and Target.

In the USA, Bachmann was one of the earliest companies to execute a licensing agreement with Union Pacific, when various manufacturers were threatened with legal action. In September 2004 Atlas Model Railroad Company, Inc. and Atlas O, LLC announced that they had signed a licensing agreement with Union Pacific Corporation to licence their corporate trademarks for the production of model railroad products. 'This agreement launches a new relationship between the Atlas companies and Union Pacific - a significant step forward that allows for co-operation while preserving company brand identity,' said CEO Dick Maddox. 'We are pleased to report that we were able to negotiate a positive agreement with Union Pacific.' This agreement will be of significant benefit to both Atlas and Union Pacific helping to preserve the quality and historical accuracy of the marks used on the production of HO, N and O scale model railroad products for consumers who seek museum quality models. The Atlas companies have since signed a licensing agreement with railroad company, CSX, located in Jacksonville, Florida.

In September 2006 Union Pacific announced that it had entered into an agreement allowing Lionel Electric Trains, the 106 year-old maker of model trains, to continue the use of Union Pacific's logos and trademarks on its products. In September 2008 a licensing agreement was

Useful Information
For more information on the products mentioned in this feature please go to:
Atlas: www.atlasrr.com

■ **Bachmann**
www.bachmann.co.uk
■ **CrossCountry Trains**
www.crosscountrytrains.co.uk
■ **Fox: Transfers**
www.fox-transfers.co.uk
■ **Precision Labels**
www.precisionlabels.com

made between Atlas and New Jersey Transit, a regional rail line operating locomotives, passenger trains and freight services in and around the New York and New Jersey area.

To prove the importance of licensing agreements to real railway companies it is worth mentioning that in September 2007 representatives of 19 model railroad companies were guests of the Union Pacific Railroad for a journey from Council Bluffs, Iowa, to Oakland, California, aboard the company's 'Heritage' fleet, which featured historic dome, sleeper, lounge and dining cars. The trip, the first of its kind, was a Union Pacific Licensing Workshop, intended to elicit feedback from the model railroad companies on how the current licensing program with UP is working, and how it could be improved. Interestingly the Atlas website (www.atlasrr. com) provides the following information: 'Products bearing American Refrigerator Transit; Chicago & Eastern Illinois (C&EI); Chicago & North Western Railway Company (CNW); The Denver & Rio Grande Western Railway Company (D&RGW); Katy; Missouri-Kansas-Texas Railroad Company (MKT); Missouri Pacific (MP); Pacific Fruit Express (PFE); Southern Pacific (SP); St. Louis Southwestern Railway Company (SSW); Cotton Belt; Texas & Pacific (T&P); Union Pacific (UP); Union Pacific Fruit Express (UPFE); Western Pacific (WP) marks are made under trademark licence from Union Pacific Railroad Company'.

So whilst a licensing agreement may be made with one parent company there may be a lot of constituent companies and their logos/liveries that fall within that agreement.

Thanks
In conclusion we would like to thank Laura Kolonski of Atlas, Dennis Lovett of Bachmann, Lee West of CrossCountry, Mike Watts of Fox Transfers and John Peck of Precision Decals for their kind assistance whilst researching the material for this article. We acknowledge their agreement to use the various quotes in the article. The views stated in this article are those from the named manufacturers, other companies may have different policies that are not covered here.

Bassett-Lowke's Northampton home at 76 Derngate, with interior designed by Charles Rennie Mackintosh. Now fully restored to its original condition, Derngate is open to the public throughout the year.

FIT FOR PURPOSE

W J Bassett-Lowke's design philosophy, 'Fit for purpose and perfection in design', is investigated by **Mike Green**, Chairman of the Bassett-Lowke Society. Images courtesy of the author and the Bassett-Lowke Society.

We tend to think of Bassett-Lowke as the guy that sold all of those expensive model trains and forget to credit him with the introduction of the OO gauge railway, the building of working architectural models which included the Singapore Mass Transit System and the Mulberry Harbour and every conceivable variety of ship. He was also a very skilled marketing person, a visionary and an outstanding designer of many things.

In attempting to understand and to try and find the source of his philosophy we have to look at his background and how he prepared himself for what he ultimately achieved. Obviously his father, who was in engineering, was a great influence to the young Bassett-Lowke since as a boy he had access to the J T Lowke works. The works was engaged in making boilers and steam fittings and he was able to build a picture of the engineering process from concept,

through design and into manufacturing. However, WJ asked his father, initially, to train as an architect and he spent 18 months working in an architectural company in Northampton. This didn't fully satisfy his ambition and he began an engineering apprenticeship with the family firm. Whilst an apprentice he studied advanced machine drawing, perspective, sound, light and heat at evening classes at the local college. After this, perhaps realising the important role that electricity would play in the future, his father sent him to Crompton Parkinson in Chelmsford to learn about the subject. So put together the knowledge he had from these experiences and you get a combination of architecture, physics, engineering and manufacturing and you can begin to answer the question about his philosophy. Added to this are the influences of the design skills of Henry Greenley who joined him in 1903, E W Twining and the early relationships with

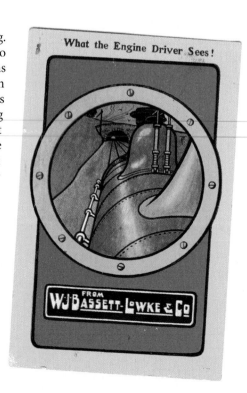

Stefan Bing and Georges Carette in Germany.

So how did the philosophy manifest itself in his achievements? The first example is his catalogues beginning in 1904-5. This was not only a brilliant marketing idea since it bought together 250 pages of everything the model engineer could possibly want but it was a wonderful piece of visual design. Many people will be familiar with the Limited Edition reprint, which in itself had a stunning front cover, but the original is embossed giving it a three dimensional feel. The company was to go on publishing and selling catalogues right up until its demise in 1965, all to a very high standard, but the most attractive are those from the pre-1938 period. The example shown is an artwork for a catalogue which was never used but beautifully designed. Did WJ do these or was it someone else? Many claim that they were the work of

Charles Rennie Mackintosh, more of whom later, but while I believe he was influenced by him they were WJ's concepts since similar catalogue artworks appeared well after Mackintosh was dead. We also see his creative designs in the other paperwork used by the company such as the letterheads and

postcards he used to deal with his customers. The postcard shown is from 1906 and the letterhead is dated 1912. The Bassett-Lowke's also sent out personalised Christmas cards every year and again I believe these were WJ's designs and ranged from sentiments of the season to cameos of his life all the way to touch on some of political views. A good range of these cards are illustrated in Janet Bassett-Lowke's book *Wenman Joseph Bassett-Lowke* and Roland Fuller's *The Bassett-Lowke Story*. The example shown with the snow scene is probably from the late 1930s when he spent some time travelling in Switzerland. All of this superb design and yet WJ was colour blind!

When WJ was married in 1916 his father bought him a small terraced house at 78 Derngate in Northampton. This began his journey into architectural design and he sought out Charles Rennie Mackintosh, the famous Scottish Architect, to completely redesign and furnish the house. Again the Janet Bassett-Lowke and Roland Fuller books have extensive photographs of the house and the examples shown from the

latter are now owned by the Bassett Lowke Society. The house is a remarkable piece of work and since Mackintosh never visited it I have to believe there is a lot of WJ's influence as well. The furniture was designed by Mackintosh and made by German prisoners of war on the Isle of Man and there is evidence that WJ visited the island at least once to check on the progress of his furniture and, being the man he was, probably added a few embellishments of his own. The house has now been fully restored to its original condition and is open to the public for guided tours for most of the year. While the Bassett-Lowkes didn't have any children of their own they liked to entertain family and friends and Derngate did not have the space they required. The plan was to build a new house with 'all mod cons' and in 1924, having lost touch with Mackintosh, WJ sought a new architect and found the German Professor Peter Behrens. The pair designed a house way ahead of its time with many new innovations and it was suitably named 'New Ways'. The house still

THIS PAGE: Bassett-Lowke depicted in miniature tin signs and an unpublished catalogue cover. The exterior of Bassett-Lowke's first home in Northampton at Derngate is seen above.

The exterior of New Ways, designed by German architect Peter Behrens.

The interior of New Ways.

has its original appearance but the interior has not been seen for many years since the owners, understandably, wish to maintain their privacy. A review of the house was published in the *Ideal Home* magazine in 1927.

We also see both of the major elements of the philosophy in the company's products since those who have owned them will say that they always were, and still are, fit for purpose all of these years later and prior to the introduction of the finer scale standards in the

standards for everyone in the model railway world and the golden age of the late 1930s with the Bassett-Lowke produced 'Princess Royal', 'Jubilee', 'Coronation' and A4 certainly met the criteria.

Finally two of the perhaps lesser known products of the company, the tin plate advertising signs and the concrete buildings were also icons of design. The tinplate signs were for buildings and generally to decorate a railway layout. The signs were either miniatures of the enamel advertising signs which adorned buildings and stations in the 1930s or the ones WJ used to promote his own company. The examples shown are the company examples and again show some beautiful designs, especially the depictions of early catalogue covers. The concrete buildings introduced in 1933 are a further example of WJ's love of contemporary design. The catalogue states that the 'Art Deco' style model of the Ashfield underground station was a collaboration between Henry Greenley and the London Transport Passenger Board.

Concrete style main line station from 1946.

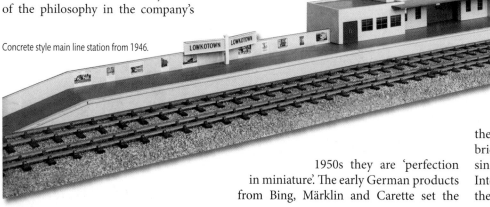

1950s they are 'perfection in miniature'. The early German products from Bing, Märklin and Carette set the

This range of buildings was clearly an attempt to modernise the attractive but dated range of brown brick buildings which had been available since the 1920s but the Second World War Intervened and by the time he introduced the rest of the range interest in O gauge was

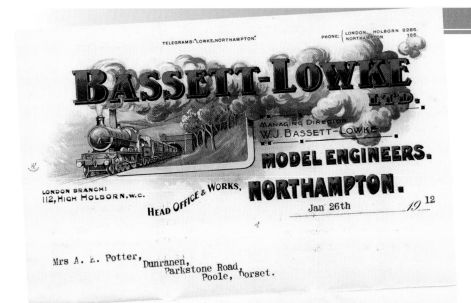

A Bassett-Lowke letterhead from 1912, and more examples of tin plate signs (below and far left). Below right is a family Christmas card from the late 1930s.

New Ways demonstrated the vision he had for modern architecture as well as some of his public duties which led to the building of the Northampton swimming baths which is again a building ahead of its time.

When WJ died in 1953 the company lost its vision and slowly went into decline. If he had survived, would the company have gone on to meet the requirements of the post-war modern age? I believe so, since WJ had always moved with the times and had changed direction several times over the 50 year history of the Company and he would have done it again.

Useful Addresses
■ **Bassett-Lowke Society**
Membership Secretary, Dept BL,
c/o Anglo Holt, 150 Birmingham Road,
West Bromwich, West Midlands B70
6QT
www.bassettlowkesociety.org.uk

■ **78 Derngate, Northampton**
Open 10.00am-5.00pm, Tuesday-
Sunday, from February to Christmas.
Tel: 0160 4603407
email: info@78derngate.org.uk
www.78derngate.org.uk

THE SONG OF THE WHEELS

WISHING YOU A MERRY CHRISTMAS

in decline. The example shown is the main line station introduced in 1946 but it only lasted until 1952.

The preparation that both WJ and his father had visualised and implemented for his mantra 'Fit for Purpose and Perfection in Miniature' clearly enabled him to achieve these goals and make him the person most remembered in the history of model engineering. His homes at Derngate and

A foreigner at Bridtorre - 26 024 is a long way from Eastfield but still looks quite at home!

BUILD THIS MICRO LAYOUT FOR LESS THAN £250!

Your complete guide to building a small scale OO gauge layout described by Peter Marriott. Photography by the author.

The origin of this layout was the arrival of the book *Building Micro Layouts* by Paul A Lunn (Santona Publications, £12.99, ISBN 978-1-907094-20-0). It had dropped through my letterbox from David Brown, editor of TRACTION magazine with a request for a review of the book. I had long admired the work of Paul and after thumbing through the book I just wanted to get on and build a tiny layout for myself.

Inspiration for this micro-layout
I found this 64-page book to be inspirational with 16 track plans plus plans for four

modules, 3D drawings of suggested layouts, model and prototype photographs. The book includes tips on using 'Y'-points and the scenic exit of the trains from the layout. Because I am a fan of one and two-car DMUs, I was not disappointed with the selection of layout projects and so in the book review that I prepared in TRACTION magazine I proclaimed 'I must say that I am already thumbing my way through the book to decide upon which layout to build first.' This article is my account of the layout that I built in the week following the writing of the review.

Another source of inspiration for this tiny layout was TRACTION magazine itself,

because over the years it has covered in words and pictures various branch lines in the South West. One article I recalled when I was considering building this micro-layout was the 'Branch to Bridport' photo feature in the August 2008 issue. There I saw Class 121 single car DMUs that offered the ideal excuse for a micro-layout. All I had to do was to locate the BR Blue Class 121 converted Lima DMU that was somewhere in the loft and Bridtorre was born.

Another source of inspiration for this layout was the two Ian Allan books by Chris Leigh entitled *GWR Country Stations* Volumes 1 and 2 that were published in

The Bachmann 'EZ Command' DCC system fits nicely behind the backscene of the tiny layout.

The landscape has been made from Woodland Scenics plaster cloth.

The road overbridge exit of the track from the layout.

A Heljan 'Hymek' indulges in some shunting.

the wires through holes drilled in the baseboard to the location of the controller. In this way the power connection is hardly visible to the eye.

Ballasting the track

We all agree that unballasted track does not look too realistic. Because I was trying to build this layout to a very tight timetable I decided to use the simplest and quickest way to install ballast. I had some Peco foam underlay pieces in stock for the points. These are a quick and easy way to ballast the track which offers quieter running characteristics than track pinned track directly to a baseboard. The one disadvantage of foam underlay is that it has a limited life and is not suitable for layouts that are envisaged to last more than a decade because it disintegrates over time.

Peco produce a 5m roll of plain track underlay but I had run out of this and my nearest model shop is 22 miles away. So for the plain track I used Gaugemaster

ballast underlay that is different from the normal foam because it has real granite bonded to the shoulders and top. I fitted the underlay to the points first and then worked between the points to 'fill in the gaps'. I found that it was better to cut less rather than more from the fill-in sections the first time. It's always easier to cut off a little bit more rather than to have to use 'fill in' sections if you have been over enthusiastic with the craft knife.

Once all of the underlay was in place, I ran a test train again to ensure that the layout still worked satisfactorily. Fortunately it did! I then used Atlas track pins at roughly 25 cm intervals to fix the track down to the baseboard. I have a small hobby hammer purchased from Hobbycraft that I use for this purpose.

The final stage of this aspect of the layout was to spray the track and ballast with Precision Paints Track Grime. This had the effect of painting the sides of the rails and visually blending the two types of underlay together.

Station platform

The top of the platform and its supporting walls were made from good quality 3mm mounting cardboard that I bought from my local Hobbycraft store. I placed the card on an A3 cutting mat and carefully and slowly cut around the card with a sharp (new) craft knife. I looked carefully at the edge of the platform and corrected some minor unevennesses with sandpaper.

The next stage was to determine the height of the platform. I stood a carriage on the track and measured to just below the step at the carriage door. Then I deducted 3mm (or whatever thickness cardboard you are using) and that was to be the height of the platform-supporting wall. Once I had decided on the height of the wall, I cut lengths of the card to form the vertical walls of the platform which were angled at the platform ramps. The walls were then fixed to the platform top by using Deluxe Materials Roket Card Glue that sets really quickly. I stood various heavy objects on the walls while upside down until the glue dried.

12 Tips for better scenery

1 Don't leave baseboard scenery flat - not even East Anglia is perfectly level! Even slight variations in the scenery do a lot to enhance the visual appearance of a layout.

2 Use a variety of scenic materials to give the scenery variety and texture.

3 Whilst not neglecting the excellent products of Woodland Scenics, Noch and other big name companies, it is also good to mix these with the products from smaller firms such as Treemendus, Geoscenics, ER Décor, miniNatur, Anita Décor in addition to natural products.

4 Use static grass if you can - the realism that 3D grass gives over 'flat' scatter material is well worth the extra time it takes. A Noch 'Grass Master' can set you back around £115, but a Gaugemaster or Noch puffer bottle is just £4.

5 Don't dismiss grass mats, some of today's products are very realistic, covering areas of ground quickly and realistically. The latest feature grasses of different heights and colours.

6 Lots of companies produce good looking trees these days. Use a few to add height to the layout but avoid 'bottlebrush' type trees - unless you are modelling the Alps!

7 Allocate an area of the layout (even just a small car park) to show off some of those excellent road vehicles available today.

8 The number of ready-made buildings available today means we can have good looking buildings on our layouts that just require 'bedding in' and a bit of weathering. The buildings can easily be 'individualised' with the addition of signs.

9 Buy PVA in large bottles - 250ml plastic bottles are too expensive per litre and you'll run out before the layout is complete!

10 Have a few rolls of plaster-impregnated cloth in stock, a mainstay in scenic modelling from Gaugemaster, Geo Scenics, Noch, Woodland Scenics and others.

11 Bachmann and Hornby now produce expanding ranges of good quality scenics which their dealers increasingly stock.

12 Use fencing, street lights, yard floodlights, road markings, figures, platform paraphernalia, posters, station signs, and road signs to add that extra scenic dimension and 'depth' to your layout.

The top surfaces of the platforms have been painted and here is a view before the fencing and other details had been added.

The Ratio signal box before detailing had taken place around it.

A few bits of goods to be moved in the goods yard plus a Land Rover by Skale Autos.

A single car DMU leaves Bridtorre.

Looking towards the station with telephone box, post box, road signs, telegraph poles with EZ Line adding the details.

The reduced height of the chimney, the figures, bushes and fencing add life to the station.

The hedging and the trees are both by ER Décor, available in the UK from The Model Landscape Company.

A Class 121 DMU looking towards the station with telephone box, post box, road signs, telegraph poles with EZ Line adding the details.

How to take better digital pictures - 1

Digital photography has encouraged more modellers to record their finished layouts or rolling stock. The arrival of digital photography has made this somewhat easier once we have mastered the skills required because for no cost (apart from the initial outlay of the camera) we can click away until we get pictures we are happy with. These tips apply to compact cameras and also Digital SLR cameras.

Get familiar with your camera and its controls as you strive to gain the most from it. It is essential to study the supplied instruction booklet.

Whilst it has always generally been better to take pictures in good daylight, digital cameras are also very good in low light situations. You might get away with a good digital picture in early evening which would not have been possible using film.

If the layout is permanently located indoors then you might need to use a mixture of daylight and artificial light when taking photographs. There are ways to compensate for artificial lighting on digital cameras. Look at your camera's manual to see if you can adjust the White Balance, this might give you a setting to use to compensate for tungsten, florescent or other lighting conditions.

One good thing is that most cameras seem to adopt common symbols, so once you have mastered one camera the next one is not such a challenge.

Bright sunlight can create shadows that do not always give the best results. But if your layout or diorama is portable you can learn to work with shadows and shade by slightly turning it around in the sun until the shadows are hidden.

Nothing mars a good digital image more than a layer of dust on the layout that can be seen in the picture. Use an air puffer to blow away any dust, cat hairs, left over scatter material or static grass fibres on the layout and rolling stock before taking the pictures. These useful tools can be bought for around £5 from specialist tool suppliers at model railway shows.

Use photographs as an aid to better modelling - for example, when you look at your pictures you may come to the conclusion that you have not included sufficient detail on the layout. You can then work up this detail and take another picture to see if you are pleased with the outcome.

How to take better digital pictures - 2

It is not necessary to have a backscene fixed on a diorama or layout to photograph it but it is always best to hide the background. A sheet of light blue mounting card will be adequate for this purpose - large sheets can be purchased from Hobby Craft or any art shop from around £4.

Overview of the station and yard.

I have a personal dislike of seeing the baseboard edge in any picture. Whilst it is unavoidable from time to time, when building a baseboard you may choose to build one that is wider rather than narrow. In this way there is less chance of the edge becoming obvious in pictures.

Use the Macro or Close Up setting on the camera where detail shots are called for. This is usually shown as a tulip on the setting dial on the camera.

Investing in a tripod is essential to achieve the best quality photos. Though the best cameras now feature some sort of image stabilisation system this can never be as good as the rock solid results that a tripod can give. Choose a tripod that enables pictures to be taken in both landscape and portrait view.

If your layout is portable and your home has a conservatory with lots of light this can be useful when the weather outside is unsuitable for photography.

Vary the angle that you take the pictures from. Try shooting the pictures below the railway line looking up, across the tracks, from the top of a building as well as a 'helicopter' shot.

Keep the camera battery topped up. There is nothing more frustrating than setting up a good picture to see the sunlight fading and the camera closing down because of a flat battery. You will probably have missed your last chance for a good picture on that day.

Set the camera to take pictures in 'Superfine' quality if you want to see them in print. Whilst this will limit the number of pictures that can be stored on a storage card, the resultant crispness of the picture image will be worth it.

Remember to back up your favourite pictures on a CD or another storage device.

Enjoy your photography and it will reward you with a good record of your hobby!

A busy detailed scene!

The hedging is by ER Décor. The figure is an old one found in my spares box.

Passenger train at the station.

'Bubblecar' and Bachmann Class 25 cross at the station throat.

A rather dirty long wheelbase Land Rover in the yard.

Evening all!

The signal indicates the DMU is about to leave.

Improving resin buildings

The Bachmann Scenecraft (N and OO), and Hornby Skaledale (OO) and Lyddle End (N scale) ranges of resin-based buildings have justifiably proved very popular with enthusiasts. These nicely detailed and painted buildings can be positioned on a layout straight from the box. Some very simple improvements can be made to the buildings to enhance their realism and to add a touch of individuality including:

■Modification, for example; reduce the height of the chimney on the Bachmann Scenecraft Market Hampton waiting room used as the main station building. Use a craft saw to remove a section of chimney, file the two cut pieces flat with a file and stick them together with Deluxe Materials R/C Modellers Craft Glue.

■ Add curtains to some windows - easily done using odd scraps of different coloured paper, thin card or tissue. A dab of PVA or Sellotape on the inside of the building will fix the curtains in place.

■On a row of terraced houses simply painting front and back doors different colours with a small paintbrush and acrylic paint improves the look.

■ Position a few birds on the ridge tiles. A variety of manufacturers including Dart Castings produce, for example, seagulls for OO scale.

■Add ivy or bushes to walls. A large number of firms make suitable material: Noch dark green leaves (Laub 07146) are ideal for ivy; Woodland Scenics Poly Fibre (FP 178) is good for bushes and creeping plants; Heki, Noch or Woodland Scenics foliage mat can be draped on the wall. Climbing roses and other flowering rambling plants can be reproduced using texture mats from 4D Modelshop; International Models retail sections of ivy mat with correct ivy shaped leaves - all fixed using a few dabs of PVA.

■Lightly weather roof and walls using a flat paintbrush lightly dipped into acrylic paint. Once the paint is applied partially rub off using a tissue so that the weathering remains in brick and tile courses.

Kit-bashing the Scenecraft building to reduce the height of the chimney.

Once I was happy that the adhesive on the platform walls had dried I painted the top with grey acrylic paint using wide flat brushes. Two coats were needed. The vertical walls were covered with Superquick stone paper attached with a frugal amount of PVA. To finish the platform I used two different colours of acrylic paint to represent a row of paving slabs and a white warning line. Both of these were also brush painted after I had run two strips of Tamiya masking tape around the edge of the platform (firstly for the paving slab line and later for the warning line). This is another task that requires a steady hand and some patience. I am always worried that the final result might have dog-legs! I worked slowly and was pleased with the resultant lines. After about a minute from painting the lines, I removed the masking tape and left the platforms to dry – do not leave the making tape on too long because it will not be so easy to remove.

Making the landscape

The embankments needed good foundations on which to fix the grass, trees, bushes, etc. On this layout I used mounting board to form the scenery contours simply because it was readily available at my local Hobbycraft store. I decided how tall the landscape would be at the rear of the layout and then cut through the cardboard with a sharp craft knife on an A3 cutting board. PVA woodworking adhesive and small blocks of timber were used to fix the landscape former to the layout.

The next stage was to 'fill' the space between the cardboard land contours. The gaps between the card pieces were filled with wads of folded and crumpled newspaper which provided support for the landscape that would be laid over the top of the paper. Once the filling material was in place, the land surface was added. I used Woodland Scenics Plaster Cloth (plaster-impregnated cloth) on the layout, cutting it with scissors into hand-sized pieces. Each piece was then dipped in a bowl of water for a few seconds and while wet was laid across the top of the newspaper; the cloth staying workable for a few minutes. I smoothed down the surface of the cloth as it dried and removed as many creases as possible, giving the landscape a smooth surface. Once fully dry (generally the next day, but within several hours if you are working in the summer) the resultant landscape is light in weight and quite rigid. I used two layers of cloth to make the landscape a lot stronger than just one layer.

When the 'land' was dry, I painted it black with acrylics to prevent the white plaster showing through the layers of scenic

BR blue days at Bridtorre.

Scenecraft Bedford with load by Ten Commandments.

Post box by Detail Matters.

Green days at Bridtorre.

More BR blue days at Bridtorre, with the Class 25 and 'Hymek' shunting the yard.

Useful websites
4D Model Shop
www.modelshop.co.uk

Anita Décor/Auhagen available in the UK from: www.internationalmodels.net

Bachmann: www.bachmann.co.uk

Berkshire Junction (EZ line) available in the UK from: www.modeljunction.info

Detail Matters: www.detailmatters.co.uk

ER Décor available in the UK from: www.modellandscapeco.com

Gaugemaster: www.gaugemaster.com

Heki available in the UK from: www.modellandscapeco.com

Hornby Skaledale: www.hornby.com

Moray Models
Detailed/weathered locos/rolling stock: www.moraymodels.co.uk

Noch: www.noch.com available in the UK from: www.gaugemaster.com

The Model Tree Shop
www.themodeltreeshop.co.uk

TRACTION magazine
www.traction.co.uk

Peco, Model Scene, Ratio and Wills
www.peco-uk.com

Railway Constructor
www.railwayconstructor.co.uk

Ten Commandments
www.cast-in-stone.co.uk

Treemendus
www.treemendusmodels.co.uk

Woodland Scenics
www.woodlandscenics.com

materials that were to be applied. Next I covered most of the steep sloping areas with Woodland Scenics Poly Fibre to represent hedging and undergrowth.

Ground cover, weeds and wild flowers
On the layout I used various layers of static grass on the level sections of the ground, static grass is a good way to cover a large area of ground quickly and realistically to provide a carpet tuft effect with grass fibres standing upright, rather than a flatter appearance as is usual with the more familiar scatter materials.

I used a Noch 'Grass Master' with static grasses made by Heki and Noch in different colours and lengths. To fix the static material to the landscape I used PVA woodworking adhesive; while the glue was still wet I shook the Noch 'Grass Master' about half an inch over the surface and watched the grasses fall into the glue in the upright position.

In other areas I brushed on a little neat PVA and sprinkled on some Woodland Scenics Fine Turf, Coarse Turf and Underbrush. When the glue had dried the excess material was shaken off.

I tried to remember to mix the colours of the materials at all stages – ground cover is never a consistent green or brown. After each layer I tipped up the baseboard to capture the excess static grass and scatter materials (when fully dry) on newspaper to save it for another day. If the layout is portable this is easier (the baseboard can be tipped upside down) than if it is permanently fixed (you may have to vacuum up the excess material).

To add further texture to the completed grass banks I dabbed a few spots of PVA glue on the landscape, at random, and attached some bushes (Auhagen Clumping) and taller grasses (Woodlands

Sea moss trees

This natural product is farmed in various countries. In appearance it's just like miniature trees with a trunk, branches and foliage. Whilst quite fragile in its raw state, by using it along with a few other products, exquisite trees can be made quickly and cheaply. Various retailers and manufacturers sell sea moss including Green Scene, International Models, Noch, Scenic Express, and ER Decor. Sea Moss can be bought in two ways – raw sea moss in boxes or packets, or as already treated trees. The first is an economical method of making trees, the second way is for those in a hurry to plant a wood or a forest!

If you buy sea moss in its untreated form you'll get pieces of all different sizes. Some will be ideal as a full (relatively small) tree in OO, a full tall tree in N or sapling in O:

■ Open the box and separate the two types of sea moss. Small pieces can be usefully used as saplings and bushes so do not throw them away.
■ Remove the large seedpods - easy to do using your fingers or a pair of tweezers.
■ Depending on the likelihood of future damage to the trees you may decide to strengthen the pieces to be used. Soaking the pieces in matt solution (such as Mod Podge available from Hobbycraft) overnight can do this - the matt solution seals and strengthens the sea moss.
■ Some modellers then spray the sea moss with paint (acrylic or similar) but this is not always necessary. The top part of the tree will be covered in foliage and if the trees are used in multiple quantities only the trunk of the tree in the foreground will be visible to viewers. The foreground tree could benefit from the painting of the trunk or alternatively Anita Décor Tree Bark or the Green Scene product could be used to bolster the diameter of the trunk.
■ Some Sea Moss trees arrive with a rather bent main trunk. This can be straightened by soaking in a solution of Mod Podge then hanging them out on the washing line, upside down, to dry. Attach a metal alligator clip to the base of the tree so that it hangs down in a vertical position.

To add the foliage use either:
■ Hairspray – choose the cheapest 'Extra Hold' type obtainable from supermarkets.
■ Scenic Cement – made by Woodland Scenics, Noch and other companies.
■ Flexible Glue - made by Anita Décor (obtainable from International Models).
■ Spray the glue over the upper part of the tree. Do this in a well-ventilated area, over a cardboard box or old newspaper. Spray the piece in various directions to get plenty of adhesive on the fine branches.
■ Sprinkle on fine scatter material. Use the finest grade of scatter material you have to hand (Woodland Scenics Fine Turf, Noch Flockage or Anita Décor Very Fine Foam are all ideal). Mix the colours a little.
■ Leave the tree to fully dry. To plant the tree drill a hole in the landscape and plant, fix with a dab of PVA.

What we found on building this micro-layout

There is nothing quite like a one baseboard layout for storage and carrying! They truly are ideal for a layout that has to be stored rather than left in one position ready to 'play with'. This layout can be picked up with one hand and moved around. It also fits flat on the floor of the boot of a medium sized hatchback car with none of the seats folded down.

For more years than I care to remember I have wanted to build a model based on a Devon branch line which I had never got round to, so this project enabled me to build one at last. So if you are like me, with many projects in your head but without the time, room, or money to build them all, perhaps a series of micro-layouts maybe ideal for you. By covering the baseboard with mounting card or similar before you begin the project, you could even use the same baseboard time and time again by simply removing the last layout's adhesive, scatter materials, etc, once the track and buildings are removed (this is generally easier than you think).

Though exponents of the art of building tiny layouts generally recommend using the smallest radius points that you can to squeeze in as much track for sidings and loops as possible, these do not always make for the most realistic looking layouts. Personally I try to use medium radius points where possible for two reasons:

■ Their visual impact is better
■ Most locomotives seem to run more smoothly through the slightly larger radius points.

I used some products that were new to me and learned some new skills on this project. These included:

■ Putting up telegraph wires using EZ wire

Scenics Field Grass) to add height to the scene.

On this layout I wanted to use a few large specimen trees to hide the 'storage siding' at the right-hand side of the layout, so I used large Sea Moss trees by ER Décor. In addition there is one Woodland Scenics Premium Tree and a silver birch by The Model Shop (4D). I drilled holes into the baseboard to take the trunks and used PVA to fix the tree into the hole.

Details

The details on the platform came from a variety of ranges. The station fencing is by Ratio, the station lamps are from the Hornby Skaledale range.

The fencing in the field and the telegraph poles are by Ratio and the road signs by Hornby (these were fixed by drilling a small hole in the baseboard and using PVA to hold the sign in place).

In the goods yard the barrels, sacks and palleted loads mainly came from Ten Commandments. Various odds and ends around the layout came from my 'spares box'. Most of the figures on the layout are from Model Scene. The figures were fixed to the layout with a dab of PVA on their feet.

The post box on a post is from specialist scenic supplier Detail Matters.

■ It was the first time I had kit-bashed a ready-made resin building

■ I used the biggest sea moss trees I could find to hide the exit track from the layout

I suppose what I did find a tad frustrating on completion of Bridtorre was that (of course) the running possibilities of the trains are very limited. I confess to not being a real fan of end-to-end layouts and prefer to see trains running through the countryside (even slowly) rather than having to move locos very short distances.

The cost of this layout was around £250.00, including the baseboard and the

It's that 'Hymek' again! This time D7040 heads through with a short passenger train.

Conclusion

To conclude, we have a small layout built in around 45 hours for about £250.00. The layout can be carried around a house by one person and can be set up in less than ten minutes.

Go on - build yourself the micro-layout that you have been promising yourself for years! It certainly is fun!

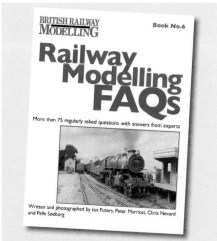

Bachmann 'EZ Command' DCC System. The layout could have been built for half that price if you used a basic DC control system, used kit or scratch-built buildings and the bridge and made the baseboard yourself.

It took me a full week of work to build the layout (in about 45 hours).

A loco-hauled passenger service replaces the usual DMU.

The large refinery at Grangemouth has always been an important source of rail traffic and remains so today. Eastfield maintained a fleet of locomotives for the petroleum sector which was utilised on Scottish petroleum traffic heavyweight Class 37, No.37 707, was present in February 1991, dressed in full Petroleum Sector livery and embellished with an Eastfield 'Scottie' dog depot plaque.

SCOTTISH DIESELS ON SHED

Nigel Burkin reflects on visits to various Scottish MPDs and the variety of traction that could once be found on shed.

Until privatisation, making casual visits to some Scottish motive power depots was relatively simple, all you had to do was turn up and ask to have a look around. Arguably, the easiest one to gain access to was Eastfield, which is no longer the place it used to be. Where extensive sheds once stood, with locomotives ready for service on freight and passenger service in the Central Belt and over the West Highland Line, you will now find extensive carriage sidings used for the stabling of ScotRail 'Turbostars', Class 156s and 158s.

Usually, a trip to Eastfield coincided with the large AMRSS Model Rail exhibition at the SECC in February, not usually the ideal time for railway photography. By

the time my group of friends and I had left the exhibition hall and travelled to Eastfield, darkness had fallen. Not to be put off, a tripod was usually included in my photographic equipment enabling photographs to be taken using available light both within the depot buildings and outside.

Other depots required a little more thought to make a visit possible and the old 'Platform 5 Publishing' books offered the addresses of officials to whom letters should be addressed in order to request passes. I was fortunate enough to visit Inverness, Ayr, Haymarket, Craigentinny and Millerhill. It was the latter depot which was the least enjoyable visit, because the depot foreman at the time was particularly

anti-railway enthusiasts and very much viewed depot passes issued from head office as an inconvenience. The limited access offered at the time of my one and only visit together with inclement weather did not produce satisfactory results!

My earliest visit to Inverness depot was in 1984 as part of the 'Mid Kylesman' rail tour which started in the Midlands with D200 in charge and finished off with a Tinsley allocated Class 37 to Kyle of Lochalsh. Part of the tour included a visit to the depot at Inverness where Class 37/0s, Class 26s and Class 27s could be observed. 1984 was well within the transition era when RETB was being introduced and Class 37s with steam heat began to replace Class 26s and 27s on services in the Highlands.

Inverness was host to numerous Class 26 locomotives which were used on services to the Far North and Kyle of Lochalsh. On my first visit to Inverness on May 19,1984, shortly after I had taken up serious railway photography (making many mistakes in the process), I was fortunate enough to be able to visit the depot. This picture shows Class 26 041 and 046 stabled between duties. They had little time left in the Highlands as RETB and Class 37/4s were not far off in the future.

These days, visits to operational depots are nearly impossible to make because of various safety rules and concerns regarding legal liability. Whilst there is no longer a depot at Eastfield, those at Inverness, Haymarket, Motherwell, Ayr and Craigentinny are still operational, although not to the same extent as before. Inverness services the Class 158s used on the Far North routes and the Aberdeen line together with maintenance of the 'Caledonian Sleeper' stock. Every night, the stock from the GNER/National Express East Coast 'Highland Chieftain' is serviced at Inverness. Craigentinny depot, which is located south of Edinburgh Waverley, remains an important servicing depot for East Coast electrics and HSTs together with the stock from the 'Royal Scotsman'. The depots at Millerhill, Ayr, Motherwell and Fort William are operated by EWS and are, to all intents and purposes, stabling points which undertake light maintenance and examinations.

Let's take a trip back in time, to when sector liveries were the norm and Class 26s were common in Scotland, with the assistance of a small selection of pictures taken on my many travels north of the border.

The depot shunter at Haymarket in January 1990 was Class 08, No.08 761 decorated in Provincial Sector livery together with a Haymarket depot badge. It was receiving attention at the time of this photograph.

Attention now shifts to Eastfield which played host to Strathclyde PTE Class 107 DMUs. Here, Nos.107 044 and 049 are receiving routine attention during the February 1991 visit.

Eastfield was famous for its varied allocation of locomotives and the West Highland 'Scottie' logo which was applied to all of its locomotives at every available opportunity. Following a visit to the Model Rail Scotland exhibition, I found myself wandering around Eastfield depot after dark with a group of friends (who were fellow members of Sunderland & District MRC) after obtaining permission from a sympathetic depot foreman. Class 26, 26 025, was present in the shed in February 1991.

It is easy to forget the variety of liveries that existed during the Sectorisation period. Class 47, 47 636 *Sir John de Graeme*, was painted in large logo livery when photographed in the shed at Eastfield in February 1991.

By 1990, Haymarket had become what it is today: a 'Sprinter' depot responsible for servicing a large proportion of ScotRail operated Class 156s, 158s and 170s. In 1990, Class 156s dominated the scene and this picture shows 156 445, which was allocated to Haymarket at the time, undergoing ultrasonic testing of its axles.

Ayr depot was an important location for maintaining those locomotives used on Ayrshire coalfield trains. It was quite normal to find a large number of Coal Sector Class 37s stabled at Ayr at the weekends. 37 376 and 37 229 were photographed on March 31, 1991.

Ayr was also host to an immaculate Class 26, 26 043 in Departmental livery on March 31, 1991.

By 1994, Class 26s had fallen out of favour in the newly privatised railway and many were stored pending developments at Inverness. One such locomotive was 26 035 which was photographed outside the depot buildings at Inverness on July 29, 1994.

READERS' LAYOUTS ALBUM

Bromsgrove

Tony Wright was very taken with Bob's highly atmospheric photos of Bromsgrove which appeared in the February 2007 issue. So much so, that he took himself to Harrow to photograph it before Bob's pictures appeared in print. The full feature made the March 2007 magazine - surely the fastest turnaround for a 'Readers' Layout' ever! Following advice from Tony, Bob later sent in some more photographs which he had taken, which graced the October 2008 *BRM*.

Cleckhuddersfax

Cleckhuddersfax is a freelance interpretation of the West Riding of Yorkshire around 1963. It has been ten years in the making, a house move setting progress back by a couple of years but allowing an enlarged version to emerge from the chaos! A double track main line is flanked by 'relief' lines which are linked by an overbridge, allowing access between the goods yard on the outer relief circuit, and the loco depot on the inner relief circuit to be operated without interrupting running on the main lines. Operation can be either as a shunting layout or just 'watching the trains'; trying to do both requires another operator! Control is analogue with complex track diagram panels and full point indication with cab control. Much work remains to be done; a diesel depot, signalling and the all important passengers.

Peter D Koch-Osborne, Penrith

ELVINLEY JUNCTION

Having featured in 'Readers' Layouts', Ian Arkley's N gauge layout now gets the full spotlight, together with some more of his photographs.

Elvinley Junction began life a couple of years ago and came together extremely quickly. The baseboard, trackwork, wiring and scenery were all complete within a few months. The finer details have been added since and will probably keep on being added as long as the railway is in existence.

Plans for the railway consisted of a rough idea scrawled on a piece of paper and the rest just came from imagination. I knew I wanted to disguise the tighter curves with tunnels and that I wanted a viaduct. The rest slotted into place without too many problems. The railway is mounted on a 4' by 8' board which can fold up against the wall.

The layout takes its name from my father's middle name 'Elvin'. I wanted to name the railway after him because of his infectious interest in railways, which has rubbed off on me over the years and (along with my mother) has been a big encouragement in my hobby from my childhood. I have fond memories of watching his OO trains as a child and of trips to the Severn Valley Railway with my family from a very young age. I started modelling railways myself in my teens and this layout is number five or six. I had a long gap away from model railways for about a decade, but my interest has been rekindled in the last few years. I constructed a small N gauge railway recently, but wanted something much bigger and with much more operating potential. This is my first attempt at a railway with point motors and is the largest I have made (so far). Over the years I have mostly worked with N gauge and started with a Fleishmann loco as a child. I think N will always be my favourite gauge, and I am glad that there have been many new models recently and that N seems to be catching up in some ways with OO.

The railway has drawn a lot of inspiration from the SVR and although it is a fictitious place, it has a distinctly Western Region vibe to it. I am not too fussy about what trains I run and have many different eras and regions, but if pushed, I would have to say that the period from the mid '50s to the late '60s is favoured.

Most of my scenery has been created from Woodland Scenics items as the colours are so realistic. Most buildings are 'Lyddle End', but I have built a few kits including some Ratio items. I laid the track on Peco foam underlay, filled the gaps with a mix of grey and brown ballast and then weathered with acrylics. This gives very quiet running. Control

A close-up of Elvinley Junction's station building, looking towards the village - the backscene looks very effective in this photo.

Another packed shed scene, though this time the motive power is all diesel.

Elvinley Track Plan

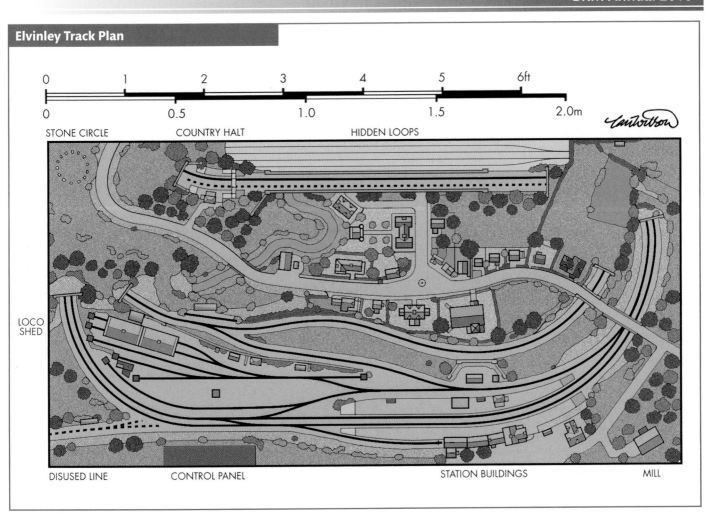

0   1   2   3   4   5   6ft

0   0.5   1.0   1.5   2.0m

STONE CIRCLE   COUNTRY HALT   HIDDEN LOOPS

LOCO SHED

DISUSED LINE   CONTROL PANEL   STATION BUILDINGS   MILL

Left: The railcar is seen passing Elvinley village,

Opposite: A busy shed scene, with plenty of steam motive power available.

Below: A bird's-eye view of the shed area, with a mixture of steam and diesel on shed. An auto-train passes by on the branch.

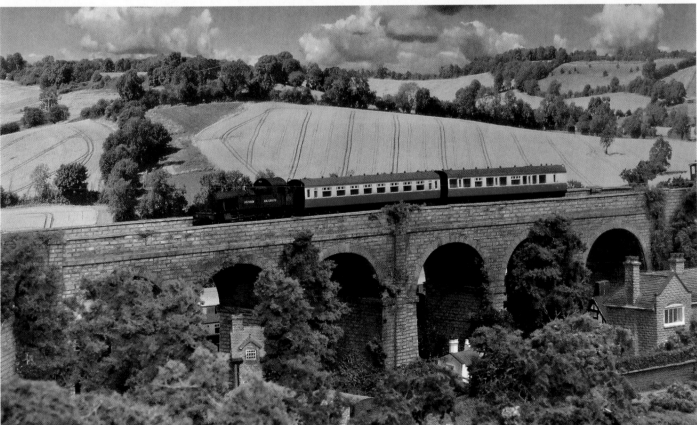

A 'Prairie' and local train pass over the branch viaduct.

diesel locomotives from Farish, Dapol, Minitrix and Union Mills and I run many different types of rolling stock.

I've recently extended the trackwork, which means I now have a siding in front of the station, and a headshunt with a steam crane in permanent residence. I also have a coal chute for the mill now which has been lashed up from card and an old girder bridge. Unfortunately all the pictures were taken before this addition.

I am a train driver for DBS (EWS) when not driving my N gauge locos, running my 5" railway in the garden or playing in one of the two bands I am currently active with! My two passions have always been music and railways and they are both very fulfilling hobbies. I would like to thank Richard Wilson at *BRM* for giving me the opportunity to share my railway with others.

A view of the road bridge which passes over the line at one end of the station.

Right: A bird's-eye view of the station as a long mixed-goods passes through. The auto-trailer is seen waiting in the bay.

is from a couple of Gaugemasters, one is a simulator controller which gives an extra dimension to DC running. I also use an electronic track cleaner by the same manufacturer. My points are controlled by a stud/probe system and I have five isolating switches for the yard. I wanted to keep wiring to a minimum and therefore opted for insulated frog points. Three trains can run continuously and I can also shunt the loco yard. There are many gradients on my upper line and I have found the best loco to deal with them has been my Farish 33, as it seems to be able to keep a pretty constant speed whether going up or down the gradients. Other stock includes many steam and

N GAUGE 'PEAK RAIL'

Darley Dale and Rowsley MPD provided the inspiration for Don
Pearson's N gauge 'modeller's paradise'.

My aims were to construct a scheme that could include the use of steam and diesel trains, with some prototypical representation, but also having a facility to allow continuous running without lapping an oval in ten seconds or so. I also considered my desire to have some fun at times and to include an aspect that was purely fictional, but embraced usage of reversing triangles, slips, gradients, and stabling for trains that are seen and not hidden behind a back scene.

The location was found in the Derbyshire Dales during a visit to friends and a ride on the Peak Rail line from Matlock to Rowsley. This line closed in 1967 as part of the Beeching restructuring of the network. Then

in 1987 efforts began to reinstate the line as far as Buxton, commencing at Darley Dale station, at that time Peak Rail's headquarters. 1997 saw further extension of the line to Rowsley and this is as far as it is today.

Rowsley was the site of the second depot constructed in 1926 as a result of congestion at the original site. Whilst all track was removed on closure after 1967, the ash pits and turntable sites were left in place, albeit filled in. Work is well under way to construct a new shed for use on the original location and also to replace a working turntable in its pit. The track plan does not conform to the original, but I feel the atmosphere of the site is very much preserved.

As a preservation society, Peak Rail has to encourage every revenue earning facility

it can find to use its lines and areas, enticing the public to join the various groups that have been formed, work as volunteers, and continue the aim of reinstating the line. This has resulted in a number of groups including the North Notts Locomotive Group, the LMS Carriage Association, Heritage Shunters Trust, and the Renown Repulse Restoration Group. There is also the Derbyshire Dales Narrow Gauge Railway based at Rowsley.

As a result of all these groups, I now find not only prototypical trains on site, but also an abundance of others who use the line. Frequent visitors make a presence and have included Class 9F 92203 *Black Prince* and 4472 *Flying Scotsman* which I was thrilled to see on one of my visits.

Research

This was my next consideration and, to me, was one of the most enjoyable aspects of my experience. I suggest that there are so many benefits to be realised, the time spent is very rewarding and can lead to a lasting association that continues to give pleasure.

I joined Peak Rail Heritage Trust, which enabled me to take copies of their *Steam in the Peak*, (now renamed *The Peak Express*) quarterly publication. From this contact was made with archivist Mick Bond. He was most helpful and referred me to articles by the late Stan Roberts on layouts he had constructed of the original Rowsley shed site and Bakewell Station. Readers may be interested to know that the Library service has a collection of all publications in an archive and so articles from out of print/unobtainable material can be obtained as photocopies from them if you know the date and name of the publication.

Matlock station building, headquarters of Peak Rail, has a shop attached and Bill Hudson, along with others, runs sales of books from here. Bill has published a book, *Through Limestone Hills* which is a fantastic reference with track plans and many scale drawings of buildings associated with the line from Ambergate to Chinley. He further mentioned that a Mr. Keith Miles

was compiling a book about his career as a 'Running Foreman' at Rowsley and gave the name of the publisher, to whom correspondence revealed his contact details. I was able quite shortly afterwards to obtain a copy of his book *Rowsley Motive Power Depot*. Visits were made to the Matlock Council Local Studies Library and I was able to peruse microfiche films of newspapers for articles about the line. These were mostly concerned with the closure, at which time much interest took place with so many jobs being lost from an area that embraced a large percentage of local employment.

The results of all this material gave me sufficient documentation to sit down and seriously consider planning the construction of my scheme. In the meantime I had built a 'fun' layout, a double oval with siding to test various construction techniques, in the areas of scenery, etc.

A question of gauge

Which gauge should the layout be modelled in was determined by the fact that from a previous foray into model railways in 1974, I already owned two N gauge Hornby Minitrix Class 42 'Warships' and a Lima Class 31. The area I wished to portray, even in N gauge, meant that considerable compression and modeller's licence would be necessary.

I am fortunate to have the complete use of a Pine log cabin for my models of some 13' 0" x 10' 0". Visiting exhibitions at which many of the excellent prototypical layouts are confined to 'end to end' with traversers did not appeal to me. My experience in membership of a club operating a layout with just a station with fiddle yards at each end found me very bored within an hour, and glad to be relieved.

I wanted to be able to store a collection of locomotives and what better than a Motive Power Depot to do this? Rowsley's MPD fitted this requirement very nicely for steam. My excursions along the line from Matlock to Rowsley soon had Darley Dale station building in my mind as the answer for a station, which also in its time incorporated some sidings and activities of interest. To attempt these in any other gauge but N would not have been possible within the constraints of space I could provide. Furthermore I did not seek to have a layout to take out to exhibitions - mine never leave home. I am very happy to entertain visitors and take pride in showing what I have been able to achieve.

This may seem selfish, but I am a member of the N Gauge Society, and of Tring & District MRC, with whom I am helping to construct Rugby Central which will go out

A 'Deltic' roars through Darley Dale in our heading photograph, whilst above Class 73 *The Royal Alex* heads a Pullman special past the brewery.

to exhibitions when it is completed. In fact it has already been shown at our annual Club exhibition, so I consider I do assist in promoting the image of railway modelling to the public and like-minded persons. I have found club membership extremely beneficial, and would suggest that all modellers will undoubtedly gain from the advice and experience of others. There are so many different approaches to each aspect of construction and I have been truly amazed at some of my achievements as a result. In my opinion clubs are all about the membership and I am now in my third club before finding the associations I am most happy with.

I have always found help and advice is freely forthcoming and this is a part of what makes this hobby so enjoyable to me.

Decisions

Having decided on building an MPD based on Rowsley and a station complex on Darley Dale, whilst still having the fun circuits to run the stock I was acquiring as each opportunity became available. At this time Graham Farish had ceased production in Poole and new owners Bachmann had not commenced supplies from China. Many second-hand items were therefore acquired.

I had the idea of making each part a self-contained project but modular (in that connection to each other is possible) by adding two linking boards, and this has worked very well for me as I have progressed. The diagrammatic plans of my scenario show these links.

Construction of Rowsley MPD commenced following a full scale plan I had made using the templates available from Peco for turnouts and Code 80 'flexitrack'. I used a baseboard of 3" x 1" framework topped with Sundeala. In retrospect, I would not use Sundeala again as my experience has shown it has bowed at joins and in the area where the cut out for the turntable fits, necessitating remedial alignments later on.

I have used Seep point motors, as I wanted the ability to indicate on the control panel the route set, and the additional inbuilt switch gave me the signal sought for this. However, again with N gauge the travel for the point is far less than, for example, OO gauge and thus it is very important to have the Seep motor centrally positioned. Even then this is not very reliable switching. I had considered Peco point motors, but these are rather large and require either an aperture cut out of the baseboard or underside mounting plates. With 23 points, even with an underside mounting plate, the likelihood of the motor fouling one of the baseboard supports was certain. Following a lecture at a club meeting which explained to me what were at the time 'Mysteries of Diodes', I made a Point Routing Selector Matrix on Veroboard, and this works very well, such that ten of the various ways through the MPD are easily selected. I also devised a way of using micro-switches to determine the turntable position having been reached.

The buildings were scratch-built using some materials from Metcalfe kits and I am very pleased with the shed to which I have added rows of lamps that work. I know they were actually gas in reality, but this is not an option with a model is it? Rowsley had a coaler that was like no other I have come across, and Keith Miles gave me a great deal of help in drawings and correspondence with this aspect and he also took the trouble to make constructive comments on photographs of progress that I sent to him. I found this most helpful in making a model which can be operated, albeit manually. I do not have the skills to automate this or the wagon tippler. My trees were in some cases made from wire and the usual flock foliage. Others were made from Seafoam that I grew myself with seeds obtained from Chiltern Seeds. These are fine for 'layouts that stay at home'. For the hills against the backscene and the gradient I used a base of expanded Polystyrene coated with plaster. The mess is quickly removed with a Vacuum cleaner and once plastered is no more.

The yard lamps were made from grain

An LMS liveried 'Crab' departs Darley Dale with a train of carmine and cream stock.

of rice bulbs fed into a slot in brass tubing, with a lampshade made from modellers clay impressed into a countersink formed in a piece of wood, and baked in an oven for 10 minutes. There are uncoupling devices in the traffic sidings, so that wagons can be sorted into lines ready for their next working. The allocation at Rowsley covered locomotives ranging from 1F 0-6-0Ts through 2, 3 and 4F/P, 5MT, 6F, 8F 2-8-0 to 9F 2-10-0s. This permits a great variety of configurations to be deployed.

With the modular concept I was able to run any locomotive or train from Rowsley MPD onto the continuous run 'fun' layout for exercise(!), whilst shunting stock around within the shed in readiness for their next working at the same time.

Construction

Construction of Darley Dale could now be considered. From Bill Hudson's book I was in possession of the full track plan as it was prior to the closures, and wanted to take this entire diagram into my project. To do this again meant compression of the platform length, but as I do not seek to run trains with more than four coaches I felt this was acceptable. Even then once I had made a track plan using Peco turnout stencils it still would not fit into the 90" length I had available. I found an interesting answer in

Fleischmann Piccolo N gauge trackwork. They have a three-way point, and additionally their points are 111mm long against Peco 124mm, all space saving qualities.

Fleischmann trackwork is preballasted even in its flexitrack lengths, but is by comparison very expensive. The other downside is that it has point motors that clip into the side of the point and these show. You can fit them upside down and they will then be contained within a cut out in the baseboard, but unless you can reach them underneath you cannot then operate them manually. Unlike Peco that can be pushed across from the top these are sprung so that this does not work and they will return to the selected position. The plus side however is that if a train is passed across a point set against its direction of travel, it does not derail the train, the light spring action allows it to pass over. The three-way point is also excellent in that if a train is sent from any branch against the set route it passes over without any problem whatsoever. The plus' were now outweighing the minus aspects and I decided Fleischmann would have my order, even though I had to wait nearly six weeks for some parts to become available. Fleischmann slips of which I used three did not give me any wiring considerations that the Peco version has, and all are so very well manufactured.

This time I used 6mm plywood on top of 3" x 1" timber for the baseboard, on a length of 90" in one piece this gives excellent strength and needs no underneath support in the middle. Initially this 'module' was at right angles to the Rowsley layout, and the track to this came up a gradient from Rowsley MPD, as Darley Dale was mounted 3" higher. The buildings were scratch-built and have internal illumination, which is a must for me whenever I can give the impression that the layout is 'alive'. Once again the help from the drawings in Bill Hudson's book and the photographs that Keith Miles the author of *Rowsley MPD* sent me were a considerable help in making it all appear, I hope, as it was. There was a footbridge in place, now removed, and the signal box has been moved to the other side of the level crossing. I made a footbridge from an N Brass kit. This was outside my experience really, but I did complete it, eventually after it had flown across the room a few times!!

The station gardens enabled me to use some skills/knowledge obtained from Roy Hickman who is in my opinion a master of the scenic arts. If you ever get the chance to see him at an exhibition I would spend some time looking at his work, and he is willing to visit your club and give private tuition sessions. To me these aspects make the whole hobby so enjoyable, in that every

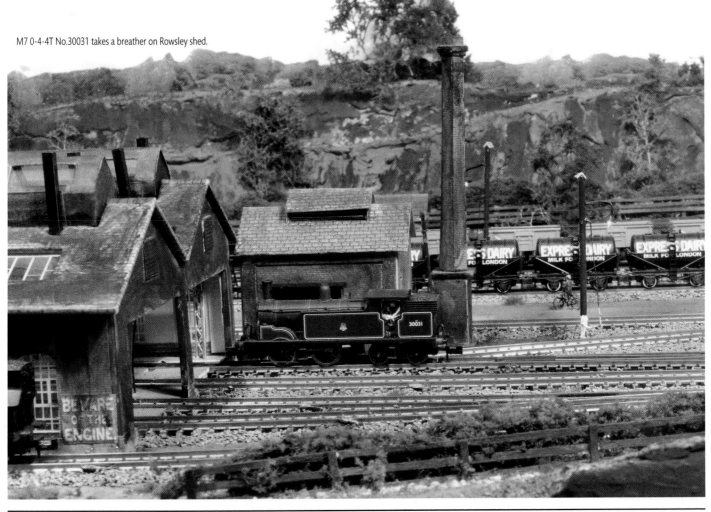

M7 0-4-4T No.30031 takes a breather on Rowsley shed.

one I have met is always more than willing to show you 'how they do it'.

Station lights were made using Ratio mouldings into which a grain of rice bulb is fitted. Run at 75% of their voltage rating they look very good to me and I have no problems with excessive heat melting the plastic either. My lamps in the sidings are made from brass tubing topped with a grain of wheat bulb and one of my lampshades previously described. I run these at 50% voltage, and to date none have expired. Other buildings are a brewery kit from Metcalfe and SD Mouldings units.

Trees are again from Sea Moss; raised areas made from expanded polystyrene plaster coated. As the track was already ballasted and I have had some problems with the usual PVA/water/washing up drops seeping into the point mechanisms, there being large areas of flat straight ballast required, I used double-sided tape and applied ballast to this with a few bits of grass, oily deposits, etc, added and am pleased with the result.

My backscenes are produced by printing in banner print from photographs taken from our local common, and using alternate mirror image prints, all line up quite well with each other. Any awkward places can be covered with a building or a tree.

Operating the layout

Operating now takes on a whole new

As dusk falls, the lights come on in Darley Dale.

aspect in that Peak Rails Preserved Line has diesel stock run on it, and even in practice at the end of BR days diesels were present on the line, including the 'Blue Pullman' (I would really like one of these). Trains could now come from the fun layout or from the MPD to Darley Dale and back again to the continuous run circuits. I can turn locomotives on the turntable after uncoupling at Darley Dale and bring back to take the next working out again. Yet, I wanted more than this and my cabin has four walls, of which only three were currently used.

After further design and planning I decided it was time for the original trial REElayout

A BR black liveried Hughes Fowler 'Crab' 2-6-0 hauls a train of tank wagons past a famous visitor - A3 Pacific *Flying Scotsman*.

The roof removed to show the detailed interior of Rowsley shed.

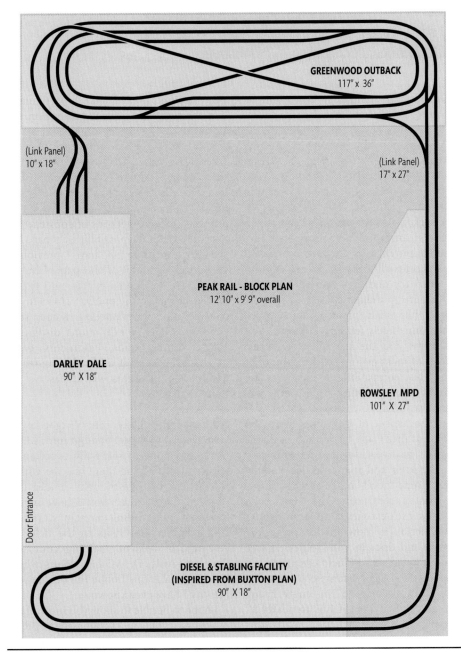

(Link Panel)
10" x 18"

(Link Panel)
17" x 27"

GREENWOOD OUTBACK
117" x 36"

PEAK RAIL - BLOCK PLAN
12' 10" x 9' 9" overall

DARLEY DALE
90" X 18"

ROWSLEY MPD
101" X 27"

Door Entrance

DIESEL & STABLING FACILITY
(INSPIRED FROM BUXTON PLAN)
90" X 18"

to go and a replacement that would link to both Rowsley and Darley Dale layouts. Once again the continuous run facility was sought plus a reversing triangle for complete trains, and a configuration such that a train can leave Darley Dale on the Down line and be returned later without reversing, on the Up line. This meant having to install a diode rectifier to overcome the short circuit that otherwise would have occurred. Additionally I made an alternative route up a gradient to bring the train in at the other end of Darley Dale that had previously been modelled as the end of the line. This probably sounds complicated, I hope the overall scheme of my track plan can help you understand this. At the same time I also planned the fourth element which I decided would be a diesel shed and stabling facility to store the diesels and complete trains awaiting their call to work. I used parts of the track plans for Buxton as a layout scheme. This would be placed along the remaining unused wall and Darley Dale moved to a new position, such is the flexibility of 'modular' layouts. I find Fleischmann extending rails excellent to use across board joins.

Okay, I accept a couple of linking sections were made to enable this. Thus I now have the situation that trains can be run around and to and from all the four layouts, and endless possibilities of running sessions are available for all scenarios.

Currently only the Rowsley and Darley Dale layouts are complete. Greenwood Outback as I have christened it is 75% finished in that the entire track, controls, etc, are in place. An amount of scenics are still in progress. However, being an impatient modeller, I have made the baseboard for the diesel stabling facility, and laid its track. This has enabled me to consider and address the revisions that are now required for the control of the whole system and interactions between the layouts. I am sure at the conclusion it is likely I will construct a whole new control panel to replace the individual ones currently in place.

Experience with various suppliers has influenced my locomotive stock, Lima, Hornby, Minitrix, Trix, Graham Farish (Poole), Farish (Bachmann), Dapol a Gem kit, a Peco 'Jubilee', and a visiting Tomix 'Bullet Train'. It's my layout and if it's in the National Museum at York, then I am happy to have it as a visitor, and the 'Bullet Train' is there - at least there is a section of it!

The dramatic improvements in quality in recent years in al gauges have undoubtedly been welcomed by most modellers. I do wish, however, that perhaps in the same way as DCC manufacturers have the NMRA Standard to work to, there might be a similar acceptance of some tolerances in certain areas. For example the back-to-back wheel

Mallard heads through Darley Dale with an express.

distance sent out varies considerably. Even the same suppliers do not seem to maintain a close tolerance throughout their releases. Current pick-up is another area that can cause poor slow running. I have added tender pick-ups to all my steam locomotives that have tenders.

Dapol's recent entrance into N gauge has shown some very interesting approaches and their 14XX is a gem of a performer. It traverses at slow speeds over all my points without hesitation, I can see that the addition of pick-ups on the rear bogie gives this enhanced power reception. It does, I regret, take off at an amazing speed at the very slightest increase in power. My experience, however, with the 45XX was disappointing as in this case the added pick-ups on the rear bogie assembly cause it to bias centrally and when reversing backwards into the branch of a point tends to derail. Only if a wagon or coach is coupled does this keep it on line. The M7 0-4-4T has no weight at 20 grams to pull any more than a couple of coaches without slipping on curves of even 12" radius.

I would like to suggest that the suppliers have a team of 'Field Testers' who have a variety of situations to be able to make relevant comments on pre-production samples so that all customers could have better experience and satisfaction. I for one would be most happy to do this for any of them.

Another wide variation is the voltage required to make a train move as well

as uncoupling standards. For example, the new generation of Farish diesels by Bachmann has a limited lift of the coupling which does not work for my uncoupling systems, whereas the steam engines do. I received a very negative response to questions raised with them about this. Similarly the variations in trackwork, slips, points, etc, between suppliers can be problematical. It is rare for me to purchase a new locomotive and find it accepts all of my trackwork without having to try and ascertain the reasons. The recently purchased Class 57 'Purple Ronnie' has sand pipes under wheels. These immediately fouled a crossover and some slips. Do the manufacturers have samples of most major trackwork on offer to fully test compatibility? Or if they are aware of incompatibility I doubt they will issue a warning.

For the aspect of buildings, here too major advances are becoming available to us. I have for some time admired Metcalfe kits, and made, as have many others some good models with these. My most recent experience has been with www.scalescenes.com from whom the material is downloaded over the Internet and once in your folders is free for use forever more. Their kits are to my mind excellent. For example I wanted a retaining wall some 36" in length rising from an initial height of 1.5" to nearly 3". The manner of construction made this

very straightforward, and I particularly like the weathered effect present on the stonework. The under arches kit offers a large range of interiors and styles. I recently made up the Diesel Depot and then made a double unit by joining two together, which won 'Best in Show' at our annual club competition.

These kits and methods of construction give adaptation possibilities that are second to none I have previously encountered. Many of the papers in the series have weathered effects, and this is an aspect that in my opinion is worthy of consideration for modellers. I have seen some creations at exhibitions displaying 100% pristine roads, pavements, walls or whatever without a blemish anywhere and life is not like this, well at least not for more than a day.

■ Thanks must go to Tony Wright for his visit, time, and expert photography, which has allowed me to share my experiences with you. I do hope there may be within this article just one thought or idea that inspires you in some way. I have myself benefited from reading magazines, articles, club membership, visits to the field for research, a weekend training course at Pecorama with Dr Michael Watts which together make this hobby the best leisure activity I have ever known.

I hope to be able to show you more of my other two layouts in a future issue of *BRM*.

The completed loco with the roof removed to show the cab interior. The crew are from the S&D Models range.

MAKING OF A CONNOISSEUR

Karl Crowther builds the Connoisseur Models O gauge 0-4-0 tank loco 'starter kit'. Photography by the author.

Having had over 30 years experience of modelling in 4mm scale (a sobering thought!), and a brief affair with N gauge/2mm scale, I thought the time was right to gain some experience of modelling in 7mm scale. I was interested to learn the extent to which my previous experience in smaller scales would stand me in good stead for working in 7mm. What better introduction could there be, therefore, than to build the Connoisseur Models starter loco kit of a private owner/industrial 0-4-0 tank engine.

The first task was to read through the comprehensive 24-page instruction booklet, which explains that the kit is aimed specifically at boosting the confidence of newcomers to the scale and is presented in the form of a tutorial exercise. An introductory background section deals mainly with how to go about soldering, which is then followed by two-pages of parts for identification and a check list, which includes photographs of both the main etch and other components such as a variety of white metal castings. The text then moves onto the assembly instructions themselves, which take the inexperienced modeller, with the aid of a comprehensive collection of annotated photographs, through each stage in the construction sequence.

Attention then turned to obtaining the recommended wheels, motor and gearset and whilst waiting for these to arrive, thought was given to exactly what I would be building. The kit has been inspired by the LSWR C14 tanks and the loco looked somehow familiar. I then noticed that the instructions mentioned it was the same prototype that inspired Tri-ang's OO gauge *Nellie* locomotive and recalled that this was one of the two locos my brother and I had on our childhood train set. Whatever happened to that little loco I don't know – I probably pulled it apart with the intention of rebuilding it into something else (and of course never did). *Nellie* spent many hours 'whizzing' around the two interconnected ovals of track that formed the layout my father had created for us. 'Whizzing' being the operative word, because I recall that the combined effects of its velocity and the sharp radii of the curves meant that every once in a while poor *Nellie* would launch herself off the layout and across the room! Having lost touch with this formative period of railway modelling interest, it seemed somehow fitting that this first venture into 7mm scale should take the form of re-creating *Nellie*. The kit, thoughtfully, also includes suitable etched nameplates for those with a similar sense of nostalgia.

As an additional challenge to myself, I also decided that for soldering I would try and make greater use of my Resistance Soldering Unit. I have possessed this for quite a while now, but have tended to use it mainly for jobs like adding etched overlays. I was interested to see how I would get on using it for the main construction, in conjunction with solder cream, instead of the conventional solder I was more familiar with. The combination offered the promise of no pre-tinning being required and little or no cleaning up afterwards, thereby representing a potential time saving. I had also acquired a miniature gas-torch and was keen to see how that could be used to help with construction. The series of annotated photographs illustrating the construction sequence will, hopefully, demonstrate how I got on.

Experiences and conclusions

Overall I found the kit straightforward to put together and for those wishing to gain experience in O gauge loco construction, the comprehensive, tutorial-style instructions should prove extremely helpful. There were relatively few occasions where I deviated from the suggested assembly sequence, or recommended techniques and these were more to suit my own personal preferences

rather than any issues I had with the instructions.

The first area was in the choice of gear mount – this in part due to my previous experiences in 4mm scale loco building. The kit's gear mount is of a width that means it will just fit in between the loco frames. This is so it can be permanently soldered to the frames, to provide strength, and prevent any tendency for the motor and mount to rotate whilst running. To enable this, the mount has to be slipped into place before inserting the driven axle top-hat bearings, which then pass through the axle bearing holes of the mount. I had not come across this approach in my 4mm scale experience and so had already fitted the driven axle bearings before even considering the gear mount. Easy removal of the top hat bearings seemed unlikely as they had purposely been made a good, tight fit in the frames - any attempt to unsolder them would probably cause them to expand and become locked in place. Fortunately I had to hand a narrower, Markits gear mount that could be used instead, which fitted comfortably in between the installed top hat bearings. To make up for the inherent loss in strength I made up an additional frame spacer from some brass sheet and installed this between the frames near to the driven axle in a position where it would not foul the Markits gear mount.

At this time I was concerned that an alternative means of resisting rotation of the motor/gear mount would be necessary. Initially I made a little 'out-rigger' to form a support for the free end of the motor shaft. This was simply fashioned from a strip of nickel-silver sheet provided with a 2mm top hat bearing that bolted onto a convenient frame spacer. In attempting to 'visualise' the forces that might be operating once the motor was running I was not completely convinced that this idea would be successful and a second potential means of restraint was included. This took the form of a little bracket, soldered onto the end of the gear mount, that could again be bolted onto an adjacent frame spacer. In practice it was found that both methods, however carefully adjusted, created unwanted additional frictional forces on the powered axle. Therefore the motor was tried under load without either restraint in place and there were no obvious signs of a tendency to rotate. In any event, the motor leads seem to provide sufficient restraint if any is required, and do so in such a way that no significant additional and unwanted frictional forces are imparted to the driven axle.

A second area where I diverged from the instructions was in the means of 'compensating' the leading (non-driven) axle. The kit can be built as a simple 'rigid' 0-4-0 but to improve current collection, it is possible to enable the leading axle to rock about its centre.

In 4mm scale, my normal way of going about this would be to provide the compensated axle with square bearings running in separately-fitted hornguides, these positioned relative to the fixed axle using the coupling rods and a set of jig-axles. After chatting to a couple of 7mm scale modellers, I decided to try out the idea of cutting a 'horseshoe' shaped groove of axle width into a pair of top-hat bearings. With these installed into the frames, making

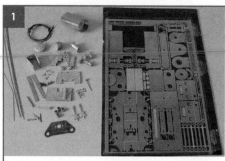

1. The contents of the kit - as can be seen, the pre-rolled boiler had unfortunately been slightly squashed in the post. Not much obvious difference, superficially, from a 4mm etched kit - just a lot bigger! 2. To keep all parts together, the castings and other components once removed from the fret were kept in this empty ice cream tub. With several modelling projects on the go at any one time I find this a helpful way of avoiding things going astray (and also a good excuse for eating ice cream!). Despite appearances, the Slater's wheels are indeed the correct ones for this kit.

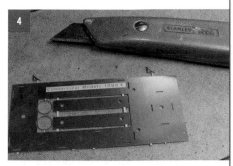

3. This general view of the workbench shows the earthed steel plate used for resistance soldering, with the probe itself just visible in the bottom left-hand corner of the picture. The magnets are for clamping items in place whilst soldering. All is relatively tidy at present, but that usually changes once construction gets underway. 4. I removed the etched parts from the main fret using a strong knife with a fresh blade. When cutting through the tabs it helps to use a firm surface such as this scrap piece of hardboard. Seen here is the footplate with a variety of other components etched into its centre. Once these have been removed, the remains of the etching tabs need carefully filing away. In 7mm scale, the etching cusp along part edges somehow seems more prominent than in 4mm, so a bit of time smoothing the edges pays dividends.

5. Here we see the footplate, valances and buffer beams cleaned up and ready for soldering. To burnish the parts in preparation I initially use fine sandpaper, followed by a glass-fibre stick. The latter tends to release tiny fragments of the material, which can be irritating if they stick in your fingers, so the use of sandpaper for the most part helps to minimise this possibility. Whatever soldering technique is to be employed, the need to have all relevant surfaces clean and properly fluxed is paramount (note that solder cream already contains flux). 6. Magnets hold the footplate and first (rear) beam in place ready for soldering. The square-sided magnets placed at the join between the two components ensure they are held at 90° to each other. If necessary, for extra security whilst soldering, the tip of an implement such as a small file can be used to help ensure the part being secured remains in position during the process.

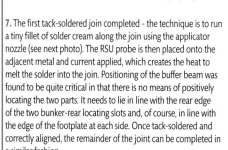

7. The first tack-soldered join completed - the technique is to run a tiny fillet of solder cream along the join using the applicator nozzle (see next photo). The RSU probe is then placed onto the adjacent metal and current applied, which creates the heat to melt the solder into the join. Positioning of the buffer beam was found to be quite critical in that there is no means of positively locating the two parts. It needs to lie in line with the rear edge of the two bunker-rear locating slots and, of course, in line with the edge of the footplate at each side. Once tack-soldered and correctly aligned, the remainder of the joint can be completed in a similar fashion.

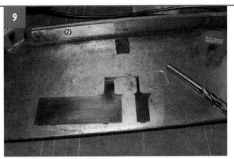

8. The two valances and the second buffer beam have now been added. The valances need to be carefully lined up relative to the outer edges of the tank-locating slots, parallel with the footplate edge. To reduce the risk of distortion from heating, it is good practice to tack-solder the two ends first, followed by the middle and so on, rather than start at one end and work all the way along in sequence. Despite that, once cooled, my footplate still developed a noticeable bow along its length and had to be carefully straightened again

using gentle finger pressure. To prevent the applicator nozzle of the solder cream from becoming clogged I inserted a mapping pin. **9.** With the tank/cab-sides cleaned up ready for soldering, the beading around the cab opening was first formed approximately to shape using a drill shank of suitable diameter. The beading was then tack-soldered into position (see next photo). **10.** Early in the learning process, and the resistance soldering here is far too messy for my liking – I did improve! It's perfectly possible to move the probe around

on the work to control the area being heated, but take care to avoid the tip making contact with the molten solder. In addition, be sure not to lift the probe whilst the power is on as arcing will occur. Here, too much solder cream may have been used on some joints, necessitating time-consuming cleaning up afterwards. As the beading projects beyond the face of the cab cut-outs, it was found helpful to insert a piece of scrap nickel-silver to maintain the correct spacing of the two components being joined.

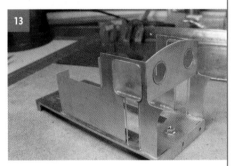

11. The tabs and slots provided for location of the tank-sides have a fair degree of slop, so careful positioning of these relative to the footplate and each other is needed. Again, tack-solder, check alignment in all planes and finally complete once satisfied. The secret is to take one's time. I found a small engineer's square invaluable for checking alignment. The cab handrails are 0.7mm brass wire, made initially over-length as recommended and held in place using a small aluminium hair-grip. Solder first at the cab cut-out and then, after checking alignment, the other end. The wire is then cut to length and tidied up with a fine file.

12. The cab front and rear have half-etched surrounds to house the spectacle rims. The rims were first tinned using an ordinary soldering iron. After fluxing the window rebates, they were sweated into place using the RSU probe (as on the right). Above and below the windows are a series of half-etched holes to enable the formation of embossed rivet detail. On the cab rear, these seemed over-etched and in some cases had come through onto the outside surface. I decided to omit this rivet detail on the cab rear and later filled in the offending holes. The cab front was fine, however and the rivets were embossed.

13. The cab rear, complete with spectacle rims, has now been tack-soldered into position. The instructions stress the need to make sure this doesn't push the cab-sides out of vertical – all was fine in this case. In hindsight, I ought to have used the etched-through rivet holes above and below the rear windows to install vertical sets of bars used on steam loco bunkers to protect the glass from breakage by coal. This is one detail that to me is obviously lacking on the completed model and not included in the instructions.

14. The kit is etched from a fairly stiff 20 thou brass, making it relatively difficult to bend evenly without introducing kinks (e.g. the bunker rear as seen here). To first soften the metal, full instructions are provided as to how one should go about this by the process of annealing - I used this miniature gas torch supplied by C&L. Given the potential fire risk, I did this over the sink in our utility room. It's amazing how malleable the metal becomes and once cooled the bunker rear was gradually formed to shape using finger pressure against an

off-cut of half-inch copper pipe. **15.** Given the rather modest length of the loco, an ordinary bench vice proved suitable for forming bends on the inner tanks (seen here). In this instance, the brass is sufficiently stiff and the half-etched fold lines are so cleanly done, it would probably have been possible to fold these parts simply by hand. Holding the top section in the vice, the side was first bent over, after which the three small tabs that support the boiler were then folded out. Note that for 90 degree bends such as this in etched kits, half-etched fold lines

are usually placed on the inside. Once completed, fillets of solder were then run along the joins.
16. The bunker rear has now been formed to shape and soldered into position, along with the tank inner portions. The probability of gap along the base of the bunker rear was highlighted in the instructions (it may have been drawn to the vertical dimension, not taking account of the effect of the curve). I soldered a piece of fret waste inside the bunker behind the gap and later made good with Milliput filler.

sure the 'horseshoe' opening faced vertically downwards, the axle would then be free to drop at either end, as necessary, to follow any minor track irregularities. For this solution to be fully effective, wiper pick-ups pressing down on the tops of the wheels would also be required. I appreciate that this is not truly three-point compensation as the axle does not actually rock, but it did seem worth a try. At least if it didn't work out, no modification to the original bearing holes in the frames would have been made and I could easily remove and discard the modified bearings and try another method instead.

In trying this out, my main concern was that of over-enlarging the diameter of the bearing holes and introducing an undesirable element of slop. Firstly, one edge of the bearing was soldered temporarily onto a piece of scrap metal sheet in order to provide a secure handle for the work. A slot was then cut into one side of the bearing, well-inside of the required width, after which it was carefully opened up with a fine file to the final size, regularly test-fitting all the time with an axle. Once unsoldered and cleaned up, the two bearings were then installed into the frames, ensuring that the slots were truly vertical. In test-running, this method seems to have worked very effectively and I have great confidence it will prove to be a success when the completed loco eventually gets put through its paces on a layout.

Other deviations from the instructions were relatively minor, primarily in the actual sequence of assembly and again down to my own preferred way of working. With assembly now complete the model now needed to be painted and in preparation it was carefully scrubbed using 'Shiny Sinks' kitchen cleaner (as in fact was done after each work session). This product has an abrasive action and is very effective at cleaning/burnishing to aid paint adhesion. An old toothbrush and small pieces of kitchen scouring pad held with tweezers are useful implements here. After a very thorough rinse to remove all residue, once dry, the model was wiped over with cellulose thinners (make sure to wear a suitable respirator mask whilst doing this) and it's surprising how much dirt still comes off the model at this stage.

The base coat was a can of Halfords grey acrylic primer, which I find an excellent paint for this purpose. After allowing this to dry thoroughly for a couple of days, the chassis was sprayed matt black, again using a Halfords can, whilst the main body colour from the Phoenix-Precision range was applied using an airbrush. After first spraying the underside of the boiler, the body was then stood on a cheap cake-decorating turntable to complete the job. Make sure an appropriate respirator mask is worn whilst spraying, even out of doors. All the remaining painting was done by brush using Humbrol enamels.

So, how did I get on with the resistance soldering? Well I have to admit that in progressing through the build I found myself reverting subconsciously to the 'old ways' of the conventional soldering iron (although something more powerful than my 25W model – say 40W, would be more appropriate for working in this scale). I think it's just a case of developing techniques and approaches that each individual modeller finds comfortable working with. I certainly make a lot of use of my RSU for attaching detail overlays, but seem to work best with a conventional iron for many aspects of the main assembly. As I say, it works for me. It was a revelation though, trying out the miniature blow-torch, which I found extremely handy for annealing parts and for soldering jobs where a large amount of heat needs to be added quickly to the work.

I think the finished model certainly looks the part and can recommend it as a means of introduction to 7mm scale modelling. For anyone moving up from 4mm and has some loco building experience already, it should prove very straightforward, whilst for inexperienced modellers in any scale, if one follows the advice provided throughout the informative instructions, building it should prove to be an educational and rewarding experience.

17. Using an off-cut of copper pipe and a computer mouse mat to roll the roof to shape (apologies for its colour!). I find that a mouse mat has just the right amount of 'give' for such operations. In this case, as the arc of the curve was relatively shallow, it was not found necessary to first anneal the metal.

18. The underside of the completed roof. As suggested in the kit's instructions, I have soldered offcuts of fret waste underneath around the edges to increase its apparent thickness (to better represent a wooden roof). The small L-shaped brackets were also bent up from fret-waste and allow the roof to be removable from the completed model – again this followed the instructions.

19. At this stage it was possible test-fit the boiler, having first rolled out the accidental distortion. The completed roof can also be seen in position.

20. Here the front and rear formers of the boiler have been soldered into position and the join completed along the bottom.

21. To solder up the smokebox I found it easier to revert back to the soldering iron, with the smokebox front pinned into a much-abused block of balsa wood I use for jobs like this. The wrapper had been pre-annealed and again formed to shape using a suitable diameter of copper tube. 22. In order to position correctly the smokebox rear, the kit thoughtfully provides a white metal spacer, which I have here glued with two-

part epoxy resin, rather than soldered into position. Before fitting, the depth of the spacer needs to be carefully adjusted by filing so that when placed upon it, the smokebox rear sits flush with the inside edge of the wrapper. Without the spacer, the task would have been rather tricky to say the least, and it also provides some useful weight at the front end.

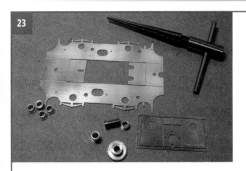

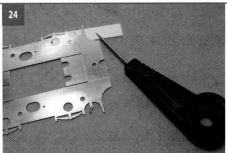

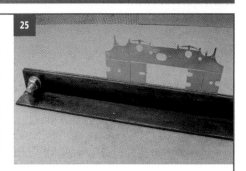

23. Attention then turned to erecting the loco frames; the basic requirements can be seen here. The holes for the driving wheel top-hat bearings are etched slightly undersize and before the frames are folded, these need carefully opening out with a reamer so they just fit. Care needs to be taken not to over-enlarge the holes – just go a little at a time, with repeated test-fitting (but don't fit at this stage). **24.** Before folding up the frames there are four sets of rivets to emboss at the

base of the guard irons. Their locations are again marked with half-etched depressions on the rear side of the metal. Using the implement shown, I pressed into each dimple to form the rivets. With a bit of care and repeating the process as necessary, it is possible to get them all the same size. To avoid distorting the front face of the metal I find it helps to work against a thick piece of scrap styrene sheet. This has just the right amount of 'give' to form the rivet and at the

same time, prevent undue distortion around the edge. **25.** Now the frames can be folded, as seen here, with the aid of a set of bending bars. To make the fold I used a metal straight edge pressed against the work from the rear, that way minimising any risk of distortion. I forgot to insert a piece of card to protect the newly-formed rivets, so I'm afraid they were squashed a little in the process – perhaps more realistic in any case though?

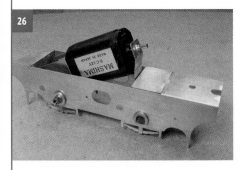

26. We jump on a little here, with frames assembled and wheel bearings and motor/gear mount test-fitted in place. Note that the alternative Markits gear mount is illustrated here, along with a supplementary bearing at the unsupported end of the motor shaft (subsequently found unnecessary - see main text). To provide a means of 'compensation' the leading pair of axle bearings have been opened out into a 'horseshoe' - a different

approach to anything suggested in the kit's instructions. **27.** The steps are made up from three separate etched parts - the instructions stress that they are vulnerable once fitted and suggest strengthening the rear with a piece of 0.9mm brass wire. As can be seen here, I decided to strengthen using a piece of fret waste as a backing plate for each step. When securing the completed items beneath the loco valances, each was first tack-

soldered in place using the soldering iron, after which a good fillet of solder cream was run around the base and then a good amount of heat applied using the RSU on its maximum setting. **28.** The basic body takes shape, now ready for detailing. Several substantial white metal castings are included to represent elements of the cab interior. Keep the work clean by scrubbing with 'Shiny Sinks' after each work session.

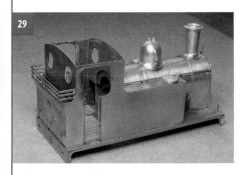

29. The castings were found to be excellent, with minimal cleaning up required. However, it pays to check in particular the fit of chimney and dome onto the boiler, as any gaps here will be extremely obvious. A small amount of treatment of the casting bases with a large round file was all that was found to be necessary. I prefer to attach castings with two-part epoxy as this allows for adjustment as the glue sets. I ran a good fillet of solder around the base of the lamp irons to make sure they were securely attached. This meant that

some cleaning-up was needed, but was considered worth the effort if it reduced the risk of them being knocked off the completed model. **30.** With the loco body now substantially complete, attention now turned back to the chassis. I wanted to test-fit the wheels so I could attach the brake gear with them in place. The loco frames are designed to accommodate coarse scale wheels and so in using Slater's wheels, it was necessary to use some of that firm's spacing washers to take up a small amount of additional sideplay. To ensure they fit into the

wheel centres, the square-ended axles need to be carefully and lightly dressed with a fine file before test-fitting. **31.** The brake gear has now been attached, but the cross-shafts still require trimming to length. Once at this stage the wheels were removed for fitting the crankpins - note that their rims have been chemically blackened. The supplementary frame spacer that I added to provide additional strength in advance of the driven axle can be seen in this view.

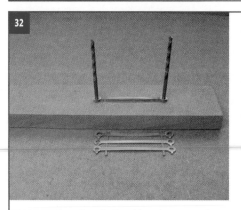

32

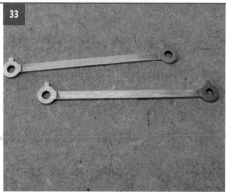

33

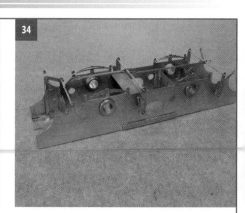

34

32. The coupling rods are laminated from three separate layers. To achieve correct alignment I used the rods to mark and then drill a pair of 2.5mm holes (the size of the bearing holes as etched) at the required spacing into a piece of scrap MDF. A pair of 2.5mm drill shanks inserted into the holes could then be used to hold the three, pre-tinned rods in alignment whilst they were sweated together. A little extra solder was introduced along the edges to achieve a strong joint. **33.** And here are the completed rods, after cleaning up with files and fine wet and

dry paper. The instructions suggest that the crankpin holes will need opening up to fit the top hat bearing bushes – better to start with the holes under-etched, minimising the risk of there being too much clearance. I was a little concerned, therefore, to discover that mine were a free fit straight onto the bushes as they were. However, when test-run, to my relief, the amount of clearance seemed to be pretty well spot-on. **34.** Here, the brake cross-shafts have been trimmed to length and a strip of copperclad glass-fibre material has been attached

to the top of each side-frame to act as mounting points for current collectors (the kit also allows for using sprung-plunger pick-ups). In this location I figured that the pick-ups would largely be hidden from view on the completed loco. This would allow them to be 'top-acting' and thereby compatible with the intended method of 'compensation', where the leading wheels needed to be provided with a downward force. The frame assembly was now ready for painting.

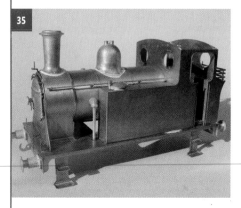

35

36

37

35. The footsteps soldered in place and the body essentially complete. The fit of the boiler castings was found to be pretty good, but a small amount of filler has been applied to some minor gaps around their bases. For this I used Milliput, applied with the shaped tip of a cocktail stick. It is possible to smooth the filler before it sets, using a small brush moistened with water. Here, however, I let the filler dry first and then dressed with my normal 'tool' of choice in such situations, a small

piece of wet-and-dry paper folded in half. **36.** Here the body has been undercoated. Placing it on this cheap cake-decorating table enables it to be easily manipulated without handling during the process. Once dry I was not happy with certain join-lines (e.g. between footplate and tank-sides and that very obvious gap around the top of the smokebox wing-plate) so these were made good with more filler and locally re-primed when this had set. **37.** After allowing the undercoat to harden

fully, the buffer beams were masked off with low-tack masking tape in readiness for applying the main body colour. It is a good idea to remove the tape as soon as possible after painting to prevent it adhering too strongly to the model. I was not worried about over-spray onto areas that would be subsequently brush-painted in black. Once the body colour had been air-brushed on, the model was then put to one side in a sealed plastic box for a good few days to allow the paint to harden.

38

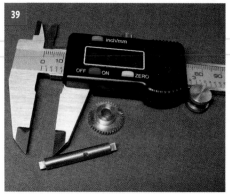

39

40

38. Whilst the body's paintwork was hardening attention turned to wheeling-up the chassis and installing the motor, etc. - a task which I prefer to do after the frames have been painted. Here are the main components ready for installation - note that the wheels are also pre-painted and weathered. The supplementary restraint I had attached to the Markits motor/gear mount can be seen in place, though it was later found to be unnecessary

and removed. **39.** Before installing the driven axle I filed a flat into it to provide something for the grubscrew of the drive gear to locate against. The position of this along the length of the axle needed to be carefully calculated and for convenience I arranged for it to coincide with one of the faces of the square axle end. **40.** The leading, non-driven axle and its driving wheels were installed first, using Slater's spacing

washers to ensure a minimum amount of side-play. The motor/gear mount unit has also been installed along with the driven axle. I test ran it before adding the other wheelset. Neither means of 'restraint' proved satisfactory, both seemed to create additional friction on the driven axle. I tried without, as I would normally in 4mm scale, and there did not appear to be any tendency for the motor/gear mount to rotate so left it like this.

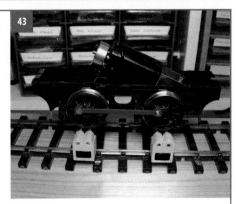

41. Happy with everything at this stage I then added the coupling rods and test-ran on a rolling road. Wires to the motor are over length and linked to the power source via crocodile clips – these will be shortened later when finally wired to the pick-up strips. **42.** The motor has now been wired-in and pick-ups added from 0.45mm straight brass wire. The latter

were adjusted to give a gentle downward tension (important in particular on the leading wheels where this pressure is required to provide the 'compensation'). At present they have been left a little over-length for subsequent trimming/shaping and will also be painted to disguise their presence. **43.** And now we see the completed chassis with its red-painted coupling rods fitted

and the crankpins trimmed to length. These were snipped off with a pair of side-cutters and carefully dressed back to the nut with a fine file. The pick-ups have also been trimmed to their final length and shape and these and their mounting strips have been painted black. A flywheel has also been fitted onto the motor shaft, secured with a spot of Loctite.

44. The completed model (prior to weathering and addition of name/numberplates etc.), awaiting test-running on an actual layout. Pre-formed coupling links are provided with the kit and rather than paint these, I chose to chemically blacken them instead. The cab windows were glazed with small circles cut from thin Perspex sheet trimmed very carefully to fit the apertures behind the spectacle rings. Using the tip of a cocktail stick, a smear of Microscale 'Kristal Klear' was then run round the inside of each opening and finally the pieces of glazing were carefully laid down in position. Once the adhesive has dried it can scarcely be noticed at all.

Useful Addresses
Connoisseur Models
■ 33 Grampian Road, Penfields, Stourbridge DY8 4UE
Tel: 01384 371418
www.jimmcgeown.com

S&D Models
■ Highbridge Works, PO Box 101, Burnham-on-Sea TA9 4WAUK
Tel: 01278 781603
www.sanddmodels.co.uk

GWR 'King' Class 4-6-0 No.6018 *King Henry VI* heads the Down 'Cornish Riviera Express' out of Horse Cove tunnel along the south Devon coast between Dawlish and Teignmouth. M C Shaw Collection

RED CLIFFS in the sunset

Michael C Shaw describes a short trip along the GWR's south Devon coastal route taken by Captain W F P Kelly and G P Keen in the 1930s. Photographs from the author's collection.

The South Devon Railway's line from Exeter to Plymouth was opened as far as Teignmouth Old Quay on May 30, 1846. The engineer was one Isambard Kingdom Brunel who decided to use the atmospheric system whereby static pumping stations exhausted a vacuum in front of, and used atmospheric pressure or pumped compressed air behind, a piston that moved in a sealed tube with an opening flap at its top, placed between two rails set at a gauge of 7' 0 ¼". The piston was in turn attached to a carriage, thus abolishing the need for a locomotive. The system was thought by Brunel to be ideal for hilly country, hence the steepness of the South Devon Banks of Rattery and Dainton remain to this day.

Sadly though, the idea was too far advanced for the technology of the day and due to the underpowered pumping engines, and the fact that the leather flap (greased by tallow) was subject to decay or being eaten by rats, the system was abandoned by the 1850s. It took

until December 30, 1846, for the line to reach Newton Abbot and July 1847 before it arrived at Totnes. The South Devon was nominally independent, but became part of the GWR on February 1, 1876, after which the narrow/dual gauge was extended as far as Plymouth between March and May 1876.

During the gauge conversion of 1892, much of the line was doubled, the last being the sections through the cliff tunnels at Dawlish which were so treated between 1902 and 1905. A second platform was also added at Dawlish which, in 1920, received a new standard-type GWR signal box. Teignmouth's 1846 structure was replaced after a fire in 1884.

Throughout its history, the line has often been damaged by winter gales and stormy seas. It received all classes of traffic, from branch line auto-trains and local passengers, to 'Castle' and 'King'-hauled titled expresses, Motor-rail services, china clay and designated freight. It also carried general merchandise, munitions and 'out of gauge' material on its

way to Devonport's Royal Dockyard, and many inter-regional services. It was also common for Southern Railway/Region trains to be diverted this way for emergency and route-learning purposes, especially from WW II onwards.

Contrary to popular belief, and decidedly hushed up during the Marple/Beeching era, the railway's passenger-carrying records peaked during 1955-8 when holiday trains would be queued in section all along the sea wall from Teignmouth back on summer Saturdays. Greater car ownership, foreign holidays and some despicable 'damping down' of demand by British Railways was aided by the wholesale decimation of the West Country seaside branch lines which further reduced demand for the main line - not much point going only part-way by train! Despite road improvements of the past 30 years traffic on this route still continues to increase.

However, the line survives and still sees considerable use today with 'Voyagers', IC125s,

diesel-hauled and DMU passenger traffic and occasional steam excursions, together with a constantly increasing freight usage. Thus the route makes a busy scene to replicate for any tail-chasing model railway with an excuse to run anything including a 'Hastings' DMU or 'Deltic'-hauled Pullman.

A trip down the line

Although time travel may eventually be possible, I suppose it might also be profoundly disturbing, as anyone who returns to old haunts might readily testify when reality fails to match a remembered historic template or rose tinted memory. What travel into the future might hold defies description, but let me take you back in my time machine in the company of Captain Kelly and G P Keen for a trip by an Up local and the Up 'Torbay Limited' in the early 1930s from West to East.

We begin our journey at Newton Abbot, its former Brunel 'barn'-type passenger station having recently been rebuilt (1927). To the right, as we board the train, is a large loco shed and repair facility, and as our 'Star' hauled express of primrose and chocolate crosses the junction with the line leading in on the left for Mortonhampstead and Heathfield, we cross the confluence of the small River Lemon and the greater River Teign on whose left-hand 'easterly' bank we now head for the sea. Here we sit on an embankment above the flood plain, with the often-flooded Newton Abbot

Leaving Newton Abbot the railway runs alongside the River Teign towards Teignmouth and Shaldon. On the far bank is the Coombe Cellars public house at Combeinteignhead, a smuggler's inn popular with 'grockles' (visitors).

Racecourse to our left. We pass over the Teign avoiding canal (site of the present-day Newton Abbot bypass) and the road to Green Hill and Kingsteignton. Here Captain Kelly leant out of our right-hand window to photograph down the Teign Valley (above) just before the line parts company with the river in the area of Lower Ware. On the right-hand bank is Shaldon and the Ness headland - note the proximity of the embankment to the river bank, they are one and the same.

We follow the old A329 (now A381) road down-river and dive under the Shaldon road which crosses the river on the famous

toll bridge with the sports ground to our left and views of Teignmouth Harbour opening to the right. Here, Keen previously photographed this very train, more normally hauled by a 'King' Class 4-6-0 and the Down version. Note the coastal sailing vessels, motor cruisers, barges and rowing boats. This area of harbour is known as the 'salty'.

We now swing left around inland of this coastal resort town and into the station and its rather cramped location, then burst out under what is now the the A379 road bridge, beside the famous red cliffs and along the sea wall, as illustrated by a 'Saint' Class 4-6-0 on

One of the GWR's 'Large Prairie' 2-6-2Ts heads a freight past the harbour at Cockwood in the summer of 1932. A brake van part way along the train suggests that this is in fact two trains combined, probably as a trip working from Hackney Yard, Newton Abbot, to Riverside Yard on the other side of Exeter.

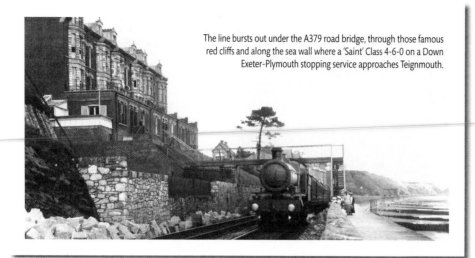

The line bursts out under the A379 road bridge, through those famous red cliffs and along the sea wall where a 'Saint' Class 4-6-0 on a Down Exeter-Plymouth stopping service approaches Teignmouth.

Another 'Castle'-hauled Down train approaches along the sea wall section at Teignmouth in 1934.

a down Exeter-Plymouth stopping service. As we head for Dawlish with the iron red Pulpit Rock clearly discernable, Keen takes two more images from the train as we get closer to Holcombe and Parsons tunnel. Observing another 'Castle' hauled train he fires off another shot as she passes, followed by a highly chancy photograph directly into the sun towards Ness Head and back down Babbacombe Bay to Teignmouth. This hauntingly beautiful image just about sums up the whole experience! There is just time to take one more image as we dash into the 513 yard Parsons Tunnel and across Horse Cove, the famous Parson and Clerk Cliff and Pulpit Rock to our right. This is followed by three short tunnels spanning the headlands of small bays - Clerk's (58 yards), Phillot (49 yards), Coryton (204 yards) - and finally Kennaway Tunnel (209 yards) and along the foreshore at Dawlish, photographed from above the tunnel mouth . We decide to break our journey at Dawlish and take some views from the lineside, surrounding cliffs and environs.

Before getting back on board, we've time for a further look around the town. Admiring the scene back towards the tunnel from which we emerged into Dawlish, we then cross over to the sea wall in time to

see two 43XX Moguls passing. Then back on the other side to see a 'Star'-hauled down express. We pop into the ornamental gardens and manage to snatch a 'Castle' class piloting a 'Star' westbound with a Down express from beside Dawlish water.

We continue through Italiante Dawlish, along the sea wall once more with the cliffs becoming less dramatic in form if not colour. Looking out from the right-hand side of our compartment, up channel, we see a less distant view across the Exe estuary and the South Devon red coast abruptly turning to the chalk and flinty white of Dorset near Beer. So this is not the Bay of Naples after all!

The view is blocked by the cliff cutting and a Class 47XX 2-8-0 on a Midland express as we curve left inland into the first dunes of Dawlish Warren, its windblown timber station platforms, buildings and four tracks awaiting the Exeter day trippers who once flocked to the spit, golf course and dunes with its ferry across to Exmouth. Our photograph shows a 'County' Class 4-4-0 on another Midland bound express.

We follow inland along the western shore of the Exe and across the harbour at Cockwood where we see a 45XX 2-6-2 hauling a typical Up goods with Exmouth as a backcloth. The

area is alive with wildfowl and wildlife. We continue through the curves to Starcross station, its atmospheric pumping station's chimney extant, and a second Exmouth ferry plying from its shore.

To our left is Powderham Castle, set against rolling wooded hills and surrounded by its deer park, and beneath us are water troughs. We head across the levels through Exminster with the Exeter canal for company, then under the A38 (also the site of the present-day M5 bridge), through City Basin Junction, the other end of the Moretonhampstead and Heathfield lines and the goods yard just past Countess Weir. Then through Exeter St. Thomas, over the Exe with views of the city's cathedral, slowing past the junction with the Southern Railway coming in from Exeter Central with an E1 banker to the right, and into the bustle of Exeter St. David's.

I do hope that local readers will forgive any important missed detail, I have not travelled this stretch of line for over 30 years or so, and much has changed since Keen's camera and my time machine passed those red cliffs in the sunset, 73 years ago! Please note the road classifications are taken from the 1936 OS map, and some have also altered over the years.

When the Great Western Railway arrived in Dawlish it was stipulated that it had to be low enough not to obstruct the view from ground floor windows in Marine Parade! Looking back towards Kennaway Tunnel from Marine Parade, two 43XX Class Moguls cross at Dawlish in the summer of 1931.

The view from a London bound train with the famous Parson and Clerk to our right. The year is 1948 and motive power is an LNER A4 Pacific taking part in the Locomotive Exchanges - the GWR Dynomometer car is at the head of the train.

A 'County' 4-4-0 emerges from the 209 yard Kennaway Tunnel and along the foreshore at Dawlish in the summer of 1931.

Another 'County' Class 4-4-0 heads a midland bound express around the curve towards Dawlish Warren during the summer months of 1933.

The power of the Great Western - summer sunlight is reflected off the paintwork of an unidentified 'Castle' Class 4-6-0 passing Riverside Yard on the approach to Exeter St. Davids. Regrettably, there is no clue in the original caption to this 1935 photograph as to why the train appears to be running 'wrong line'.

A last look at Dawlish from an almost deserted ornamental gardens. Even the famous black swans are not around to watch *Pendennis Castle* and an unidentified 'Star' Class 4-6-0 double-heading a Down train in 1931.

THREE GRESLEYS

Building three 7mm scale Gresley non-corridor coaches from a variety of kit parts, described by **Tony Geary**. Photography by the author.

The charm of secondary lines in the early '60s is that ancient vehicles still hung on to provide the services for a while, before they were all swept away as DMUs and the Mk.1 coach building program progressed. To populate the line that one day I hope to build, based on the GN Derbyshire extension, it was clear that some Gresley 52' non-corridor coaches would be required. A range of 7mm scale modular kits are available from Ian Kirk, the sides of which are made up from standard door and window components.

After some research, I decided to use a variety of parts, to include the Kirk body, united with Newbold underframes and Just Like The Real Thing bogies. Also, Sidelines components would be used for the underframe fittings and the seats. This was going to be an 'All Nations' project! The three vehicles I would be building would be a Diagram 65 brake third, Diagram 57 full third and a Diagram 129 full brake. I elected to build the coaches with the roof fixed to the sides, this five-sided box would then trap the separate interior, with its floor,

seats and partitions, to the underframe. For reference I used the Michael Harris books, *LNER Standard Carriages* and *LNER Carriages*. These are very good research aids, full of useful information.

Bodyshell

The body is as good a place to start as anywhere, and has the benefit of fairly quick visible results. Basically the coach sides come as a set of door and window modules and it's a messy process to cut them from the sprues with a razor saw and

The three completed Gresley non-corridor coaches.
Tony Wright

scraping with a craft knife better than a file to clean them up, as they seemed to bow in under filing, meaning that not enough material was removed. The finished result does depend upon the preparation, so it's worth spending some time on cleaning up the surfaces that form the joins and getting the components square. The sides were left to set whilst I concentrated on other work. The coach ends incorporated the buffer beams, and these needed to be cut off as I was using brass underframes. There was a faint moulding line about 2mm below the lower beading edge and I cut along there with the razor saw. The full brake and the brake end are narrower than the normal coach as they are 8' 6" wide instead of 9' 0", so the equivalent of 3" had to be removed from each side of those ends. That's where my 7mm scale rule came in useful. The other thing that needed doing, was to cut the two windows in the brake end of the brake third. This was done by drilling four small holes in each corner and using a piercing saw to join them up. Some beading for the outside of these was added with some plastic strip. One way to strengthen the sides, I suppose would be to add a continuous sheet of plastic card inside along the sides below window level – I didn't do that! But what I did do was to glue in the

centre partition in the compartment coach and a couple of stretchers in the full brake to prevent the sides from squeezing in too much during handling. The brake third was made up as two separate assemblies for the compartment section and the brake. To fit the roofs, I placed the side and end assemblies into the upturned roofs to work out how much to cut off. It's always best to be cautious and not remove too much. The ends were cut off with the trusty razor saw and the gutter trimmed with a sharp craft knife. I overdid it on one coach and had to re-instate it with some Slater's plastic strip.

What did I say about being cautious?

It's always useful to keep a variety of this strip in stock, ready for any occasion, including over-zealous cutting. The roof is designed to glue on to the top of the sides as a butt join, so to eliminate the chance of any gaps, and draughts on the passengers, I cemented a strip along the inside of the coach above the top of the windows. This also created a rebate that would help align the roof and keep it in place. The roof was fixed on after the ventilators (Sidelines), rainstrips and destination brackets made from that ever useful plastic strip had been added. There were a few gaps between the tops of the end mouldings and the underside of the carriage

clean up the mouldings with a craft knife. The plastic debris seems to get everywhere, so after all the cutting and filing was done, I had a good tidy and a vacuum up before the domestic authorities homed in. If I had planned ahead, I would have drilled the sides for the commode handles at this stage, but I hurried 'cos I wanted to see the completed sides! The sides are assembled using 'MekPak' on a sheet of plate glass with a straight edge used as a guide for the top edge of the sides and doors. Care had to be taken there to ensure that the edges of the components were as square as possible, otherwise it is very easy to end up with a banana shaped side, or the other risk is that a cumulative error causes the joins between the doors and windows to increasingly move away from being vertical. After a later inspection, I found that I had to break apart and re-work a couple of them. I found that the window frame portions responded to

Cleaning up and mating up the sides – there is an awful lot of mess!

Assembling the ABS Fox bogies for the full brake, they seem to have an earlier parentage!

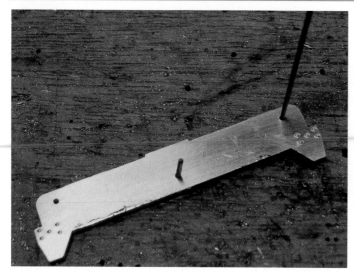

Soldering together the queen post stretchers for the underframe. Brass wire is inserted into the alignment holes.

Making up the battery boxes, a strip of thick card is used to control the position of the handles as they are soldered from the inside.

The Sidelines brake cylinders being assembled.

Gluing together the side components, the strip of wood is used as a guide to align the top edge of the parts.

The brake compartment assembled as a unit - it is narrower than the coach body and a stretcher to provide strength is evident.

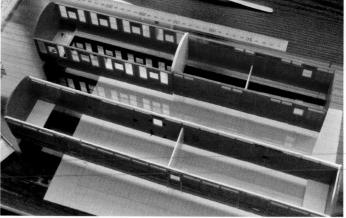

The bodies assembled, the method of attaching to the underframe can be seen with the plastic stretchers and brass plate at the far end.

roof; I filled those with some cellulose filler, that is not really advisable of course as it reacts with the plastic surface. After this, I fitted the Laurie Griffin commode handles and retained them with 'Zap' CA. Originally, I was going to leave the moulded door handles - but this was to change!

The interior floor was made up from thick plastic card (1.6mm, I don't know how many thou that is!) as were the many compartment partitions. The seating was cut from Sidelines

mouldings. The floor is retained in place at each end by a brass 'U' shape bracket that fits in the end of the coach. This is glued to a 20mm wide plastic card stretcher with 'Evostik'. 8BA nuts are soldered inside this bracket and this assembly holds the body onto the underframe and also serves to clamp the floor in place. The seats seemed a little low, so I measured the first class carriage seat (complete with luggage racks and mirror!) that I have set up in my study

and decided to add some plastic strip to the bottom of each to raise them up a little.

About the last thing I added was the Laurie Griffin lamp irons, two on the end of each coach.

Chassis

The Kirk kits come with a plastic chassis, that, I'm sure is adequate, but my own personal taste is for a brass underframe. Newbold models produce versions suitable

The body mounting plates are glued in with Evostik, some plastic strip has been added to the top edge of the brake vehicle to create a more positive location for the roof.

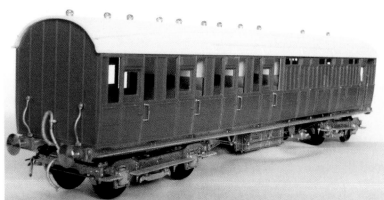

The completed brake vehicle, well, one compartment partition to add and the alarm gear.

A close up of the truss rods and vacuum cylinder.

A completed JLTRT bogie with the stepboards added. The outer brakes are Sidelines castings.

An underside view – the 1.6mm copper wire along the centre represents the steam heating pipe.

RIGHT Behind the buffer beam – the springs were salvaged from a scrap computer keyboard. The vacuum pipe is made from 1.7mm copper wire from electrical cable.

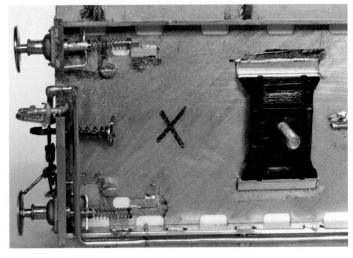

for truss rod or turnbuckle versions of the underframes. All three vehicles in my project are turnbuckle versions. The etches follow a pretty standard design for this sort of thing – fold-up solebars with overlays and cut-outs and markings for the various underfloor fittings. The first job was to use a big file and remove any etching cusps that would be visible, ie: the outer edge of the solebar flange. After this, the hardest part was to fold up the lower flange of the solebar. It's very narrow and my homemade bending bars struggled to grip it. Some judicious work with some smooth jawed pliers saw the remaining portions folded up. I eventually managed to get rid of the worse wiggles by going back over it with the pliers a few times to get it all straight. I basically followed the instructions (for once!) and

the etches are nicely designed. They fold up neatly and everything fits, the etched battery box goes together particularly well. The queen posts are created by laminating several layers of etchings and the threaded posts that fit into them and support the truss rods ate up my stock of 14BA nuts – eight for each coach! One minor issue that I found was that the slots and tabs didn't quite match for one of the queen posts – easily rectified with a file. I decided to use Sidelines castings for the underframe fittings, vac cylinder, dynamo, buffers and hose connections. They were all soldered into place with 145° solder. I was in a bit of a dilemma here, when my coaches eventually reside on my railway, it would look better to have the hoses connected, but whist being shown off and visiting other lines, it's easier

to have them frozen in place as if the vehicle is standing in a siding idle. I don't know, so I took the male prerogative to take the easy road and hope for the best! They are frozen in place - I can always change them later. The underframe instructions suggest using O gauge PCB sleeper strip for the step boards and annoyingly these coaches have stepboards everywhere. The strip I obtained was double sided and seemed a little too thick, so I carefully split them in half with a Stanley knife. I used a big file again to round off the outer edge and corners. The underframe etch provides etched brackets to support them. One has to be careful here, the half-etch for the fold can be very weak and the stepboard, once in place, can easily just fold up when gripped, as they are the first things that the pinkies come in

The battery boxes.

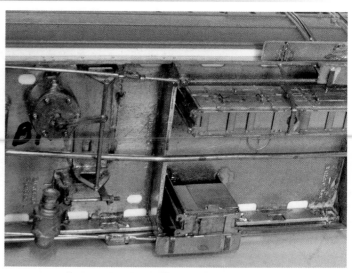

Underside of the brake vehicle showing the dynamo arrangement and shortened battery box. I'll have to straighten that wonky step!

The full brake.

The full third showing the alarm gear at the end of the coach.

touch with when picking up the coach. To reinforce them, I drilled 0.6mm holes into the solebar below a number of the brackets and soldered in brass wire supports to make the whole assembly more robust. When filed down slightly they are quite discreet. The full brake vehicle differed in that it had separate sets of boards under the doors rather than a continuous one running the full length of the

coach, so wire supports were added for all of those. The Sidelines cast buffers were cleaned up in the mini drill, a cross hole was drilled and a brass wire 'L' soldered into place. This acted as a positioner to control the amount that the buffer projects. A spring mounted on the buffer tail reacts against a holding post made up from scrap etch. Finally the prominent vacuum pipe that runs along the

solebar was added and retained in place by split pins, at least it would hide any wiggles in the solebar angle on that side of the coach! The Sidelines lost wax brass vacuum pipes are supplied straight and they had to be gently reformed (bent) into the angled pipe typical of these coaches. I should have made up some brass bosses to mount the bogies on, but I couldn't resist using the plastic centres of some redundant Kirk 4mm bogie frames as they seemed to be just the right depth. The truss rods were added as per instructions, although it was more practical to split the fold up turnbuckle into three separate pieces and solder them together that way.

Bogies

There are a number of 7mm Gresley bogie kits around, I went with the JLTRT ones; the main reason was that I knew the castings would need little cleaning up, and I was right. The only thing they do lack is brake gear and although on these type of bogies it is fairly well hidden, I really wanted to represent the outer brakes that can just be seen and used Sidelines brake castings to do the job. The bogie castings assembled well, the only point to watch was that with the central bolster and end castings in place, the sideframes remained parallel. I guess there might have been some shrinkage discrepancies with larger castings, which can happen, but this was easy enough to resolve once I had worked out what the problem was. I liked the way the axleboxes are free to move in the hornguides. I had to carefully counterbore the backs of them to allow the top hat bearings to fit 'inside' them so that the Easybuild wheels would rotate freely. Not a big problem.

The full brake had Fox bogies and ABS produce a suitable white metal kit which assembled up without any problem. Unusually the vehicle I was modelling had a stretcher bar between the axlebox retainers. This was not common, but I fancied a feature

of interest! This was achieved by hand-drilling into the castings and springing some brass wire in. I embossed some rivets on some suitable brass strip and used it for the axlebox retainers. I invested in a GW riveting tool some time ago, if you are going to do much 7mm kit building, they are an invaluable tool, forming good rivet heads without distorting the surrounding material. I had mine as a birthday present from Mrs G. No one else in the family understood what it was!

Light springs were used on all of the bogies between the head of the 4BA screw and the underside of the bogie to try and eliminate any wobble, time will prove if it works.

Painting and finishing

With a house move in the offing, I might be getting closer to building the railway, but I had a number of projects that had reached the painting stage, so I decided to hold that work until after the move. However in the meantime it meant that I could take the coaches to various running sessions and iron out any problems before they were painted. They seemed to run ok and are surprisingly weighty considering that the body is all-plastic.

After visiting a few shows and private railways, I decided that I couldn't live with the moulded handles. Other people had replaced them with brass ones on their coaches! So one afternoon I carefully carved them off. It wasn't as hard as I thought it would be. I fitted Griffin brass ones and they do the job nicely, and I can sleep at night knowing that the coaches look better. Unfortunately this led on to dissatisfaction with the hinges and I copied the method passed to me by Andrew Baldwin at the Telford O gauge show. This was to make hinges from .020" x .020" Evergreen strip for the top and middle hinges – the lower ones are .020" x .060" and are carefully trimmed to shape after they have been allowed to set for a day. The hinges are set on the joint line with plenty of solvent to make sure they fix securely. Some of Andrew's superb rolling stock can be seen on the Editor's Gifford Street layout from time-to-time (*we might even persude him to write about them sometime! - Ed.*).

I finally got to the stage where the coaches could be painted; so they were broken down into the various sub-assemblies and cleaned with 'Jif 'in the kitchen sink. This was followed by a good rinsing and then they spent 24 hours in the airing cupboard to dry out. I was lucky enough to get some good sunny dry days to work outside and spray the underframes with Halfords primer, and after inspection, this was followed by Satin Black. Later on, before re-assembly, these parts were sprayed with a

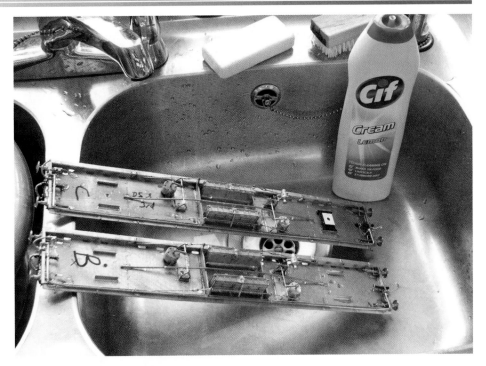
Cleaning the underframes prior to painting.

This old projector stand is ideal for spraying models – nice weather!

The door hinges have been added – that looks a lot better!

Spraying the coach bodies with undercoat in the workshop.

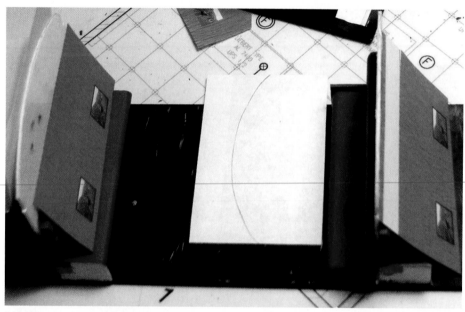

Adding the printed compartment partitions.

Close up of glazing and weathering.

weathering mix. I like the original carmine livery that these coaches had in the early 50s, and this livery survived in some cases to quite late on. I decided to have one coach in this livery, although I'm not sure any survived until 1962! I sprayed the coaches with Halfords primer and used Just Like The Real Thing aerosol cans for the main colours. This always sprays well and gives a good finish. I was probably pushing the limits as the temperature was struggling to get above 12°. This all turned out to be a long drawn-out process as we were well in to the autumn and I had to wait for suitable warm days to paint and find time between working on the house. The usual sequence of numbering and varnishing with Precision Paints satin varnish followed.

The coaches were weathered down by painting on diluted matt black and then wiping it off – a frightening process! Hopefully this captures the neglected sooty appearance that I desire. Also a variety of passengers was added. The Slater's ones seem somewhat diminutive compared with some of the other offerings available. However they provide some life to the coach and justify the continuation of the Nottingham Victoria to Derby Friargate service.

Almost the last task was to fit the windows, which took an age, as each window fits inside a rebate on the inside of the coach body. These were mass-produced by cutting strips of glazing material, then parting off individual panes. Some of the vertical rebates are quite shallow, so it was difficult to hide the edge of the 'glass'. I used Cobex, from Comet Models, it's quite a hard material and resists scratching more than normal clear plastic and looks more glass-like, but it doesn't take solvent quite so easily. I used G-S Hypo Cement, which has a very fine applicator tube which minimises the amount of glue smudging. This sticks, rather than melts the two surfaces together, so the windows are a little fragile. One has to accept that there will be a failure rate, so I cut a good number of spare panes. When the coach was fully glazed, I inspected and popped out any that had smudges or were a poor fit - a bit of a pain, but you know your mates will happily point out any bad workmanship!

Conclusion

It was a form of kit-bashing to put these coaches together and it was interesting sourcing the various parts, so that made it a bit of a challenge, half of the problem was knowing where to get parts from and if they exist at all! That knowledge only came from visiting a few O gauge shows and taking to chums. The plastic makes a considerable mess when being worked, and it sticks to everything, but I think I got away with it – no domestic wrath! Care has to be taken with the

The finished full brake.

The completed Brake Third.

modules to create a coach side that is straight in both planes. With the modular approach to these panelled coaches, it might well be possible to go through the diagram book and use different combinations to produce other coach variants, I've done that with Gresley coaches in 4mm scale in the past. It will be atmospheric to see them trundling along behind an elderly J6 or an L1. I would like to do some more really, and I guess it would be quicker now I know all the snags.

I also used this project to assist one of my chums into model making, as it covered all three common disciplines, working in plastic, white metal and brass. That was a useful exercise. This was a project that took over a year, due to the house move and working on other projects. Now all I have to do is build some steel panelled vehicles to keep them company. I think they will probably be less work - I hope!

Parts List

■ **Body/roof**
Ian Kirk
www.speedy231278.demon.co.uk/ik/

■ **Underframe**
Newbold Models
newbold@modelrail.net

■ **Fox bogies**
ABS
01202 672 891
www.keykits.net/

■ **Oval mirrors**
CPL
01635 44 001 (evenings only)

■ **Wheels**
Easy Build
www.easybuildcoaches.co.uk

■ **Commode handles/lamp irons**
Laurie Griffin
www.lgminiatures.co.uk

■ **Black paint**
Halfords

■ **Just Like The Real Thing**
Maroon/crimson paint/Gresley bogies
www.justliketherealthing.co.uk

■ **Couplings**
Premier Components

■ **Vents/seats/vacuum cylinder/ dynamo/buffers**
Sidelines
01228 521671
www.sidelines.freeserve.co.uk

READERS' LAYOUTS ALBUM

King's Cross

Paul Walker's superb N gauge model of the Cross first came to light in the March 2007 issue. As a dyed-in-the-wool Eastern Region fan, Mr Wright was soon off to photograph it - and what excellent pictures it made! Paul was also lucky to bump into Richard Dockerill, our N gauge correspondent, at a Harrogate show in 2006 and Dicky has, since then, produced a fair amount of the superb rolling stock featured on the layout.

Haunting Hollowbeck

In 1962, Hollobeck Shed used to serve a brewery on Tyneside. Now the beer goes by road but the shed is used by BR as temporary cover for Percy Main depot, which suffered a fire at this time. This scenario is ficticious of course, but it provides an opportunity to showcase a fleet of unglamorous and dirty locos applicable to the period: - and in chunky O gauge. This 18' exhibition layout runs from a fiddle-yard (inside the brewery) to a turntable - negotiating an ashpit, coal stage, signal box and two-road depot building on the way. Locos depicted include J27, Q6, WD, V3, Ivatt 4, K3, J72, J94 and some early green diesels. All kit-built with some classes duplicated to add authenticity.

David Wellington, Driffield

READERS' LAYOUTS ALBUM

Beeley

Brian Lee first sent us photographs for the July 2007 magazine. Having been a modeller for many years, dabbling in both EM and P4, Brian finally settled for traditional OO for his Mk.3 version of Beeley. All of Brian's layouts have an interesting history - we'll be covering them and their creator in a future edition of *BRM*. It was only recently that I worked out why the layouts were so named!

Country Sidings

My layout is N gauge measuring 6' x 2' and all buildings are scratch-built. I get a lot of enjoyment from the layout and cannot resist adding to it. My 12 year-old grandson also gets a lot of pleasure from it when he stays here.

David Hartshorne, Perton, South Staffs

WIN A MICRO LAYOUT!

You could win this ultra small-space layout worth £250 in our easy-to-enter competition!

Not everyone wants a large layout or has the space for one so scenic expert Peter Marriott is on hand in the *BRM Annual* to show you how to build a micro layout for under £250 in less than a week!

But if the thought of building a layout doesn't appeal, why not try to win it in our easy-to-enter competition? Measuring a compact 4' x 2' (approx) it can be set up and running in less than ten minutes. To enter, simply answer the following question correctly - but you'll have to read the article beginning on page 90 first to find the answer!

Q: What is the name of the station on the *BRM* micro layout?

A: Bridge End
B: Bridtorre
B: Bridport

Send your answer on a postcard or back of a sealed envelope, together with your name, address and daytime telephone number, to: Micro Layout Competition (BRM0160), British Railway Modelling, Warners Group Publications plc, West Street, Bourne, Lincs. PE10 9PH to arrive no later than January 31, 2010. We regret that due to the nature of the prize, this competition is open to UK residents only.

There is no cash alternative to the prize offered and no correspondence will be entered into. Our usual terms and conditions apply, see: www.brmodelling.co.uk

* By entering this competition you automatically agree to receive correspondence from Warners. If you do not wish to receive any correspondence please put a cross on the top right hand side of your entry.

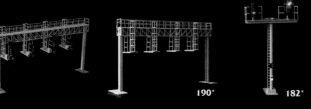

Get all your questions answered and improve your layout

Order any of the products shown below and we'll deliver them to your door at no extra cost, *plus* if you are a *BRM* subscriber quote your subscriber number while calling and we'll give you **£2.00 off** the listed price*.

BRAND NEW

More than 75 regularly asked questions with answers from experts.

This book has been produced to answer many of the frequently asked questions that beginners and those already active in the hobby ask from time to time. We have written and photographed the book to be as helpful and comprehensive as possible within its 120 pages. The questions that the book sets out to answer are those that have been put to the writers at various times.

We are aware that there are many more detailed questions that modellers have. We have concluded many of the answers in this book with a list of suggested additional sources of information.

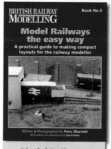

BRITISH RAILWAY MODELLING — Book No.6

Railway Modelling FAQs

More than 75 regularly asked questions with answers from experts

Written and photographed by Ian Futers, Peter Marriott and Pelle Søeborg

only £14.99

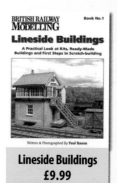
Lineside Buildings
£9.99

Scenic Modelling
£9.99

Model Railways
£9.99

Scratch-Built Buildings
£9.99

Modern Wagons
£11.99

Right Track 1
£15.60

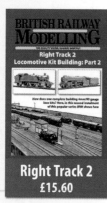
Right Track 2
£15.60

Right Track 3
£17.50

Right Track 4
£18.50

Right Track 5
£16.60

Right Track 6
£18.50

Right Track 7
£18.50

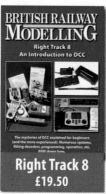
Right Track 8
£19.50

Right Track 9
£19.50

Right Track 10
£22.00

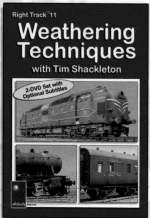

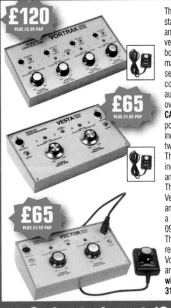

364 - 370 SMITHDOWN ROAD, LIVERPOOL, L15 5AN

TEL: 0151 - 733 3655 FAX: 0151 - 734 4040

WWW.EHATTONS.COM

Hatton's — Established 1946

OPENING HOURS

8.00am to 6.00pm - MON to SAT   10.00am to 4.00pm - SUNDAY

All shown items in stock on 16/09/09

Most prices valid until 13/01/10, though some may change on 11/12/2009. errors excepted

UK POSTAGE £4 PER ORDER

£2 POSTAGE FOR SINGLE DIECAST ITEM

Next Day Delivery £7 (same day dispatch)
We must receive order by 2.00pm for same day dispatch. Weekends do not count.

5800+ ITEMS AVAILABLE

WWW.EHATTONS.COM

PRE-ORDERS ALSO TAKEN

N Gauge

Dapol - Steam locos

ND023 45xx straight sided 2-6-2 tank loco 4527 in GWR livery (list £65)........ **BARGAIN** £35
ND024 45xx straight sided 2-6-2 tank loco 4571 in British Railways livery (list £65) .... **BARGAIN** £32
ND064B Class Ivatt 2-6-2 loco 41271 in BR black with early crest - Push-Pull £52
ND090 Class 9F "Evening Star" 2-10-0 92220 BR green with late crest & BR1G tender double chimney........£105
ND104a 14xx 0-4-2 Tank with top feed 1438 in BR black with early emblem. Final run ever - ltd edition of 250........£34
ND104b 14xx 0-4-2 Tank with top feed 1414 in BR black with early emblem. Final run ever - ltd edition of 250........£34

Train Packs

ND080/3 Train pack with Class 14xx 0-4-2 loco 1467 in GWR green & autocoach in chocolate & cream with GWR crest. Due Jul/Aug 09 ..£49
ND080/4 Train pack with Class 48xx 0-4-2 loco 4865 in GWR shirtbutton green & autocoach in chocolate & cream with shirtbutton logo...£49
ND084E Class 35 Hymek diesel trainpack D7099 in BR blue and 6 x silver 6 wheel milk tank wagons (all weathered) £119

Diesel locos

ND021a Class 73 Electro-Diesel 73114 "Stewarts Lane" in Mainline blue livery (list £75)........ **BARGAIN** £35
ND102 Class 66 diesel 66 725 "Sunderland" in GBRF livery........£49
NEW **ND108** Class 66 66181 in EWS livery........£59
NEW **ND109** Class 66 66222 in EWS livery........£59
NEW **ND110** Class 66 66152 in DB Schenker livery........£59

DMU's

ND073d Class 221 4 car Super Voyager DMU 221144 "Prince Madoc" in Virgin trains livery........£105
ND081b Class 156 2 car DMU 156492 in "Northern Rail" ex First 'Barbie' livery (dummy)........£40
ND083A Class 156 2 car DMU 156506 in "Strathclyde P.T." livery £104
ND083B Class 156 dummy car 156435 in "Strathclyde P.T." livery..£40
ND087b Class 221 Super voyager unit 221135 "Cross Country" (list £119)........ **BARGAIN** £89

Coaches

NC045D Gresley third class coach in LNER Teak livery £20
NEW **NC051c** Mk3 Coach First Class (FO) Blue Grey without buffers £17
NC052d Mk3 Coach Second Class (SO) in Virgin Trains livery with buffers. Another version of NC052a........£18
NEW **NC052e** Mk3 Coach Second Class (SO) in Intercity livery with buffers. Second version of NC052b........£18
NEW **NC052f** Mk3 Coach Second Class (SO) in Blue Grey livery with buffers. Second version of NC052c........£20
NEW **NC053c** Mk3 Coach Second Class (SO) in Blue Grey livery without buffers........£17
NEW **NC053d** Mk3 Coach Second Class (SO) in Virgin Trains livery without buffers. Second version of NC053a........£18
NEW **NC053e** Mk3 Coach Second Class (SO) in Intercity livery without buffers. Second version of NC053b........£18
NEW **NC053f** Mk3 Coach Second Class (SO) in Blue Grey livery without buffers. Second version of NC053c........£18

Accessories Railway related

NC040a Light Bar coach lighting unit for modern coaches/multiple units (Class 156/MkIII 'Plug&Play')........£5

Gaugemaster Controls - DCC Decoders

DCC23 1A 2 function decoder with 6-pin NEM 651 plug for direct insertion. N gauge suitable........£22

Graham Farish - Steam locos

371-932 8750 class 0-6-0 Pannier tank 8759 in BR black late crest .£42
372-002 Hall class 4-6-0 4965 'Rood Ashton' in GWR green £57
372-003 Hall class 4-6-0 4979 'Wooton Hall' in BR green late crest .£57
372-052 Class 4F 44027 Fowler 0-6-0 & tender BR black early emblem£55
372-053 Class 4F 44422 Fowler 0-6-0 & tender BR black late crest £55
372-227 Midland Crab 2-6-0 42765 in BR lined black early emblem £68
372-355 Class A4 60017 'Silver Fox' BR lined green late crest.....£71
372-380 Class A3 4-6-2 60065 "Knight of the Thistle" in BR green with late crest (list £92) .... **BARGAIN** £58
372-529 4MT tank 81030 BR lined black late crest........£55
372-530 4MT tank 80048 BR lined black early emblem weathered..£55
372-575 Rebuilt Royal Scot 4-6-0 46159 "Royal Air Force" with LMS smoke deflectors & tender in BR green with late crest (DCC ready) .£76
372-576 Rebuilt Royal Scot 4-6-0 46106 Gordon Highlander with BR smoke deflectors & tender in BR green with early crest........£76

372-577 Rebuilt Royal Scot 4-6-0 6115 "Scots Guardsman" with LMS smoke deflectors & tender LMS black £76

372-601 V2 2-6-2 60807 & tender in BR lined black with early emblem (list £92.20)........ **BARGAIN** £62
372-602 V2 2-6-2 4844 "Coldstream" & tender in LNER Doncaster green (list £92.20)........ **BARGAIN** £62

Diesel locos

371-015 Class 08 diesel shunter BR Blue livery £45
371-016 Class 08 diesel shunter EWS livery........£45
371-017 Class 08 diesel shunter Railfreight Distribution livery £45
371-028 Class 20 Diesel D8307 in BR blue with headcode box (Weathered)........£56
371-050A Class 04 diesel shunter D2264 in BR green £38
371-052 Class 04 diesel shunter 11217 BR black with early emblem£38
371-077 Class 25/3 diesel D7646 in BR two tone green £59
371-130 Class 33 diesel 33002 'Sea King' BR civil engineers dutch (yellow/grey) (list £68.75)........ **BARGAIN** £39
371-160 Class 37/4 diesel 37431 'Bullidae' Intercity Mainline (list £80.25)........ **BARGAIN** £44
371-177 Class 40 diesel D351 in BR green with centre head code box (list £78)........ **BARGAIN** £57
371-233 Class 47 diesel 47306 'The Sapper' Railfreight Distribution (list £78.35)........ **BARGAIN** £39
NEW **371-278** Class 55 Deltic 55008 'The Green Howards' BR blue £62
371-350 Class 60 diesel 60052 "Glofa TWR" in EWS livery £61
371-351 Class 60 diesel 60078 Mainline blue (list £87.65)**BARGAIN**£48
NEW **371-380A** Class 66 diesel 66098 in EWS livery........£75
NEW **371-382** Class 66 Diesel 66412 DRS Malcolm Rail £75
NEW **371-383** Class 66 diesel in DB Schenker livery £72
371-391 Class 66/4 diesel 66411 'Eddie the Engine' DRS/Stobart rail £65
371-451 Class 37/0 D6707 BR green late crest split head code boxes£59
371-452 Class 37/0 diesel 37238 BR blue centre head code boxes .£59
371-453 Class 37/0 D6826 BR green late crest centre head code boxes £59
371-585 Class 46 diesel D163 "Leics & Derbys Yeomanry" BR green £61
371-586 Class 46 diesel 46053 in BR blue £56
371-602 Class 42 Warship diesel D814 "Dragon" in BR green £63
371-650 Class 57/3 57301 "Scott Tracy" in Virgin Trains livery £61
371-651 Class 57/0 diesel 57003 "Freightliner Evolution" in Freightliner livery (list £84.55)........ **BARGAIN** £42
371-652 Class 57/6 diesel 57602 "Restormel Castle" in First Great Western livery (list £80.55)........ **BARGAIN** £44
371-825 Class 47 diesel D1500 with 4 character headcode in BR two tone green with half yellow ends £64
371-826 Class 47 diesel 1764 with 4 character headcode in BR two tone green with full yellow ends £64
371-827 Class 47 diesel 47035 with domino headcode in BR blue with full yellow ends........£64
371-828 Class 47 47404 'Hadrian' with marker light headcode BR blue £64

Electric locos

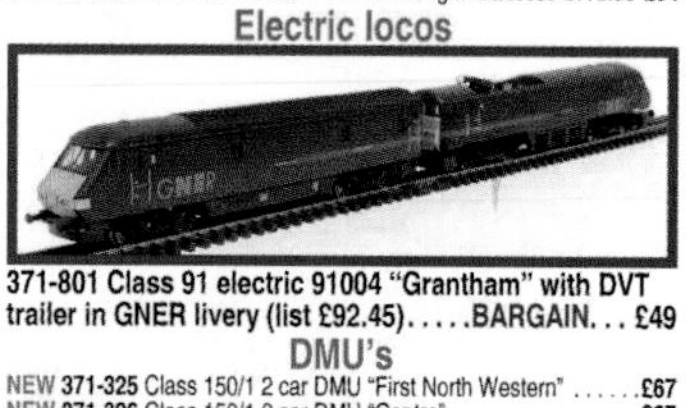

371-801 Class 91 electric 91004 "Grantham" with DVT trailer in GNER livery (list £92.45).....BARGAIN... £49

DMU's

NEW **371-325** Class 150/1 2 car DMU "First North Western" £67
NEW **371-326** Class 150/1 2 car DMU "Centro"........£67
NEW **371-327** Class 150/2 2 car DMU "Arriva Trains Wales.......£67
371-425 Class 170/1 2 car DMU Midland Mainline(list £84.50)**BARGAIN**£61
371-427 Class 170/4 2 car DMU in Southwest Trains livery £69
371-428 Class 170/4 3 car DMU in Scotrail livery £84
371-429 Class 170/2 2 car DMU in One railways livery........£66
371-430 Class 171/7 2 car DMU Southern........£79
371-555 Class 158 2 car DMU Arriva Trains Wales........£69
371-675 Class 220 001 'Maiden Voyager' Virgin trains 4 car unit ...£88
371-678 Class 220 4 car Voyager DMU in 'Cross Country' livery ...£88
371-876 Class 108 2 car DMU in BR blue £68

371-877 Class 108 2 car DMU BR blue & grey livery. £68

HST trainpacks

371-475A HST 125 3-car set in Midland Mainline new livery (list £101.10)........ **BARGAIN** £49
371-479 HST 125 3 car set Intercity swallow(list £101.10)**BARGAIN**£59

Coaches

NEW **374-102C** Mk1 RMB mini buffet car M1821 in BR (M) maroon £12
NEW **374-116A** Mk1 RU Restaurant Car BR Maroon £13
NEW **374-151A** Mk1 FK First Corridor BR Green £13
NEW **374-152A** Mk1 FK corridor first W13137 in BR (WR) chocolate/cream........£14
NEW **374-153B** Mk1 FK First Corridor BR Maroon £13
374-241 Mk1 BSP Pullman 2nd class bar car in blue/grey £12
NEW **374-271A** Mk1 57ft Suburban BR Maroon £13
NEW **374-281A** Mk1 57ft Suburban Composite BR Maroon £13
NEW **374-291A** Mk1 57ft Suburban Open Second BR Maroon.....£13
374-325A Mk3 2nd class coach in "Midland Mainline" 2002 Pullman livery (list £14.60)........ **BARGAIN** £8
374-400A Mk3 TGS guard 2nd in "Midland Mainline" "Pullman" livery (list £14.60)........ **BARGAIN** £8
374-525 Mk4 TSOD 2nd open 75ft coach in "GNER" livery (list £14.60)........ **BARGAIN** .. £7.50
NEW **374-702B** Mk2 65ft RFB Restaurant First Buffet BR Blue & Grey £13
374-727B Mk2F TSO 2nd open 65ft coach in BR blue/grey £12
374-800 Mk1 restaurant car RFO in BR blue/grey........£11
NEW **374-802A** Mk1 restaurant car RFO in BR crimson & cream...£11

Wagons

NEW **373-008A** Bulk Powder PCA Wagon 'ICI' White........£7
NEW **373-030A** Bulk aggregate hopper PGA wagon "British Industrial Sand"........£7
373-032 Bulk aggregate hopper PGA wagon "VTG" light grey (list £7.80)........ **BARGAIN** .. £4.50
NEW **373-506A** 46T GLW HEA Hopper Wagon BR Coal Sector Grey £7
NEW **373-600B** 46t VGA Sliding wall van "EWS" (weathered) £7
373-602B 46t VGA Sliding wall van "Railfreight Distribution" (weathered) £8
NEW **373-625B** 31 Ton OBA Open Wagon EWS £8
NEW **373-626B** 31 Ton OBA Open Wagon 'Railfreight'........£8
NEW **373-627B** 31 Ton OBA Open Wagon 'Plasmor Blockfreight' Weathered........£8
NEW **373-628B** 31 Ton OBA Open wagon with high ends EWS.....£8
NEW **373-776A** 45 Tonne GLW TTA Tank Wagon 'Esso'........£8
373-801A 100 tonne glw HHA bogie hopper wagon with hinged exterior doors 'Freightliner'........£15
373-850A Pack6 Pack of 6 x 373-850A 102 Tonne glw HTA bulk coal hopper EWS........£99
373-925 30 ton bogie bolster wagon in BR gulf red........£10

373-926 30 ton bogie bolster wagon BR grey & load £9.50

373-927 30 ton bogie bolster wagon in GWR grey with load £10
NEW **373-950A** HFA hopper wagon with dust cover Transrail (weathered)£8
373-951A HFA Hopper Wagon with railfreight coal sector markings and Mainline branding (weathered) (list £9.45)........ **BARGAIN** .. £7.50
NEW **374-752B** Mk2 65ft FO First Open BR Blue & Grey........£12
377-000 40 Tonne Sealion YGH Bogie Hopper Wagon Olive Green £15
377-001 40 Tonne Seacow (Ex Sealion) YGB Bogie Hopper Wagon Departmental Dutch........£16
377-002 40T Seacow (Ex Sealion) YGA Bogie Hopper Wagon EWS£15
377-027 5-plank wagon "George Lovegrove"........£4
377-100 90 tonne GLW JGA bogie hopper 'RMC'........£18
377-176A 7 Plank Wagon With Coke Rail BR Grey........£6

377-225Z 6 X BR grey 16 Ton weathered steel mineral wagons with end door & different run no. Ltd ed of 500 £37.50

377-552 31 Tonne OCA dropside open wagon in 'EWS' maroon £8

Train Sets - analogue control

370-025 Basic complete 0-6-0 starter steam train set with 3 wagons £43
370-250 Diesel tanker freight complete train set with Class 47 (list £129.95)........ **BARGAIN** ...£109
370-251 Diesel fuel freight complete train set with Class 37 in Railfreight Distribution £114

Stations & Buildings

379-200 4 x Platform sections (red brick)........£6

Hornby - Stations & Buildings

NEW **N8017** Cotswold Stone Walls - Pack 1........£5
N8019 Cotswold Stone Walls - Pack 3........£5
N8020 Granite Stone Wall - Pack 1........£5
N8021 Granite Stone Wall - Pack 2........£5
NEW **N8022** Granite Stone Wall - Pack 3........£5
N8030 Wooden standalone garage - Lyddle End "Village & Town" £3.50
N8073 Mid terraced house (right hand) - Lyddle End "Village & Town" .£7
N8077 Country Fire Station - Lyddle End "Village & Town" range...£13
N8850 Lyddle End East Engine Shed - Lyddle End "Station Life" ...£23

Trackside Accessories

N8571 Road over bridge - Lyddle End Range........£17
N8745 Corner walls x 2 - Lyddle End "Gasworks" Range £5

Oxford Diecast Ltd - Cars

NEW **N105004** Ford Anglia 105E in Grey/White £2.50
NEW **NJJ003** Jowett Javelin in Maroon........ £2.50
NEW **NMMT002** Morris Minor Traveller in Trafalgar Blue £2.50
NEW **NSS002** Humber Super Snipe in Silver Grey £2.50

Buses

NEW **NOB005** Bedford OB Coach in Macbraynes livery........£4
NEW **NRM005** Routemaster Bus in LT Silver Jubilee livery £5
NEW **NRM006** Routemaster Bus in Blackpool livery........£5

Commercial & public services

NEW **NFX4002** FX Taxi in Evening News livery £2.50
NEW **NMM052** Morris Minor Van in BRS Parcels Livery........ £2.50

Peco - Steam locos

NL-27 0-6-0 Collett & tender in BR black........£115

Stations & Buildings

NB-27 Platform Edging (Concrete)........£2
NB-80 Diesel Depot Kit £10

Track & Points

SL-310 Rail Joiners/Fishplates for N & 009 gauge (24 per pack) . £1.50

Track & Points - Setrack Code 80

ST-1 Standard straight track........ £0.90
ST-11 Double straight track £1.10
ST-12 No.1 radius double curve........£1
ST-15 No.2 radius double curve........ £1.25
ST-21 Add on Level crossing for ST20........£3
ST-5 Setrack right hand point with insulfrog........£6
ST-6 Setrack left hand point with insulfrog........£6
ST-7 Setrack short crossing........£6

Track & Points - Streamline Code 55 Finescale

SL-300F/B 30 * 1 yard (91.5cm) lengths of Finescale Nickle Silver flexible track........£68
SL-E390F Finescale double slip with electrofrog........£27
SL-E391F Finescale right hand small point with electrofrog £7
SL-E392F Finescale left hand small point with electrofrog £7
SL-E396F Finescale left hand medium point with electrofrog £8

Track & Points - Streamline Code 80 Universal

SL-300/B Box of 25 yard (91.5cm) lengths of Wooden-sleeper Nickle Silver flexible track........£52
SL-300/S 1 yard (91.5cm) length of Wooden-Sleeper Nickel Silver Flexible track £2.60
SL-387 Left hand curved point with insulfrog........£8
SL-389 Left hand large point with insulfrog £8
SL-395 Right hand medium point with insulfrog........£7
SL-396 Left hand medium point with insulfrog........£7
SL-397 Y Point with insulfrog........£7
SL-E395 Right hand medium point with electrofrog........£7
SL-E396 Left hand medium point with electrofrog........£7
SL-E397 Y point medium radius with electrofrog........£7

OO Gauge

Bachmann - Steam locos

NEW **30-041Steam** 0-6-0 Industrial steam loco "Digby" DCC fitted (unboxed)........£23
31-059 J72 class 0-6-0 tank loco 69022 in BR black with late crest .£39
31-115 Standard 4MT 75027 single chimney in BR lined green with late crest with BR2 tender (weathered)........£74
31-116 Standard 4MT 75069 double chimney in BR lined green with late crest & BR1B tender £70

31-118 Standard 4MT 4-6-0 75033 single chimney loco in BR lined black with late crest and BR2 tender ... £70

31-175 Jubilee 45611 'Hong Kong' BR green early emblem 4000 gallon riveted tender £71
31-176DC Jubilee 45562 'Alberta' BR green late crest 4000 gallon flush tender (DCC on board)........£80
31-185 Jubilee 5563 'Australia' LMS crimson with Fowler tender ...£71
31-186 Jubilee 45587 'Baroda' with Fowler tender in BR lined green with late crest £80
31-210 Patriot class 4-6-0 45503 'The Royal Leicestershire Regiment' in BR green with early emblem........£78
31-211 Patriot class 4-6-0 45543 'Home Guard' BR green late crest £78
31-212 Patriot class 4-6-0 5541 'Duke Of Sutherland' LMS crimson £78
31-284 Parallel boiler Scot 4-6-0 46165 'The Rangers (12th London Regiment)' in BR green with early emblem £57
31-475A G2A 0-8-0 49064 BR Black Late Crest with back cab tender (list £91.60)........ **BARGAIN** £69
31-476 G2A (Super D) 0-8-0 9449 LMS black tender without back cab £89

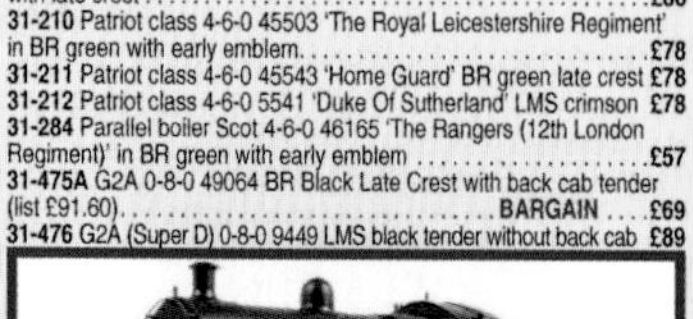

31-477DC G2A (Super D) 0-8-0 49361 BR black late crest (DCC on board)........ £78

31-478 G2A 49287 BR Black Early Emblem without back cab tender £74

31-550A Gresley V2 2-6-2 4771 "Green Arrow" LNER Doncaster Green (National Collection)........£72
NEW **31-563** V2 60865 BR Lined Green with late crest........£69
31-711 B1 1189 'Sir William Gray' LNER apple green........£55
31-712 B1 61000 'Springbok' BR lined black early emblem........£58
31-855A J39 0-6-0 and flat sided tender in BR black early emblem .£48

31-952 A4 4-6-2 4468 "Mallard" with valances & tender in LNER garter blue £68

32-000DC Hall class 4-6-0 5927 'Guild Hall' BR green late crest hawksworth tender (DCC on board)........£68
32-129 45xx 2-6-2 Prairie tank 4557 BR lined black early emblem (list £59.60)........ **BARGAIN** £37
32-135A Class 4575 Prairie tank loco 5565 in GWR green........£59

32-164 N Class 2-6-0 31406 & tender in BR lined black with late crest & standard 4MT chimney £60

32-212 Class 57XX 0-6-0 Pannier tank 5757 in BR black late crest .£49

32-213DC Class 57XX pannier tank 7788 GWR green (DCC on board)........ £59

32-259 WD Austerity 2-8-0 90630 loco & tender in BR black with late crest (lightly weathered)........ £83

32-278 K3 2-6-0 61823 with stepped 4200 gallon tender in BR lined black with late crest (list £87.85) .... **BARGAIN** £52

32-279 K3 2-6-0 1935 with Group Standard 4200 gallon tender in LNER Doncaster green livery £66

32-300DC Collett Goods 2244 & churchward tender in BR lined green with late crest (DCC on board)........£73
32-351DC Standard 4MT 2-6-4 tank 80140 in BR lined black with late crest (DCC on board)........£70
32-358 Standard class 4MT 2-6-4 tank 80118 in BR lined black with early emblem £60

32-504 Standard class 5MT 73014 & BR1 tender in BR green with late crest (list £89.25) .....BARGAIN... £59

32-506 Standard class 5MT 73110 "The Red Knight" & BR1f tender in BR lined black with late crest £70

32-507 Standard class 5MT 73050 with BR1G tender in BR lined black with late crest (weathered)........ £74

NEW **32-558 Class A1 60115 'Meg Merrilies' BR Lined Green Early Emblem £88**

32-578 Ivatt Class 4 43038 loco & tender in BR lined black with early emblem (list £81.95) ..BARGAIN... £59

32-580 Ivatt Class 4 2-6-0 43019 in BR lined black with late crest (weathered) £69
32-585 Ivatt class 4 2-6-0 43106 BR black with late crest & tablet catcher (list £85.35) .... **BARGAIN** £52

364-370 SMITHDOWN ROAD, LIVERPOOL, L15 5AN
TEL: 0151 - 733 3655 FAX: 0151 - 734 4040
INFO@EHATTONS.COM

UK POSTAGE £4 PER ORDER
All items actually in stock on 16/09/09

UK2013 Dennis Trident/Plaxton President d/deck bus "Brighton & Hove" (list £24.99) ..... **BARGAIN** £17
NEW **UK5023** Mercedes Citaro rigid - Metrobus route X26 ..... £32
UK5110 Mercedes Benz Citaro articulated bendy bus "London Central" (list £30) ..... **BARGAIN** £20
UK6011 Dennis Enviro 400/Alexander d/deck bus "Stagecoach (East Kent)" (list £30) ..... **BARGAIN** £14
UK6012 Dennis Enviro 400/Alexander d/deck bus "Stagecoach (Newcastle)" (list £30) ..... **BARGAIN** £15
NEW **UKVAN1006** Mercedes Sprinter Traveliner Minicoach - plain white to allow modification £8

Dapol - Wagons
B734 Grampus wagon in BR black (unweathered) £11
B734 SPEC 4 Grampus wagon DB990173 in weathered BR olive green Hattons Limited Edition of 250 ..... £12
B737 Passenger fruit 'D' wagon in GWR shirtbutton livery £15
NEW **B747f** Telescopic steel hood wagon 33.70.0899.024.0 Tiphook £22
NEW **B747g** Telescopic steel hood wagon 33 80 4667 023 Tiphook £22
NEW **B747h** Telescopic steel hood wagon 33 80 4667 046 Tiphook £22
B762 6-wheel milk tank in UD Livery £9
NEW **B766** 7 Plank wagon in Glazebrook livery - with 9 ft w/b chassis £7
NEW **B767** 5 Plank wagon in Marshall livery with 9ft w/b chassis £7
NEW **B772** 7 plank wagon in John Yates livery £7
NEW **B773** Breakdown Van in Frodingham livery £8
NEW **B775** Rectangular Tank Wagon in Walkers livery £10
B775b - v2 Container for Spine Wagon - Twin pack of 40' containers 'msc' and blue "ITALIA" £10

Accessories Railway related
NEW **B807** Dapoil - low viscosity lubricant for Dapol locos £3

Spares & Repairs
B803 Track cleaner (B800) accessory pack £9
B804 Track cleaner (B800) replacement track cleaning pads £5
B805 100ml of track cleaning fluid for the B800 Track cleaner £7

Track Maintenance Vehicles
B800 Non-motorised OO Track Cleaner with motorised cleaning heads and vacuum £52

EFE Diecast Buses & Vehicles - Buses
NEW **14702** Leyland National MkII "Portsmouth City Transport" £21
19304 Atkinson Artic Flatbed 'J & A Smith of Maddiston Ltd' £18
20007 Leyland Titan PD2/12 (Orion) d/deck bus "Plymouth City Transport" £14
20134 Bedford OB/Duple 1950's (Winchester) "Southern National" . £18
22717 Alexander Y Type "Fife Scottish" £21
NEW **23207** AEC RF MkII "London Country N.B.C." £21
NEW **23709** Alexander Fleetline d/deck bus "Glasgow Corporation" £21
25305 AEC Duple coach "Wilts & Dorset" £18
26805 Leyland Duple half cab 1940's coach "Ribble" £15
27312 Leyland TD1 Closed Rear "Fishwick & Sons Ltd" £17
30703 AEC Renown d/deck bus "South Wales" £17
32205 Bristol RELH Coach 'United N.B.C' £21
NEW **33101** RMC Routemaster Open Top "First London" £20
NEW **33102SB** RMC Routemaster Open Top "First London Showbus 2009" £23
34102 AEC RT Bus "London Country" £20
34103 AEC RT Bus London Transport (Last Day) £21
34204 AEC RLH Bus "London Transport" red £19
34205 AEC RLH Bus "London Transport" green £20
34301 AEC RT 2 Bus "London Transport" £19
34903 Leyland Olympian Coach "Eastern National" £21
36201 RMA Routemaster and trailer - British European Airways £26
NEW **36601** Plaxton SLF MkII Dart 2 door "Transdev" £21
NEW **36701** Plaxton SLF Dart MkII "Bus Eireann" £21
36901 AEC Park Royal Renown low height d/deck 'Devon General' £21
37101 ERF KV 4 Axle Dropside 'Asscociated Lead' £18
NEW **99647** Leyland National Mk2 Long & Trailer "British Railways Sealink" (operated by Western National) £22
99923 Maidstone and District 2 d/deck bus set £35

Commercial & public services
13702 Atkinson 8 wheel tanker lorry "Texaco" £17
30103 AEC MkIII 4 axle tanker 'Pickfords' £18
32702 Trader 2 Axle Flatbed 'Milk Marketing Board' £18
33301 AEC Ergo artic tanker in "Leather Chemicals" green & silver livery £15
34402 AEC Mammoth Major 8 MkV 4 axle flatbed "British Road Services" £15
NEW **35003** AEC Mandator Articulated Flatbed "J & A Smith of Maddiston Ltd" £18
36401 Foden S24 artic flatbed 'Robsons of Carlisle' £16

London Underground Tube Train
99931 4 car 1938 tube stock London Transport underground train in Metropolitan East London livery, not motorised £108

Heljan UK - Diesel locos
1706 Class 17 Clayton diesel Ribble Cement (ex-D8568). Limited edition of 1000 ..... £89
2606 Class 26 BRCW Sulzer diesel D5320 in BR blue with full yellow ends (list £79) ..... **BARGAIN** £43

2610 Class 26 BRCW 26028 BR blue full yellow ends, boiler tank & blanked cab doors (list £79)BARGAIN. £47
2611 Class 26 BRCW Sulzer diesel 26031 in BR blue with full yellow ends, boiler tank and blanked cab doors (list £79) .. **BARGAIN** £47
2612 Class 26 BRCW Sulzer diesel 26027 in BR blue with full yellow ends (list £79) ..... **BARGAIN** £47
2613 Class 26 BRCW Sulzer diesel 26029 in BR blue with full yellow ends (list £79) ..... **BARGAIN** £47
2630 Class 26 BRCW Sulzer diesel 26037 in Railfreight Red Stripe livery (list £79) ..... **BARGAIN** £48
2631 Class 26 BRCW Sulzer diesel 26025 in Railfreight Red Stripe livery with West Highland terrier depot crests (list £79)**BARGAIN** ... £49
2632 Class 26 BRCW Sulzer diesel 26046 in BR blue with full yellow ends (list £79) ..... **BARGAIN** £51
2633 Class 26 BRCW Sulzer diesel 26038 in Engineers "Dutch" grey & yellow livery (list £79) ..... **BARGAIN** £50
2634 Class 26 BRCW Sulzer diesel 26032 in Railfreight Red Stripe livery (list £79) ..... **BARGAIN** £49
2635 Class 26 BRCW Sulzer diesel 26041 in Railfreight grey livery with large logo (list £79) ..... **BARGAIN** £49
2636 Class 26 BRCW Sulzer diesel 26024 in BR blue with full yellow ends & West Highland terrier depot embelishment (as preserved) (list £79) ..... **BARGAIN** £48
2637 Class 26 BRCW Sulzer diesel 26043 in Engineers "Dutch" grey & yellow livery with Eastfield depot plaques (list £79) . **BARGAIN** £51
2720 Class 27 BRCW Sulzer diesel D5356 in original BR green (list £79) ..... **BARGAIN** £49
2721 Class 27 BRCW Sulzer diesel D5362 in BR green with small yellow warning panel (list £79) ..... **BARGAIN** £49
2722 Class 27 BRCW Sulzer diesel D5348 in BR blue with full yellow ends and cabside windows (list £79) ..... **BARGAIN** £49
3325 Class 33/2 diesel 33201 in Engineers grey (list £79)**BARGAIN** £39
3330 Class 33/2 diesel 33211 in Railfreight Distribution sector livery (list £79) ..... **BARGAIN** £39
3332 Class 33/2 diesel 33201 in Engineers grey & yellow "Dutch" livery (list £79) ..... **BARGAIN** £39
3333 Class 33/2 diesel 33204 in Railfreight Triple Grey livery with Mainline branding (list £79) ..... **BARGAIN** £39
3351 Class 33/1 diesel 33101 in Engineers grey (list £79)**BARGAIN** £41
3353 Class 33/1 diesel 33116/D6535 in BR Blue "Hertfordshire Rail Tours" (as during 1990's) (list £79) ..... **BARGAIN** £47
3354 Class 33/1 diesel 33103 "Swordfish" in Fragonset livery (list £79) ..... **BARGAIN** £44
3355 Class 33/1 diesel 33103 Civil Link "Dutch" (list £79)**BARGAIN** £42
4677 Class 47 diesel 47321 Railfreight Distribution(list £89)**BARGAIN** £54
5304 Class 53 diesel D1200 'Falcon' in BR blue with full yellow ends (weathered). Ltd Edition of 1200 (list £129) ..... **BARGAIN** ... £106
5803 Class 58 diesel 58037 in red stripe Railfreight grey (version 2) (list £89) ..... **BARGAIN** £57
5805 Class 58 diesel 58050 "Toton Traction Depot" in Mainline blue (version 2) (list £89) ..... **BARGAIN** £49
5806 Class 58 diesel 58009 in Railfreight sector grey with "Mainline" branding. Version 1 (list £89) ..... **BARGAIN** £49

5807 Class 58 diesel 58024 in EW&S maroon & gold livery. Version 1 (list £89) ..... BARGAIN... £49
5808 Class 58 diesel 58041 in Railfreight Red Stripe livery (version 2) (list £89) ..... **BARGAIN** £49
5809 Class 58 diesel 58048 in Railfreight coal sector "Coventry Colliery" (version 2) (list £89) ..... **BARGAIN** £52

Wagons
4095Dutch Pack of 4 Dogfish ballast wagons in 'Dutch' Engineers grey with ballast loads £43
NEW **4097** Pack of 4 Dogfish ballast wagons in 1960's/70's engineers liveries (1 Gulf red, 2 black, 1 Olive) £49
NEW **4098** Pack of 4 Dogfish ballast wagons in sectorisation engineers liveries (3 Dutch and 1 Loadhaul) £49
5008 Cargowaggon 2797699 in Blue Circle Cement yellow & blue livery (weathered) (list £30) ..... **BARGAIN** £19
5102 Cargowaggon IPE/IGE557 bogie flat 4647 035 (ex works) £20
NEW **5105Hel** Cargowaggon IPE/IGE557 bogie flat 4747 xxx with Corus Rail brandings £27
NEW **5106** Cargowaggon IPE/IGE557 bogie flat 4747 000 in ex-works Cargowaggon livery £27
NEW **5107** Cargowaggon IPE/IGE557 bogie flat 4747 028 in weathered Cargowaggon livery £31
NEW **5108Hel** Cargowaggon IPE/IGE557 bogie flat 4647 041 in ex-works Cargowaggon livery with load £31

Scenic Accessories/Scenery
NEW **2501** Local Railway Station Kit (list £26.75) .. **BARGAIN** £16

Trackside Accessories
8900 Container crane terminal with operating crane (OO & HO gauge, DC/AC/DCC operation) £385

Hornby - Steam locos
H763Loco GWR 0-4-0 steam loco 105 ..... **BARGAIN** £17
R2164U J83 class 0-6-0 tank 8469 in LNER green (Weathered) (Unboxed) £27
R2339 Class A4 4-6-2 4468 "Mallard" & tender in LNER blue (loco has DCC socket) £102
R2403 Grange class 4-6-0 "Derwent Grange" in BR black with early logo (list £95) ..... **BARGAIN** £65
R2441 Class A1 4-6-2 4472 "Flying Scotsman" in LNER (NRM) £95
R2455 Castle class 4-6-0 "Pendennis Castle" & tender in BR livery (list £93.50) ..... **BARGAIN** £59
R2459 Castle class 4-6-0 "Wellington" & tender in GWR livery (list £93.50) ..... **BARGAIN** £69
R2483 AIX class 0-6-0 "Piccadilly" Terrier tank in LBSC livery £53
R2534A Class 2721 0-6-0 Pannier 2748 in GWR Brunswick green (list £45.75) ..... **BARGAIN** £26
R2543 Castle class 4-6-0 4081 "Warwick Castle" loco & tender in BR green with early emblem (list £106.50) ..... **BARGAIN** £69
R2548 Grange class 4-6-0 6816 "Frankton Grange" & tender in BR black with early emblem (weathered) (list £113.99) **BARGAIN** £59
R2551 Castle class 4-6-0 5077 "Fairey Battle" & tender in BR green with early emblem (list £95) ..... **BARGAIN** £63
R2606 BR (Late) Rebuilt Battle of Britain "Sir Trafford Leigh Mallory" (list £116.50) ..... **BARGAIN** £87
R2608 BR (Late) Rebuilt West Country "Yes Tor"(list £116.50)**BARGAIN** £86
R2618X Class 7MT Britannia 4-6-2 "Lord Rowallan" & tender in BR with late logo. (DCC on board) £119
R2626X M7 class 0-4-4 tank loco in BR with late crest. (DCC on board) (list £95) ..... **BARGAIN** £68
R2628X Royal Scot class 4-6-0 "Black Watch" & tender in BR green with early crest (DCC on board) (list £112.99) ..... **BARGAIN** £89
R2629X Royal Scot class 4-6-0 "The Kings Royal Rifle Corps" & tender BR early crest (weathered) (DCC on board) (list £112.99)**BARGAIN** £78
R2631X Royal Scot class 4-6-0 6133 "The Green Howards" & tender in LMS black (DCC on board) (list £112.99) ..... **BARGAIN** £78
R2632 Rebuilt Patriot class 4-6-0 "Sir Frederick Harrison" & tender in BR early emblem. (DCC ready) (list £102.50) ..... **BARGAIN** £66
R2636X Stanier 4P tank 2 cylinder 2-6-4T in BR Lined black with early emblem (DCC on board) £71
R2637X Stanier 4P tank 2 cylinder 2-6-4T in BR Lined black with late crest (weathered) (DCC on board) £74
R2674 Class 3F Jinty 0-6-0 steam loco in LMS crimson £26

R2683 Caledonian Single Class 4-2-2 14010 LMS lined black Limited Edition of 2000(list £85.49)BARGAIN . £58
R2684 A4 Class 4-6-2 "Mallard" 70th Anniversary loco 4468 and tender in LNER blue. Ltd edition of 5000 (gold plated parts) £120
R2685 1948 Nationalisation WC "Bude" with Stanier tender. Limited edition of 2000. DCC Ready, not DCC fitted (contrary to box) £84
R2688 Class A4 4-6-2 "Sir Nigel Gresley" loco & tender in LNER blue (70th Anniversary ltd edition of 2008 in older style box) £109

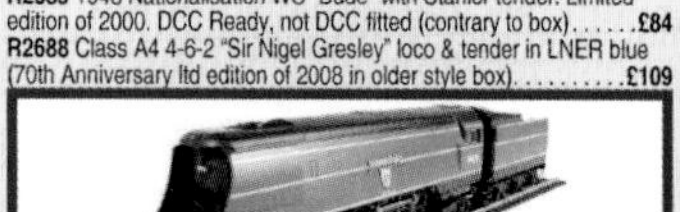

R2691 West Country Class 4-6-2 "Torrington" 34031 loco & tender SR Malachite green (list £119.49)BARGAIN . £69

R2692 Battle of Britain Class 4-6-2 "Sir Eustace Missenden" 34090 loco with wide cab & tender in BR Malachite livery (list £119.49) ..... BARGAIN... £74

R2709 Rebuilt Battle of Britain Class 4-6-2 "Sir Frederick Pile" 34058 loco & tender in BR green with late crest (list £123.25) ..... BARGAIN... £72
R2710 Merchant Navy Class 4-6-2 "Blue Star" 35010 loco & tender in BR green with late crest (list £119.49) ..... **BARGAIN** £69
R2711X Class T9 4-4-0 steam loco 729 in pristine 1936 Maunsell SR green. Narrow cab & 6-wheel tender. DCC Fitted £99
R2712X Class T9 4-4-0 steam loco 30724 in pristine 1949 early emblem BR lined black. Narrow cab & water cart tender. DCC Fitted £87
R2713 Class T9 4-4-0 steam loco 30310 in pristine 1958 early emblem BR lined black. Wide cab & water cart tender. DCC Ready £89
R2714 Standard Class 4 75005 4-6-0 steam loco in BR black with early emblem. BR2 tender. DCC Ready £86
R2714X Standard Class 4 75005 4-6-0 steam loco in BR black with early emblem. BR2 tender. DCC Fitted £89
NEW **R2715** Standard Class 4 75062 4-6-0 steam loco in BR black with late crest. BR2A tender. DCC Ready £82
R2717 BR 7P6F Late Britannia BR Green 70015 "Apollo" (DCC Ready)£89
R2717X BR 7P6F Late Britannia BR Green 70015 "Apollo" (DCC Fitted) £96
R2721 Class A4 BR Late green "Sparrow Hawk" non corridor tender £109
R2724 N15 Early BR Green 30800 "Sir Mileaus de Lile" (DCC Ready) (list £106.49) ..... **BARGAIN** £69
R2724X N15 Early BR Green 30800 "Sir Mileaus de Lile" (DCC Fitted) (list £122.75) ..... **BARGAIN** £86
R2725 N15 Class 30450 "Sir Kay" in BR green with late crest (DCC Ready) (list £106.49) ..... **BARGAIN** £64
R2725X N15 Class 30450 "Sir Kay" in BR green with late crest (DCC Fitted) (list £122.75) ..... **BARGAIN** £69
R2726 Patriot Class 45536 BR Early Green "Private W Wood VC" (DCC Ready) (list £102.75) ..... **BARGAIN** £62
R2727 Patriot Class 45528 BR Late green "R.E.M.E" (DCC Ready) (list £102.75) ..... **BARGAIN** £58
R2728 Royal Scot Class 46120 "Royal Inniskilling Fusiliers" BR Green (DCC Ready) (list £102.75) ..... **BARGAIN** £62

R2728X Royal Scot Class 46120 "Royal Inniskilling Fusiliers" BR Green (DCC Fitted)(list £119.49)BARGAIN £69
R2730 Stanier 2-6-4T 4MT 2484 in LMS black (DCC Ready) (list £85.49) ..... **BARGAIN** £54
R2730X Stanier 2-6-4T 4MT 2484 in LMS black (DCC Fitted) (list £102.75) ..... **BARGAIN** £65
R2732 Stanier 2-6-4T 4MT 42616 in BR late black (DCC Ready) ... £68
R2732X Stanier 2-6-4T 4MT 42616 in BR late black (DCC Fitted) .. £75
R2733X SR Class M7 (DCC Fitted) £89

R2734X M7 BR early black 30056 (DCC Fitted) (list £108.49) ..... BARGAIN... £64
R2735 M7 BR late black 30036 (DCC Ready) £89
R2736 Castle class 7013 BR late green "Bristol Castle" with Collett tender & 5-pole skew motor (list £106.50) ..... **BARGAIN** £57
R2738 BR 2-6-4T Fowler 4P 42315 BR early black £79
R2739 Class 2721 GWR 0-6-0PT BR green 2764 ..... £36
R2740 PO WPR 0-6-0ST "No 18" £47
R2741 Class A1X BR 0-6-0T Terrier 32662 ..... £44
R2743 Schools Class 4-4-0 steam loco 30915 'Brighton' in BR (Late) Green with Lemaitre blast pipe. DCC Ready £99
R2744 Schools class 4-4-0 steam loco 30932 'Blundell's' in BR Black with standard tender. DCC Ready (list £108.49) ... **BARGAIN** £79
R2744X Schools class 4-4-0 steam loco 30932 'Blundell's' in BR Black with standard tender. DCC Fitted £92
R2779 Class A4 LNER Blue 4484 "Falcon" £53
R2785 BR Class 9F 92220 BR green "Evening Star" - Railroad range £52
R2799 AIX class 0-6-0 Terrier tank "Brighton" in LB & SCR livery (Collectors Centre Special Edition of 1500) £47
R2823 BR Princess Elizabeth Late Crest -Pete Waterman Collection £102
R2826 Class A4 60013 "Dominion of New Zealand" & tender in BR lined green with early crest £131

NEW R2828 GWR "Duke of Edinburgh" Dean Achilles Class £79
R2840 Class M7 SR Maunsell Green 42 - DCC Ready £94
NEW **R2882** S & Djr Jinty 0-6-0 3f Locomotive £23
NEW **R2999U** S & DJR 0-6-0 Class 3P Jinty loco 24. DCC Ready. Unboxed £26

Train Packs
R2379A Eurostar 6 Car Train Pack £116
R2467 Pendolino train pack (4 car). DCC ready £89
R2467X Pendolino train pack (4 car). DCC on board £109

R2663A Class 90 & 3 Mk3 sleepers Caledonian Sleeper train pack "First Scotrail"(list £125.49) BARGAIN... £79
R2669 Class 08 shunter in BR red, 2 x open wagons & 1 x box van £26
R2706 GWR "The Flying Dutchman" train pack Royal Sovereign + 3 coaches. Limited edition of 2000 ..... £140

Diesel locos
R2428 Class 50 diesel 50037 "Illustrious" in early BR blue (list £95) ..... **BARGAIN** £59
R2486 Class 50 diesel 50013 "Agincourt" in early BR blue livery (list £95) ..... **BARGAIN** £57
R2490 Class 60 diesel 60078 in Mainline livery £68
R2521 Class 59 diesel 59102 "Village of Chantry" in ARC livery (list £62.50) ..... **BARGAIN** £39
R2523 Class 67 diesel electric 67005 "Queens Messenger" in Royal Train livery £65
R2639 Class 60 diesel 60 014 "Alexander Fleming" EWS/Trainload £76
R2640 Class 60 diesel 60 066 "John Logie Baird" in Trainload Coal livery with Transrail branding (list £102.50) ..... **BARGAIN** £65
R2641 Class 50 diesel 50 020 "Revenge" BR blue large logo & arrows £76
R2646 Class 56 diesel 56049 BR Railfreight red stripe livery (1987) DCC ready (list £102.25) ..... **BARGAIN** £62
R2646X Class 56 diesel 56049 BR Railfreight red stripe livery (1987) (DCC on board) (list £118.50) ..... **BARGAIN** £62
R2647 Class 56 diesel 56128 "West Burton Power Station" in Railfreight Coal sub-sector livery. DCC Ready (list £102.50)**BARGAIN** . £62
R2649 Class 31 diesel 31165 in BR Blue (list £95) . **BARGAIN** £60
R2650 Class 66 diesel "Joseph Arnold Davies" Medite (list £74.25) ..... **BARGAIN** £41
R2656 Class 73 diesel in BR green E6001 (list £70.99)**BARGAIN** .. £42
R2676 Class 06 diesel shunter in BR blue £17
R2677 Class 47 diesel loco in Virgin Trains livery £34
R2746 Class 60 diesel EWS 60029 "Clitheroe Castle" £86
R2747 Class 60 diesel BR Railfreight Petroleum 60062 "Samuel Johnson" (list £108.49) ..... **BARGAIN** £72
R2748 Class 50 diesel 50011 BR Large logo "Centurion" (list £108.49) ..... **BARGAIN** £64
R2750X Class 56 diesel 56103 EWS "Stora" (DCC Fitted) (list £125.25) ..... **BARGAIN** £69
R2751 Class 56 diesel 56003 Loadhaul (DCC Ready) (list £108.49) ..... **BARGAIN** £64
R2751X Class 56 diesel 56003 Loadhaul (DCC Fitted) (list £125.25) ..... **BARGAIN** £69
R2752 Class 56 diesel 56032 Railfreigh Metals "Sir De Morgannwg County of South Glamorgan" with Toton decal (DCC Ready) (list £108.49) ..... **BARGAIN** £59
R2753 Class 31 diesel 31296 in Railfreight Construction with Immingham decal (list £108.49) ..... **BARGAIN** £65
R2754 Class 31 diesel in BR Railfreight grey with red stripe 31 105 (list £108.49) ..... **BARGAIN** £65
R2760 Class 20 Bo-Bo diesel 20118 in Railfreight Red Stripe livery as preserved at the South Devon Railway (list £62.49) **BARGAIN** . £39.50
R2761 Class 20 diesel BR Blue (list £62.49) ..... **BARGAIN** . £39.50

R2764 Class 67 67018 diesel "Rapid" in EWS (list £80.25) ..... BARGAIN... £45

R2765 Class 73/1 electro-diesel 73108 BR Civil Link (Dutch Livery) (list £70.99) ..... BARGAIN... £34
R2766 Class 73/1 electro-diesel NSE 73 129 "City of Winchester" (list £70.99) ..... **BARGAIN** £39
R2767 Class 73 electro-diesel 73204 BR InterCity "Stewarts Lane" (list £70.99) ..... **BARGAIN** £39
R2780XS Class 60 60048 diesel electric in EWS livery with DCC sound fitted £189
R2781XS Class 56 diesel 56127 in BR trainload coal livery with sound & working fans £189
R2793 Class 50 diesel 50048 "Dauntless" in original Network Southeast livery (list £108.49) ..... **BARGAIN** £64

NEW R2803XS Class 31 31233 diesel in Railfreight Subsector Petroleum with DCC sound £168
R2861 Class 59 diesel in Hanson Aggregates 'Yeoman Endeavour' £64
NEW **R2871** Class 08 diesel shunter in EWS livery £62
NEW **R2879** Class 55 Diesel Deltic loco in BR Blue (list £43.99) ..... **BARGAIN** £34
NEW **R2883** Class 60 Diesel EWS 'The Territorial Army Centenary' £119

Electric locos
R2663A Loco Class 90 electric in "First" livery from Caledonian Sleeper pack. Unboxed ..... **BARGAIN** £44
R2755 Class 86 electric 86259 BR electric blue (Preserved) "Les Ross" (list £68.49) ..... **BARGAIN** £44
R2772 Class 87 electric 87004 "Britannia" in BR Blue livery £53
R2787 Class 87 electric 87010 "King Arthur" in BR InterCity Swift .. £54

DMU's
R2508A Class 121 single car DMU (Bubble car) in Network SE livery 55 025 (list £70.99) ..... **BARGAIN** £45
R2509A Class 121 single car DMU (Bubble car) in BR green livery . £58
R2579A Class 101 3 car DMU in BR blue £73
R2644 Class 121 single car DMU 55020 chocolate/cream (list £70.99) ..... **BARGAIN** £45
R2693 Class 156 2 car DMU in "One" livery (list £91.25)**BARGAIN** . £51
R2696 Class 101 2-car DMU Scotrail SPT 101692 (list £91.25) ..... **BARGAIN** £52
R2698 Class 101 3-car DMU in BR Blue/Grey(list £91.25)**BARGAIN** £48
R2700 Class 142 pacer 2 car DMU in Arriva livery £54
R2756 Class 153 single car DMU 153379 in Central Trains livery (2000-2008) DCC Ready £54
R2756X Class 153 single car DMU 153379 in Central Trains livery (2000-2008) DCC Fitted £67
R2758 Class 153 single car DMU 153323 in North West Trains blue with Northern branding livery (2000-2008). DCC Ready £54
R2759 Class 153 single car DMU 153311 in Regional Railways (was announced as Arriva Wales) livery (1989-2000's) DCC Ready £55
R2769 Class 121 bubblecar Chiltern Railways 121020 (list £70.99) ..... **BARGAIN** £39
R2771 Class 121 bubblecar DMU in BR Green £56
R2792 Class 153 DMU 153374 East Midlands blue, red & yellow (previously Wessex Trains) £59
R2792X Class 153 DMU 153374 East Midlands blue, red & yellow (previously Wessex Trains) (DCC Fitted) £67
NEW **R2869** BR Crimson & Cream diesel railcar express £60
R2876 GWR diesel railcar "Express parcels" £62

HST trainpacks
R2701 Class 43 HST Power (W43055) & Dummy-car (W43054) pack in original BR Blue livery (1977-mid 1980's). DCC Ready £118
R2701X Class 43 HST Power (W43055) & Dummy-car (W43054) pack in original BR Blue livery (1977-mid 1980's). DCC Fitted £131

NEW R2705 Class 43 HST Power & Dummy-car pack - Grand Central livery (DCC Ready) £106
NEW **R2705X** Class 43 HST Power & Dummy-car pack - Grand Central livery (DCC Fitted) £118

Coaches
R2663A Coaches 3 * Mk3 "First" sleepers from "Caledonian" train pack. Unboxed ..... **BARGAIN** £42
R4086H MK2E standard 2nd coach "Virgin" red £20
R4087G Mk2 Virgin Open Brake Standard Coach £19
NEW **R4116B** Mk1 Parcels Coach BR Green No.(Southern Region) £20
R4155 LMS TPO operating Royal mail coach set £32
R4179 Gresley 61ft corridor 1st class coach E11018E in (ex LNER) BR crimson & cream (list £34.50) ..... **BARGAIN** £18
R4182 Gresley 61ft corridor 1st class sleeper coach in (ex LNER) BR crimson & cream (list £33.65) ..... **BARGAIN** £14
R4232A LMS standard period 3 Stanier corridor brake 3rd class coach in crimson 5619 ..... £31
R4234 BR (ex LMS) corridor 1st class coach in maroon (list £34.50) ..... **BARGAIN** £23
R4260B BR 61ft 6in corridor brake composite in BR maroon £38
R4261A BR 61ft 6in corridor 1st class coach in BR maroon SC 11026 E (list £38.25) ..... **BARGAIN** £17

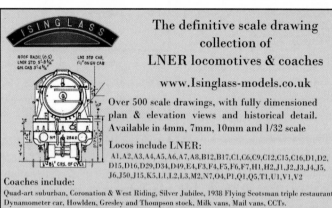

IF YOU WANT TO BUY TOP QUALITY MODEL RAILWAYS AT PRICES YOU CAN AFFORD

**LOOK AT MY WEBSITES
WWW.RAYMANSFIELDMODELRAILWAYS.COM
WWW.MODELRAILWAYSMART.COM**

IF YOU WANT TO BE EMAILED THE MOMENT NEW STOCK ARRIVES, REGISTER YOUR EMAIL ADDRESS AT TRAINMASTER47120002000@YAHOO.CO.UK

NEW STOCK ARRIVING EACH WEEK

I ALSO TAKE PART EXCHANGE OR BUY ALL TYPES OF MODEL RAILWAYS IN ALL GAUGES FROM Z TO 5 INCH GAUGE. IF YOU WISH YOU CAN BOX IT UP AND SEND IT TO ME FOR A VALUATION THE SAME DAY.

WE DO: WEATHERING, RESPRAYS, NAME AND NUMBER CHANGES, PAINTING AND LINING, KIT BUILDING REPAIRS, SERVICING OLD LOCOS

**TEL 01279 417646 OR 07811 453306
43 EASTPARK HARLOW ESSEX CM17 0SE**

www.raymansfieldmodelrailways.com
www.modelrailwaysmart.com

PayPal®   PayPal®